Evident

Evidentiary Foundations
Irish Edition

Liz Heffernan
LLB, LLM, BL, JSD,
Lecturer and Fellow, Trinity College, Dublin

Ray Ryan
Barrister-at-Law

Edward J Imwinkelried
Edward L Barrett Jr Professor of Law,
University of California, Davis

Published by
Tottel Publishing Ltd
Maxwelton House
41–43 Boltro Road
Haywards Heath
West Sussex
RH16 1BJ

Tottel Publishing Ltd
Fitzwilliam Business Centre
26 Upper Pembroke Street
Dublin 2

ISBN 978 1 84592 787 5
Original edition published by
Matthew Bender & Company, Inc.

Authorised derivative work published by
Tottel Publishing Ltd

British Library Cataloguing-in-Publication Data
A catalogue record for this book is available from the British Library

Typeset by Marie Armah-Kwantreng, Dublin, Ireland
Printed and bound in Great Britain by
Athenæum Press Limited, Gateshead, Tyne & Wear

ACKNOWLEDGEMENTS

We would like to express our gratitude to Professor Paul O'Connor of UCD Law School who was instrumental in the genesis of this book. Several individuals provided assistance, guidance and support along the way. We are particularly grateful to Mr Niall Buckley BL, Mrs Helen Bradford BL, Mr Des Ryan, Professor Hilary Delany and Mr Conor McAuliffe. We are also much indebted to Ms Sandra Mulvey and the staff at Tottel Publishing, to Marie Armah-Kwantreng for typesetting the text and Andrew Turner for drafting the index.

CONTENTS

TABLE OF CASES

A

B

C

Q

R

S

TABLE OF STATUTES

Statutory Instruments

ABBREVIATIONS

CCA – Court of Criminal Appeal

CJ(E)A 1924 – Criminal Justice (Evidence) Act 1924

CEA 1992 – Criminal Evidence Act 1992

CA 1997 – Children Act 1997

CJA 1999 – Criminal Justice Act 1999

CJA 2006 – Criminal Justice Act 2006

CJA 2007 – Criminal Justice Act 2007

CPA 1865 – Criminal Procedure Act 1865

CPA 1993 – Criminal Procedure Act 1993

J – Judge

O – Opponent

P – Proponent

W – Witness

Chapter 1

INTRODUCTION

1.01 BACKGROUND

This text is designed as a practical guide to the application of the Irish law of evidence. The origins of the text lie in Professor Imwinkelried's extensive experience teaching evidence and trial practice to students in American law schools. Responding to recurring complaints from evidence students that they could not develop a working understanding of the evidentiary doctrines discussed in class, Professor Imwinkelried resolved to prepare a comprehensive set of simple foundations that would enable students to convert classroom theories into concrete, practical courtroom scenarios. That set of foundations, based primarily on the United States Federal Rules of Evidence, became the first edition of *Evidentiary Foundations* (1980). Now in its sixth edition, *Evidentiary Foundations* has been an invaluable resource for generations of American law students and trial lawyers.[1] This text extends Professor Imwinkelried's concept to an Irish audience by providing a collection of foundations for the introduction of various items of evidence in the Irish courts.

There are certain limitations inherent in a project of this kind. First, this is an Irish edition of an American text and the American influence is discernible throughout. Were this project an exclusively Irish undertaking, the final draft might well have assumed a different hue. At the same time, this edition is grounded in Irish law and practice and in light of the significant differences between the Irish law of evidence and its American counterparts (both federal and state), the text departs substantially from Professor Imwinkelried's original in terms of structure, content and form.

Second, the sample evidentiary foundations that lie at the heart of the text are designed to illustrate the *potential* application of evidentiary doctrines in practice. They do not purport to be prescriptive and should be read as possible rather than probable (much less mandatory) courtroom strategies. We acknowledge that in contemporary Irish practice counsel may examine witnesses, and judges may respond to submissions, in ways other than those represented in the sample foundations. Our intention throughout is to remain

1. *Evidentiary Foundations* (6th edn, LexisNexis, 2005).

true to Professor Imwinkelried's primary objective of demystifying and contextualising the law of evidence.

Third, there are many evidentiary issues that have been the subject of case law and comment in the United States but on which Irish law and practice remain silent. We have endeavoured to acknowledge in the individual sample foundations the few occasions on which we have borrowed ideas from this more developed American practice.

Finally, the events and persons described in the sample foundations are entirely fictitious and do not represent actual events or persons in any way. To underscore this point, and at the risk of trivialising the fact patterns to some degree, we have deliberately chosen 'unreal' names for the various characters, based on themes such as colour or common objects.

1.02 FORMAT

Most sections of the text use the following format. First, each section opens with a summary of an evidentiary rule or practice incorporating references to the governing statutes and case law. Second, the text breaks the rule or practice down into a numbered list of the elements that embody a proper foundation for the admission of evidence. These elements comprise the facts and events which constitute the foundation. Finally, the section contains a sample or hypothetical foundation for the evidentiary rule or practice. Each question in the body of the sample foundation is numbered; the number corresponds to the element of the foundation to which the question relates. Thus, the numbered foundation demonstrates how each element in the evidentiary rule or practice converts into concrete questions in the courtroom.

Some of the foundations are drafted in the context of a criminal jury trial; others assume the more informal procedure of a civil bench trial (a trial by judge or judges alone). In the latter instance, where the judge is both finder of fact and arbiter of the law, some elements of the foundation for the introduction of an item of evidence may be simplified or dispensed with.

The following terminology is used in the sample foundations:

- P. Proponent (party proposing the introduction of an item of evidence).
- O. Opponent (party opposing the introduction of an item of evidence).
- W. Witness.
- J. Judge.

1.03 LAYING AN EVIDENTIARY FOUNDATION

1.03.1 Procedure

For our purposes, the most important procedural requirement is that the party presenting an item of evidence must ordinarily lay a foundation for its admission into evidence. Whenever the law of evidence makes proof of a fact or event a condition precedent to the admission of an item of evidence, that fact or event is part of the foundation for the admission of the evidence. For example, a party seeking to introduce a letter must present proof of its authenticity before offering the letter into evidence. The law of evidence makes proof of authenticity a condition precedent to the letter's admission and, consequently, proof of the letter's authenticity is part of the letter's 'foundation'.

The trial judge has discretion to deviate from this procedural requirement; the judge may vary the order of proof and admit the evidence on the condition that the party will establish the foundation at some later stage in the proceedings. However, proof of the foundation before admission of the evidence is usually the more logical approach. If the judge admits the evidence subject to subsequent proof of the foundation and the party later fails to present the necessary proof, the judge will be in an awkward position. In a jury trial, the judge will have to instruct the jurors to disregard evidence they have already heard. If the judge believes that the instruction will be ineffective and the jurors will be unable to put aside the evidence, the judge may have to grant a mistrial. Hence, whenever possible, the party presenting an item of evidence should establish the foundation or predicate when asking the court to admit the item.

Any item of evidence potentially implicates several evidentiary rules and may require more than one foundation, depending on its use at trial. For example, in laying the foundation for a document, the proponent must demonstrate that the document is relevant and authentic but he or she may also be required to lay a foundation showing that the document satisfies the rule against hearsay and the best evidence rule. Multiple foundations are analogous to the analysis of conditions in contract cases. The plaintiff must demonstrate that every condition precedent or concurrent has been either fulfilled or excused. Similarly, the proponent of evidence must show that every foundational fact has been established under the applicable rules.

1.03.2 Practical matters

Professor Imwinkelried offers three cardinal rules for drafting a line of questioning: simplicity, brevity and preparation. First, always use the simplest, most easily understood term. Counsel must communicate effectively with lay witnesses and jurors and this requires use of lay diction. Jonathan Swift quite properly condemned the lawyers of his day for using 'a peculiar Cant and Jargon of their own that no other mortal can understand …'[2] and, in the present day, many lawyers are guilty of the same literary sin. It is essential to bear in mind that the examination of witnesses is a test of communicative skill rather than vocabulary.

Second, counsel should strive to make each question as short as possible. Rudolph Flesch has pointed out that there is an inverse relation between the length of a sentence and its comprehensibility: the longer the sentence, the lower the level of comprehension on the part of the audience.[3] Leading psychological studies suggest that the maximum length of a written sentence should be 25 words; if the sentence is any longer, comprehension drops off markedly. Moreover, it is more difficult for an audience to absorb a spoken sentence as opposed to a written sentence. Consequently, many experienced lawyers strive to limit the length of their questions so as to ensure that the witness and jurors are able to follow them.

The third cardinal rule is preparation. Both counsel and the witness must be well prepared for trial. If counsel falters or pauses too long during direct examination, the examination loses its flow and rhythm. If the witness appears uncertain during questioning, at the very least, the judge or jurors will doubt the quality of the witness's memory. To avoid these and related pitfalls, counsel generally meets the witness before trial to review the witness's proposed testimony.[4] When preparing for trial, the witness may refresh his or her memory by reading over any pre-trial statement that he or she made at the time of the material events.[5]

---

2. *Gulliver's Travels* cited in Seldes (ed), *The Great Quotations* (Kensington, 1993) 670.
3. Flesch, *The Art of Plain Talk* (Harper, 1946) 120–133.
4. Assisting the witness prepare for trial must not rise to the level of coaching. *DPP v Donnelly* (22 February 1999, unreported) CCA; *R v Richardson* [1971] 2 QB 484.
5. Such as a statement made to the gardaí. *DPP v Donnelly* (22 February 1999, unreported) CCA.

Chapter 2

WITNESSES

COMPETENCE AND COMPELLABILITY

2.01 BACKGROUND

Some evidentiary rules have the effect of keeping a prospective witness out of the witness box altogether; the rules governing competency and compellability can prevent a person from testifying in proceedings at all.[1] The application of these rules ordinarily turns on the prospective witness's status rather than the content of his or her contemplated testimony. A witness is competent if he or she is capable of understanding the oath and of giving a rational account of events relevant to the proceedings. A witness must be competent in order to be compellable. Compellability refers to the authority of the court to force the witness to testify. Special statutory rules govern the competence and/or compellability of certain categories of witness such as the accused in a criminal proceeding,[2] the spouse of an accused in a criminal proceeding,[3] children,[4] persons with mental disabilities,[5] diplomats[6] and bankers.[7] Otherwise, the Irish courts operate on the pragmatic assumption that a witness is competent and compellable.

If the competency of a witness is challenged by a party or raised by the court itself, the party calling the witness has the burden of establishing that the witness is fit to testify. The issue is determined by the trial judge after the witness has been examined by the party calling him or her (or the judge) and possibly cross-examined by the party contesting competency. The party

---

1. See generally McGrath, *Evidence* (Thomson Round Hall, 2005) ch 3B; Fennell, *Law of Evidence in Ireland* (2nd edn, Tottel Publishing, 2003) ch 5; Healy, *Irish Laws of Evidence* (Thomson Round Hall, 2004) ch 2.
2. Section 1 of the CJ(E)A 1924.
3. Sections 20–26 of the CEA 1992.
4. Sections 27 and 28 of the CEA 1992; s 28 of the CA 1997.
5. Sections 27(1) and 27(3) of the CEA 1992; s 27(1) of the CA 1997.
6. Section 5 of the Diplomatic Relations and Immunities Act 1967.
7. Section 6 of the Bankers' Books Evidence Act 1879, c11, as amended.

calling the witness may also adduce independent evidence of competency. In a criminal jury trial, the accused may elect to have the hearing of the legal argument, known as *voir dire*, on competency conducted outside the presence of the jury.[8]

2.02 CHILDREN

2.02.1 The law

Historically, a child was competent to testify only if he or she possessed sufficient knowledge to understand the nature and consequences of the oath.[9] Statutory reform permitted the child witness to provide unsworn, rather than sworn, testimony at trial thereby removing the need for the court to grapple with the troublesome question of the child's understanding of the existence of a deity and the need to testify truthfully.[10] Today, a child under 14 years of age may testify otherwise than on oath or affirmation in both criminal and civil proceedings provided that the child is capable of giving an intelligible account of events that are relevant to the proceedings.[11] Similar provisions govern the competency to testify of a witness with a mental disability.[12]

2.02.2 Elements of the foundation

Where a party challenges the competency of a child witness, the party calling the witness has the burden of demonstrating that the child is capable of giving an intelligible account of events that are relevant to the proceedings. The foundation might include the following elements:

1. The child has the capacity to observe.
2. The child has the capacity to remember.
3. The child has the capacity to relate.

---

8. *AG v Lanigan* [1958] Ir Jur Rep 59.
9. *R v Brasier* (1779) 1 Leach 199; *R v Hayes* [1977] 1 WLR 234.
10. Section 30 of the Children Act 1908, c 67.
11. Section 27(1) of the CEA 1992; s 28(1) of the CA 1997.
12. Section 27(3) of the CEA 1992 and s 28(3) of the CA 1997.

2.02.3 Sample foundation

The fact scenario is a personal injury action arising from a road traffic accident at a junction. The plaintiff, the proponent, calls a child who witnessed the collision.

P. As his next witness, the plaintiff calls Master Alan Ash.
O. Judge, I object to any testimony by this child on the ground that the child is not competent to be a witness. I request that the child be examined concerning his competency.
J. I'll grant your request.
P. Judge, may I conduct the initial examination of Master Ash?
J. You may.
P. *(To the witness)* What is your name?
W. Alan Ash.
P. Where do you live?
W. I live at 12 Tree Terrace in town.
P. Alan, How well do you see? (1)
W. Fine. I have no problems seeing.
P. Do you need to wear glasses? (1)
W. No.
P. How well do you hear? (1)
W. Very well.
P. How old are you? (2)
W. I'm seven.
P. When is your birthday?
W. In December. Just after my Dad's birthday.
P. How many brothers and sisters do you have? (2)
W. I have one sister.
P. What is her name? (2)
W. Amy.
P. How old is Amy? (2)
W. She's two.
P. What school do you go to? (2)
W. The National School.
P. Where is your school? (2)
W. At the end of our road.
P. What class are you in? (2)
W. First Class.

P. Who is your teacher? (2)
W. Miss Olivia Oak.
P. What subjects do you learn in school? (3)
W. We have English.
P. What do you learn in English? (3)
W. We read books and poems. We do spelling.
P. Does your teacher, Miss Oak, give you English tests? (3)
W. Yes.
P. How do you do in your English tests?
W. Well. I got all the questions right last time.
P. Alan, what is a 'car'? (3)
W. It's a thing you drive around in. My Dad has one. It takes you places.
P. What does 'fast' mean? (3)
W. It's the same thing as quick.
P. What is a 'junction' on a road?
W. It's where roads join up.
P. I have no further questions for Master Ash about his competency.
O. I have no questions. I renew my objection on the ground that this child is too young to be a witness in these proceedings.
P. Judge, Master Ash's answers to my questions clearly demonstrate his capacity to observe, remember and relate.
J. I agree. The court will hear the witness's unsworn evidence.

2.03 MENTAL DISABILITY

2.03.1 The law

The law governing the competency of a person with a mental disability to testify is similar to the law governing the competency of a child witness. A person who is 14 years or older and who has a mental disability is competent to give unsworn testimony in criminal[13] or civil[14] proceedings provided that he or she is capable of giving an intelligible account of events relevant to the proceedings.[15] Where the competency of the witness is challenged by a party

13. Section 27(3) of the CEA 1992.

14. Section 28(3) of the CA 1997.

15. *O'Sullivan v Hamill* [1999] 3 IR 9.

to the proceedings, one possible response by the party calling the witness is to present expert medical evidence. The opinion of a qualified expert is presented in order to satisfy the court either: (1) that the witness does not have a mental disability and, consequently, is competent to testify on oath as an ordinary witness; or (2) that the witness has a mental disability but is nevertheless capable of giving an intelligible account of material events and, consequently, may give unsworn testimony to the court. The party challenging the competency of the witness may present its own expert evidence on the matter.

2.03.2 Elements of the foundation

The party tendering the witness (the proponent) seeks to demonstrate that:

1. The proponent's witness is a qualified medical expert.
2. The proponent's witness has examined the prospective witness.
3. The prospective witness has a mental disability.
4. The prospective witness is capable of giving an intelligible account of relevant events:
    a. The prospective witness has the capacity to observe;
    b. The prospective witness has the capacity to remember;
    c. The prospective witness has the capacity to relate.

The opposing party (the opponent), who is presenting its own expert evidence to challenge the competency of the prospective witness, seeks to demonstrate the following:

5. The opponent's witness is a qualified medical expert.
6. The opponent's witness has examined the prospective witness.
7. The prospective witness has a mental disability.
8. The mental disability interferes with one or more of the prospective witness's testimonial qualities such as perception or memory.

2.03.3 Sample foundation

The fact situation is a prosecution for assault causing bodily harm. The prosecution calls Mr Stephen Stone as a witness. Mr Stone has told the gardaí that he witnessed the assault; his window overlooks the park where the assault took place and he saw the accused attack the alleged victim. Defence counsel objects to any testimony by Mr Stone on the basis that Mr

Stone is not a competent witness. The prosecution has presented expert evidence in support of its claim that Mr Stone is competent. Defence counsel now calls Dr Raymond Rock, a psychiatrist based in London.

O. *(To the witness)* What is your name?
W. Raymond Rock.
O. Where do you live?
W. I live at 32 Riverside Close, in London.
O. What is your occupation? (5)
W. I am a physician.
O. Where are you licensed to practice medicine? (5)
W. In the United Kingdom.
O. When did you obtain your licence to practice? (5)
W. Approximately 10 years ago.
O. What medical school did you attend? (5)
W. University of London.
O. In what field of medicine do you specialise? (5)
W. Psychiatry.
O. What is the subject matter of your specialty? (5)
W. A psychiatrist studies the diseases and disorders of the mind.
O. What special training do you have in psychiatry? (5)
W. I spent three years as a resident in psychiatry at Birmingham Hospital.
O. What is your current professional position? (5)
W. I am a consultant in psychiatry at St. Philip's Hospital in London.
O. How long have you held that position? (5)
W. Three years.
O. Who is Stephen Stone? (6)
W. He is a man that I interviewed recently.
O. Why did you interview him? (6)
W. I was asked to do so by the defendant's solicitor.
O. When did this interview take place? (6)
W. Approximately three months ago.
O. How long did the interview last? (6)
W. About two hours.
O. What was Mr Stone's appearance at the time of the interview? (7)

W. It was rather unkempt. He was rather dirty.
O. What was his general attitude? (7)
W. At first, he seemed rather distant and detached. He became rather excited and angry whenever I tried to question him about certain subjects.
O. What were those subjects? (7)
W. Subjects like social interaction, being in public places, encounters with strangers and physical violence.
O. What, if anything, did he say during the interview? (7)
W. At first he just told me to keep my distance.
O. What did he say then? (7)
W. He said that this city was full of criminals. He said it was full of what he called 'men in black', meaning men in black clothing, carrying sticks. He said the streets weren't safe, and no one could be trusted. He said that as long as he could remember someone had tried to rob him or beat him up every time he went outside. He said that every bone in his body had been broken.
O. Did he say anything else? (7)
W. He asked if I was one of them. He asked if I was going to hurt him.
O. How would you characterise his statements? (7)
W. They were delusional. A delusion is a belief that a rational person would not entertain under the same circumstances. The person persists in the belief although all the evidence is to the contrary.
O. Why did he have this belief? (7)
W. He said that voices told him that the men in black were taking over the city. They told him that no one was safe and that he should not trust anyone.
O. Who were these voices? (7)
W. He did not know.
O. How would you characterise those statements? (7)
W. They are hallucinations; he has auditory experiences when in fact there is no voice or sound.
O. What did you do after you interviewed Mr Stone? (7)
W. I tried to gather his history.
O. What do you mean by 'his history'? (7)
W. The background of his illness. You trace the history of an illness through the years and its various stages.

O. How did you gather Mr Stone's history? (7)

W. I spoke with Mr Stone's general practitioner, Dr Pauline Pebble, and obtained copies of Mr Stone's medical files. I also spoke with Mr Stone's sister, Ms Sylvia Stone.

O. What is Mr Stone's background or history? (7)

W. He has been treated for mental illness for several years and was hospitalised for a period of four months in 2002. Evidently, he has made numerous complaints to the police about assaults against himself and against others, and in each case the investigation has shown that the complaint was groundless.

O. What, if any, diagnosis have you reached of Mr Stone's psychiatric condition? (7)

W. I would diagnose his condition as a schizophrenic reaction of the paranoid type.

O. What does that mean? (7)

W. A schizophrenic person has a form of split personality. He or she lives in two worlds – one the fantasy world, the other the world of reality. They have lost contact with reality to a severe extent. Mr Stone's disorder manifests itself in paranoid beliefs that other men are persecuting and constantly attacking him.

O. What leads you to this diagnosis? (7)

W. The irrational nature of his statements for one thing. I also considered his appearance and attitude. I attach particular importance to his delusions and hallucinations. His history confirms the diagnosis.

O. Dr Rock, in this case Mr Stone wants to testify about an assault he allegedly observed. What effect, if any, would his psychosis have on his ability to accurately observe an encounter between two men? (8)

W. The psychosis grossly interferes with that capacity. He is going to see things that did not actually happen – just as he hears voices when they are not there. Every encounter, particularly a physical encounter, tends to become an assault in his mind.

O. What effect, if any, would his psychosis have on his ability to accurately remember a physical encounter between two men that he had observed? (8)

W. It's going to severely distort the memory process. A psychosis of this magnitude is going to attack his abilities to perceive and remember. His purported recollections will be untrustworthy. In the process of remembering, he'll embellish the encounter.

O. Thank you, Dr Rock.

2.04 SPOUSE OF AN ACCUSED

2.04.1 The law

Historically, the spouse of an accused was not competent to testify at the trial of the accused. By virtue of the 'union of the person' between husband and wife, the spouse was viewed by the courts as indistinguishable from the accused. An exception was made in cases where the accused was charged with physical or sexual assault against the spouse; as the alleged victim of the crime, the spouse was deemed competent to testify for the prosecution. Statutory intervention came in the form of s 1 of the Criminal Justice (Evidence) Act 1924, which rendered the spouse a competent but not compellable witness for the accused. The modern rules governing the competence and compellability of the spouse of the accused are contained in Part IV of the Criminal Evidence Act 1992. A spouse, or a former spouse,[16] is now both a competent and compellable witness for the accused unless the spouse is jointly charged in the proceedings.[17] A spouse or former spouse is competent to testify for the prosecution[18] unless he or she is jointly charged in the proceedings.[19] A spouse or former spouse is not generally compellable at the behest of the prosecution; however, he or she may be compelled to testify for the prosecution in relation to certain sexual offences and offences involving violence as specified in the Act.[20] The spouse of an accused is competent to testify for a co-accused,[21] and is compellable at the behest of a co-accused in the same circumstances that he or she is compellable for the prosecution.[22]

16. Section 20 of the 1992 Act. A former spouse includes a person whose marriage to the accused has been the subject of a separation agreement, a judicial separation or a decree of divorce.

17. Sections 21 and 23 of the 1992 Act.

18. Section 21.

19. Section 25.

20. Section 22 as amended. The former spouse is compellable only in relation to the offences stated in s 22 and provided that the marriage was subsisting at the material time.

21. Section 21.

22. Section 24.

2.04.2 Elements of the foundation

The fact scenario below involves a criminal proceeding in which the prosecution is seeking to compel the spouse of the accused to testify. The prosecution must show the following:

1. The witness spouse is married to the accused.
2. The offence with which the accused is charged is an offence specified in s 22 of the CEA 1992 as amended.
3. The alleged victim of the offence is the spouse, a child of the spouse or the accused, or a person under 18 years.

2.04.3 Sample foundation

Mr Noel Navy is charged with two counts of assault. The indictment first alleges that on 1 January 2007, the accused assaulted his wife, Mrs Nuala Navy. The prosecution (the proponent) has called Nuala Navy to the stand.

O. Judge, I object to any testimony by this witness on the ground that she is not a compellable witness for the prosecution.

J. Is the witness present in court?

O. Yes, she is.

J. *(To the witness)* Mrs Nuala Navy? Could you step forward please?

P. Judge, the witness may be compelled to testify at the instance of the prosecution under s 22 of the Criminal Evidence Act 1992. May I put some preliminary questions to the witness to establish this?

J. You may. *(To the witness)* Mrs Navy, counsel for the prosecution will now ask you some questions so that I can determine whether you should testify in these proceedings. Please answer those questions.

P. Mrs Navy, isn't it true that, on 30 August 2004, you married Mr Noel Navy? (1)

W. Yes.

P. Isn't it also true that Noel Navy is the accused in this case? (1)

W. Yes.

P. Isn't it correct that there have been no judicial separation or divorce proceedings since the marriage? (1)

W. Yes.

P. Isn't it also the case that there have been no annulment proceedings since the marriage? (1)

W. Yes.

P. Mrs Navy, isn't it correct that your husband, Noel Navy, is charged with committing an assault? (2)

W. Yes.

P. And isn't it true that you are the person who has been named as the victim of the assault? (3)

W. Yes.

P. Thank you Mrs. Navy. Judge, the witness's answers demonstrate that she is a compellable witness for the prosecution. She is married to the accused and is herself named as the alleged victim of a violent offence.

J. I agree. You may proceed with the examination-in-chief.

THE EXAMINATION OF WITNESSES

2.05 BACKGROUND

Witnesses play a central role in the conduct of civil and criminal trials as the primary source of the information on which courts base their decisions. In our adversarial system of trial, counsel do not argue a case in the literal sense before the finder of fact; instead, counsel elicit relevant testimony from individuals with firsthand knowledge of the matters at issue.[23] Typically, the witness presents the court with an account of facts that are in dispute although sometimes the function of the witness is limited to introducing and authenticating an independent item of evidence such as a document. For lawyers preparing for settlement and/or trial, identifying potential witnesses and securing an account of their evidence constitute vital preliminary steps. Where a case goes to trial, the witness may be called to testify in court: the witness will be called to the stand, administered with the oath or affirmation[24] and then questioned by counsel. In a limited range of

23. It is only in opening the case and in closing argument that counsel addresses the finder of fact directly on the merits of the case.

24. Oaths Acts 1888, c 46, and 1909, c 39; Ord 39, r 18 of the Rules of the Superior Courts as amended. There is statutory authority for the admission of unsworn evidence in certain circumstances. See eg ss 27(1) and (3) of the CEA 1992 and ss 28(1) and (3) of the CA 1997 (evidence of children and persons with a mental handicap).

specified circumstances, the need for an in-court appearance may be dispensed with and the witness permitted to testify via live video link from a location outside the courtroom.[25] Exceptionally, the evidence of a witness may be admitted in the form of an affidavit[26] or written statement without the witness participating in the oral proceedings at all. However, the presentation of live testimony in court remains the overwhelming preference of the law; without it, the other parties may not have the opportunity to test the evidence through cross-examination and the finder of fact may not have the benefit of observing the demeanour of the witness firsthand.

The examination of a witness in court unfolds in three stages. First, the party who has called the witness to testify conducts examination-in-chief. Counsel puts a series of questions to the witness with the objective of securing a factual account that will support the party's cause. Next, counsel for the other party (or parties) will be given an opportunity to cross-examine the witness. Finally, after cross-examination, counsel representing the party who called the witness may re-examine the witness.

2.06 LAYING A FOUNDATION DURING EXAMINATION-IN-CHIEF

2.06.1 The law

Before presenting evidence during examination-in-chief, examining counsel should lay a foundation, adhering to the cardinal rules of simplicity and brevity discussed in **1.03** above. A trial judge is not strictly bound by the substantive rules of evidence when determining a preliminary question concerning the admissibility of an item of evidence.[27] Suppose that a party is offering a witness's statement made prior to trial under an exception to the rule against hearsay. Part of the foundation for the exception to the rule against hearsay is proof that the witness is unavailable at trial. Because the

---

25. See eg s 13 of the CEA 1992 (witnesses including children testifying in relation to certain sexual and violent offences); s 29 of the CEA 1992 (witnesses located outside the State); s 39 of the CJA 1999 (intimidated witnesses).

26. Order 40, r 1 of the Rules of the Superior Courts provides that evidence may be given by affidavit but that the court may order the attendance in court of the person making the affidavit for purposes of cross-examination.

27. *DPP v Cash* [2007] IEHC 108 (28 March 2007).

judge is not constrained by the rule against hearsay when considering the preliminary question of whether the witness is unavailable, the proponent could lay the necessary foundation by asking a member of the gardaí on the witness stand to relate a third party's statement that the witness said she was moving to Australia. If the proponent attempted to present the third party's statement to the jury during the trial, the statement would be inadmissible hearsay; the third party was outside the courtroom when he or she made the statement and the proponent would be offering the statement for the truth of the matter asserted. However, the rule against hearsay does not strictly constrain the judge's determination of the preliminary question.

The contours of examination-in-chief are circumscribed by various rules of which counsel should be aware.[28] The witness may only testify as to facts of which he or she has personal, firsthand knowledge, ie facts which the witness has seen, heard or otherwise perceived.[29] Furthermore, the witness must limit his or her testimony to facts as opposed to inferences that may be drawn from facts or the witness's opinions or beliefs.[30] Counsel may not put leading questions to the witness whether in the form of questions that suggest the desired answer or questions that assume the existence of facts in dispute.[31] Nor may counsel generally ask the witness about any statement made on a previous occasion that is consistent with his or her testimony at

28. Most of these rules also apply during re-examination.

29. Information which the witness has acquired secondhand will generally be caught by the rule against hearsay. See **Chapter 6**.

30. The rule against opinion evidence is subject to significant exceptions: where the witness is an expert, where the witness is authorised by statute to offer an opinion and where fact and opinion are seemingly inseparable. See **Chapter 4**.

31. Since the witness is expected to provide favourable testimony during examination-in-chief, the danger is that the witness will probably follow counsel's lead. Suppose that the plaintiff is suing the defendant for personal injuries arising out of a car accident. The plaintiff alleges that the defendant was speeding. The plaintiff's brother was a witness to the accident and is called by the plaintiff to testify. Counsel would be leading the witness if he or she were to ask, 'Isn't it true that the defendant was travelling at 100 kilometres per hour?' There is a serious risk that the witness, the plaintiff's brother, will simply follow counsel's lead rather than attempt to testify accurately. A non-leading question, such as, 'In your opinion, what was the defendant's speed?' would be more appropriate. The ban on leading questions during examination-in-chief is not absolute. Thus, counsel may lead the witness in relation to preliminary matters such as the witness's occupation and the setting of the scene.

trial.[32] The witness may refresh his or her memory by referring to a note made contemporaneously with the events at issue in the proceedings.[33] If a witness gives testimony unfavourable to the party who has called the witness, counsel may attempt to repair the damage by calling other witnesses. Counsel may not attempt to discredit the witness unless the judge determines that the witness is hostile.[34]

2.06.2 Practical matters and sample foundation

Counsel should ensure that the substantive rules of evidence are met even where it is not strictly required. Even if the law allows a party to disregard those rules when laying an evidentiary foundation, such action may prompt an objection from an opposing party. Examination-in-chief provides an opportunity for the witness to tell his or her story. The ideal examination-in-chief is a flowing, uninterrupted exchange between counsel and witness, free from the distraction of objections. Every time counsel disregards a substantive evidentiary rule when putting foundational questions to the witness, he or she runs the risk that the opponent will interrupt with an objection.

Similarly, counsel should refrain from using leading questions during examination-in-chief again so as to reduce the risk that the examination will be interrupted by an objection. A further practical consideration against the

32. The rule against narrative, as it is known, is subject to exceptions the most notable of which are the exception in relation to a pre-trial identification of the accused (see eg *DPP v Cahill and Costello* [2001] 3 IR 494; *AG v Casey (No 2)* [1963] IR 33) and the doctrine of fresh complaint (see eg *DPP v MA* [2002] 2 IR 601; *DPP v Brophy* [1992] ILRM 709).

33. *DPP v Clifford* [2002] 4 IR 398; *Northern Banking Co v Carpenter* [1931] IR 268; *Malahide v Cusack* [1864] 17 IR CLR 213.

34. Where the judge has determined that the witness is hostile, counsel representing the party who has called the witness may conduct examination-in-chief in the manner of cross-examination. One way in which counsel may seek to contradict the witness is by showing that the witness made a statement on a previous occasion that is inconsistent with his or her present testimony. The procedure for challenging a hostile witness with a previous inconsistent statement was set down in s 3 of CPA 1865, and the judgment of the Court of Criminal Appeal in *AG v Taylor* [1974] 1 IR 97. Part III of the CJA 2006 makes more radical provision for the admission into evidence of the previous statement of a witness who is unco-operative at trial. See **6.09**.

use of leading questions is the need to provide a witness with sufficient opportunity to speak. Questions which lend themselves to 'yes' or 'no' answers may unduly restrict the witness and leave the judge and jury with the impression that counsel is putting words in the witness's mouth. Astute jurors may even infer that counsel lacks faith in the witness and, consequently, discount the witness's credibility. If the witness projects honesty and intelligence, counsel should capitalise on those strengths by asking open-ended, non-leading questions.

A useful rule of thumb to avoid leading a witness is to begin as many questions as possible with the words: 'who,' 'what,' 'which,' 'when,' 'how' and 'why.' Clearly, some variation in the phrasing of questions is desirable; beginning *every* sentence with one of these words could make examination-in-chief annoyingly monotonous. When eliciting background information about the witness, counsel may prefer imperative to interrogatory sentences, eg 'Please tell the court where you work.' In order to highlight the subdivisions of examination-in-chief, counsel may employ an occasional declarative sentence, eg 'Now I would like to ask you some questions about what happened at the hospital.' Of course, the ban on leading questions is not absolute and, in practice, there are times when the use of gently leading questions will be permitted.

The following hypothetical scenario is based on a relatively straightforward negligence claim arising out of a road traffic accident that took place on 9 February 2007. The plaintiff, Mr Ben Blue, alleges that the defendant, Ms Greta Green, was negligent and that this caused the collision. No personal injuries were suffered, and the claim is for compensation for damage to the plaintiff's vehicle, loss of use of the vehicle whilst it was being repaired and related loss of earnings. Mr Blue takes the stand to testify on his own behalf and is examined-in-chief by his counsel. The purpose of the examination in chief is, broadly speaking, to elicit evidence that the plaintiff sustained the loss and damage complained of as a result of the defendant's breach of duty.

P. What is your name?

W. Ben Blue.

P. I think you are thirty years of age, is that correct?

W. That's correct.

P. Do you drive?

W. Yes, I have been driving for over ten years.

P. What is your occupation?

W. I'm self-employed; I'm a painter and decorator.

P. Apart from the collision that is the subject matter of this case, have you ever been involved in any collision or accident in a car?

W. Never.

P. Mr Blue, do you recall the events of the morning of Friday, 9 February 2007?

W. Yes, I do.

P. Please tell the court what you were doing on that day.

W. I was driving to a job I had to do in a house in Notown in Dublin. I set off in my car at about 8:30 am.

P. Where were you coming from?

W. From Anytown, where I live.

P. What were the weather conditions like?

W. It was a bright, dry day.

P. Did anything unusual happen during your journey?

W. On Somewhere Street a green Opel Corsa crashed into my vehicle.

P. I see. Just explain for the judge the scene on Somewhere Street, immediately prior to the collision.

W. The street was empty, there were no other cars except the green Opel Corsa.

P. Is Somewhere Street well known to you, Mr Blue?

W. Yes, very well known to me. I have driven down it probably hundreds of times.

P. Is it a one-way street?

W. Yes.

P. And where was this green Opel Corsa in relation to your car?

W. It was stationary, on the left-hand side of the road as I drove up behind it.

P. Did you notice anything unusual about that car?

W. Yes, I specifically recall that the hazard lights were on.

P. What speed were you travelling at?

W. Roughly 35 kms per hour.

P. Is there a designated speed limit in that area?

W. It's a 40 km per hour zone.

P. Did you drive past the green Opel Corsa?

W. I attempted to but suddenly from nowhere that car swung into me without notice.

P. Just explain to the judge exactly how the impact occurred, Mr Blue.
W. Basically the driver of the green Opel Corsa just turned to the right and ran straight into the front left-hand side of my car.
P. Did you feel the impact?
W. Yeah, I was a little bit shaken.
P. What happened next?
W. We both stepped out of our vehicles.
P. Did you talk to the driver of the other vehicle?
W. Not really, she seemed pretty distressed. She was very apologetic and kept saying sorry.
P. Why do you think she said that?
W. I think she knew that she was at fault and she was genuinely sorry.
P. Did you exchange insurance details at that point?
W. Yes.
P. Did you report the matter to the gardaí?
W. Yes, I walked down to Somewhere Street Garda Station to report the accident.
P. Thank you very much Mr Blue.

2.07 LAYING A FOUNDATION ON CROSS-EXAMINATION

2.07.1 In general

Where one party calls a witness to give evidence, any other party to the proceedings has the right to test that evidence by cross-examining the witness and by presenting its own independent evidence.[35] Cross-examination has been characterised as 'the greatest legal engine ever invented for the discovery of truth'[36] and 'an essential ingredient in the concept of fair procedures'.[37] Generally, any person who has presented evidence to the court, whether in the form of live testimony or an affidavit or other sworn statement, may be cross-examined by any other party or parties. As Fennelly J stated in *DPP v Kelly*: 'It is axiomatic that every witness must submit himself to the rigours of cross-examination, to having

35. *DPP v Kelly* [2006] 3 IR 115; *Re Haughey* [1971] IR 217.
36. Wigmore, *Evidence* (3rd edn, Little Brown) vol V, p 29.
37. *Donnelly v Ireland* [1998] 1 IR 321 at (*per* Hamilton CJ).

his evidence questioned, tested, challenged and contradicted and his credit impeached.'[38] However, a criminal defendant may not be compelled to testify; consequently, if a criminal defendant elects not to take the stand and testify in his own defence, he or she may not be cross-examined by the prosecution or any co-defendant.[39]

The general rules for laying a foundation for the introduction of evidence extend to cross-examination. The trial judge may be reluctant to permit cross-examining counsel to introduce an item of evidence on the condition that the foundational proof for its admissibility will be provided at a later point in the examination. The witness is often hostile to cross-examining counsel and the judge is more sceptical of counsel's assurance that, ultimately, the witness will provide the necessary, favourable testimony. Simplicity and brevity, the guiding norms of examination-in-chief, apply with even greater force during cross-examination. Counsel should strive to frame questions that are clear and short so that the witness can neither plead a lack of understanding nor strain to misinterpret a question. In addition to knowing the general rules for laying foundations, counsel must be familiar with several special rules that apply during cross-examination.

2.07.2 Legal rules

Counsel seeks in cross-examination to test the credibility of the witness and the veracity of the testimony given during examination-in-chief and, at the same time, to procure from the witness any facts that may assist his or her party's case. As Hardiman J observed in *Maguire v Ardagh*: 'Cross-examination is a special skill and usually an acquired one, of which a thorough knowledge of the facts of a particular case is merely the foundation.'[40] The scope of cross-examination is not limited to matters raised during examination-in-chief and may extend to any matter that is material to the proceedings. Since the witness is frequently averse to cross-examining counsel, the law permits leading questions on cross-examination,

---

38. [2006] 3 IR 115 at 136.

39. Nevertheless, evidence of a previous statement or admission made by the accused and relevant to the proceedings may be offered by the prosecution or any co-accused. Where the accused takes the stand and testifies in his or her own defence, any subsequent cross-examination is governed by the special rules laid down in s 1 of the CJ(E)A 1924.

40. [2002] 1 IR 385 at 705. In that case, the Supreme Court confirmed the constitutional pedigree of the right to cross-examine. See also *O'Callaghan v Mahon* [2006] 2 IR 32; *DPP v Kelly* [2006] 3 IR 115.

although counsel should refrain from questions that are unduly argumentative. The trial judge has a discretion to exclude questions which he or she considers to be improper, oppressive or irrelevant.[41]

One of the ways in which counsel may challenge the credibility of the witness is by revealing any errors or inconsistencies in the witness's testimony. Indeed, counsel may go further and seek to contradict the witness by establishing that the witness made a statement on a previous occasion which is inconsistent with his or her testimony at trial.[42] In proceedings arising out of a road traffic accident, assume that the witness testifies during examination-in-chief that the defendant's car was travelling at 100 kilometres an hour just before the collision. Cross-examining counsel may legitimately attempt to force the witness to concede the fact of a prior inconsistent statement. Counsel might ask in cross-examination: 'Isn't it true that you told your neighbour, Mrs Laura Lavender, at a party last Sunday that the defendant's car was travelling within the speed limit of 60 kilometres per hour?'

2.07.3 Practical matters and sample foundation

The need for cross-examining counsel to exercise restraint during cross-examination may be driven by practical as well as legal considerations. For example, an excessively aggressive or argumentative line of questioning may prompt a heated exchange between counsel and the witness and, in the context of a jury trial, may cause the lay jurors to sympathise with the lay witness. Unless the witness has a particularly abrasive personality, provoking an argument with the witness may be counterproductive. For example, if counsel appears to dominate the exchange, the jurors may infer that counsel does not want the witness to tell the whole truth. Conversely, if the witness appears to dominate, the jurors may conclude that counsel is diffident – perhaps because he or she lacks faith in his or her case.

As a general proposition, counsel should use leading questions on cross-examination. The skilful use of leading, non-argumentative questions may enable cross-examining counsel to virtually testify for the witness.

41. *DPP v DO* [2006] 2 ILRM 61; *O'Broin v Ruane* [1989] IR 214. Any answers given in cross-examination on collateral matters are generally deemed to be final. Thus, cross-examining counsel may not call additional evidence to contradict the witness. See *AG v Hitchcock* (1847) 1 Exch 91.

42. Sections 4–5 of CPA 1865; *DPP v McArdle* (13 October 2003, unreported) CCA.

Questions may be prefaced with phrases such as: 'Isn't it true …?' or 'Isn't it correct?', which enable counsel to exert control over the witness's testimony. For example, if counsel wishes to refer to a prior inconsistent statement, he or she might ask: 'Isn't it the case that, immediately after the altercation, you told the garda officer that the laneway was so dark that you could not identify your attacker?' The same effect may be achieved by appending interrogatory phrases (eg 'Isn't that true?' or 'Isn't that the case?') to the end of declarative statements. Thus, as an alternative, counsel might ask: 'Immediately after the altercation, you told the garda officer that the laneway was so dark that you could not identify your attacker. Isn't that the case?' Ordinarily, counsel should avoid giving the witness any opening, such as the opportunity to explain provided by the question, 'Why?' Of course, there may be occasions when counsel may wish to use non-leading questions. For example, if counsel suspects that an adverse witness has memorised his or her testimony, counsel may choose to pose an open-ended, non-leading question that will give the witness another opportunity to repeat the story verbatim. Counsel may then argue in closing argument that the jury heard a rehearsed script rather than live testimony. In other instances, if counsel is confident that the topic is safe, gently leading questions may be used, beginning with such words as 'Is,' 'Was' or 'Did.'

Finally, it is important to remember that ordinarily counsel's demeanour and tone should be cordial even when posing narrowly phrased, leading questions. Some measure of co-operation on the part of the witness is required if counsel is to elicit helpful concessions on cross-examination. If counsel's demeanour is combative or aggressive, the witness is likely to put up his or her defences, making it very difficult for counsel to procure favourable information. Exceptionally, counsel may choose to make a show of righteous indignation at an opposing witness caught in an obvious lie; in contrast, when counsel is using an opposing witness to lay an evidentiary foundation, the wisest course of action is to be cordial and polite. If a witness's cooperation is required in laying the foundation, that cooperation should be secured before any attack is made on the witness.

The following is a continuation of the fact scenario set out at **2.06** above regarding the collision that took place on Somewhere Street. The plaintiff, Mr Ben Blue, is now being cross-examined by counsel for the defendant, Ms Greta Green. Broadly speaking, counsel for the defendant will aim to impeach Mr Blue's credibility by highlighting that Mr Blue's testimony on examination-in-chief was misleading and deficient in a number of important respects. This is done with a view to ultimately inviting the judge, as finder of fact, to conclude that the accident was caused by the careless driving of the plaintiff, and not by an action or omission of the defendant.

P. Mr Blue, you said in your direct evidence that you've been driving for over ten years, correct?
W. Correct.
P. But you don't have a full driving licence, do you?
W. No, I'm still on a provisional licence.
P. And did you not think that was something that should have been mentioned to the judge in your direct evidence?
W. I just didn't think of mentioning it.
P. Why is it that after ten years of driving you still don't have a full licence?
Have you done your driving test, Mr Blue?
W I've done the test twice but failed it both times.
P. I see. So you're in court suing the defendant after a road traffic accident and you 'didn't think of mentioning' to the judge that you're a learner driver.
W. Yeah.
P. Incidentally, why didn't you have L plates on your vehicle on 10 February 2007?
W. I must have forgot to put them up.
P. I want to suggest to you Mr Blue that your account of the collision on 10 February 2007 is entirely false.
W It isn't.
P I suggest that the collision was caused by you endeavouring to execute a highly dangerous overtaking manoeuvre.
W. I wasn't; it happened just as I've said.
Q. Ms Green will give evidence presently, Mr Blue, and it will be her evidence that she duly indicated and moved out from the kerb, and it was at that point that you shot up on her outside giving her no chance to avoid colliding with your vehicle. What do you say to that?
W. That's not true.
Q. Ms Green will also say that her hazard lights were never on. You've invented that to try and make your story more plausible, haven't you?
W. No, her hazard lights were definitely on.
P. I want to suggest to you that immediately prior to the collision you were talking on your mobile phone.

W. I wasn't. I never use my phone in the car.

P. Ms Green will say that she saw you talking on the phone straight after the collision, and that when you got of your vehicle you were just finishing off a phone call.

W. I completely deny that, it's not true.

P. Ms Green will also deny that she ever said sorry or said anything from which you might understand that she thought she was at fault. I put it to you that your account of the conversation that took place is false.

W. It's the truth.

P. I put it to you, Mr Blue, that this accident was caused by your reckless driving.

W. I reject that.

SPECIAL MEASURES

2.08 BACKGROUND

Statutory changes in the rules governing the competence and compellability of witnesses reflect evolving attitudes regarding the role of the witness in the trial process and the capacities required to undertake that role. A further motivation for reform has been increased recognition that testifying in court may be a daunting, traumatising experience for particularly vulnerable categories of witness. The application of technology to legal proceedings has led to the adoption of certain special measures designed to address these concerns. Legislation permits certain witnesses to give evidence by live television link from a location outside the courtroom. For example, this facility may be extended to victims of sexual and violent offences,[43] children,[44] persons who are in fear or subject to intimidation,[45] and persons situated outside the State.[46] Other special measures include the giving of evidence through intermediaries,[47] and removal of the requirement that the witness identify the accused at a criminal trial.[48]

43. Section 13(1) of CEA 1992.
44. Section 13(1)(a) of the 1992 Act and s 21(1) of the CA 1997.
45. Section 39 of the CJA 1999.
46. Section 29(1) of the 1992 Act as amended.
47. See eg s 14(1) of the 1992 Act.
48. See eg s 18 of the 1992 Act.

2.09 EVIDENCE BY VIDEO LINK

2.09.1 The law

Section 13(1) of the Criminal Evidence Act 1992 makes provision for a witness to give evidence via a live television link in proceedings for violent or sexual offences. In the case of a child witness, the use of a live television link is permissible 'unless the court sees good reason to the contrary'.[49] Where the witness is 18 years or over, the party tendering the witness must apply to the court for permission to use a live television link.[50] The legislation does not specify the grounds on which the court might grant such permission but one likely factor is the risk that the witness will suffer psychological trauma if required to testify in court.[51] One way in which a party may satisfy the court of the need for a live television link is through the use of expert medical testimony.

2.09.2 Elements of the foundation

The party seeking the leave of the court should demonstrate the following:

1. The witness is a qualified medical expert.
2. The witness has examined the prospective witness.
3. The prospective witness is likely to suffer trauma if forced to testify in open court.

2.09.3 Sample foundation

The fact scenario is a prosecution for rape. The prosecution allege that Mr Henry Holly assaulted and raped his neighbour, Mrs Irene Ivy, in her house in the early hours of a Sunday morning. The prospective witness is the victim's 19-year old daughter, Ms Isabelle Ivy, who was present upstairs in the house at the material time. The prosecution has made a pre-trial application for leave to allow the prospective witness to testify via live television link. The application is supported by the following affidavit of a psychologist, Dr Bartholomew Berry.

49. Section 13(1)(a) of the 1992 Act.

50. Section 13(1)(b) of the 1992 Act.

51. McGrath, *Evidence* (Thomson Round Hall, 2005) para 3.130.

AFFIDAVIT OF BARTHOLOMEW BERRY

I, Bartholomew Berry, Consultant Psychologist, of Broad Street, Suburbia, aged eighteen years and upwards, MAKE OATH, and say as follows:

1. I am a consultant psychologist employed at St Jude's Hospital, Dublin, and I also have a private consultancy practice. I say that I hold degrees in psychology from The National University, and the International University. I qualified as a clinical psychologist in 2000, and have been working as a consultant in St Jude's Hospital since September 2001.
2. I say that I have given evidence before the courts of Ireland on a number of occasions, and that I have testified in trials in the Central Criminal Court on seven occasions.
3. I beg to refer to the proceedings entitled *DPP v Henry Holly*, Record No 2008 1234, which proceedings I understand are currently before this Honourable Court. I make this affidavit for the purposes of outlining to this Honourable Court the professional view that I have arrived at in light of consultations that I have conducted with the daughter of the Complainant in this case, Ms Isabelle Ivy, and specifically, regarding the psychological impact that giving evidence in the abovementioned proceedings may have on Ms Ivy.
4. I say that I first met with Ms Ivy on 21 January 2008, in a consultation room at St Jude's hospital. Ms Ivy had been referred to me by her General Practitioner, Dr Michael Mistletoe. I say that this was to be the first of three lengthy consultations that I had with Ms Ivy.
5. I say that I found Ms Ivy to be a highly articulate and intelligent young woman. It was plain to me, however, that she has undergone a degree of psychological trauma in recent times, and this has caused her to have a nervous and somewhat fragile mental disposition. In particular, she became visibly distressed and very emotional when I raised the subject of her mother having been assaulted and raped in the family home.
6. I say that it was immediately obvious to me that the circumstances of the assault and rape of the Complainant had caused considerable angst, stress and psychological trauma to Ms Ivy. It became clear to me that Ms Ivy has been preoccupied with this vicious attack on her mother since the day of its occurrence, and that Ms Ivy's trauma in

this regard has been compounded by the prospect that she will have to give evidence at the trial of the accused in the Central Criminal Court.

7. I say that the prospect of having to give evidence in open court was a source of grave concern to Ms Ivy. On no less than three occasions she broke down when I discussed this prospect with her. She stated that she was 'petrified' at the prospect of having to give evidence in court, and that she would not be able to cope. Ms. Ivy on one occasion became uncontrollably distressed at the prospect of having to give evidence in open court where the accused would be present.
8. I say and believe that, owing to the ongoing psychological trauma being experienced by Ms Ivy, it would potentially have a very bad effect on her psychological well-being if she was required to give evidence in open court. I say and believe that it would be greatly in Ms Ivy's interests if she was permitted to give evidence via live television link, as provided for in the Criminal Evidence Act 1992. I say and believe that this would greatly lessen the likelihood of Ms Ivy experiencing further and/or aggravated psycholigical trauma.

SWORN by the said A Psychologist this day of 2008

Before me

Practising Solicitor/Commissioner for Oaths

and I know the deponent.

CREDIBILITY AND CHARACTER

2.10 CREDIBILITY

After a witness has taken the stand and been administered with the oath, counsel representing the party calling the witness immediately begins examination-in-chief. As soon as the witness answers the first question in examination-in-chief, his or her credibility becomes an issue in the case.

The party tendering the witness naturally wants to build up the witness's credibility in the eyes of the finder of fact, whereas the opposing party or parties want to undermine that credibility. The general common law rule is that a party may not bolster the credibility of his or her own witness until such time as the witness's credibility has been challenged by an opposing party. In other words, a party generally should not anticipate an attack on the witness's credibility by building it up during examination-in-chief. The rationale is the need to ensure that the attention of the finder of fact, particularly a jury, is focused principally on the factual issues in the case. Where the credibility of the witness is attacked in cross-examination, the party who called the witness may attempt to repair the damage in re-examination. A challenge to the credibility of a witness may emerge in a context other than cross-examination; the opposite side may present extrinsic evidence, such as the testimony of other witnesses, to undermine the credibility of the witness. Similarly, rehabilitation of the credibility of the witness may be sought through the testimony of other witnesses.

The next two subsections concern certain exceptions to the general common law rule, ie instances in which a party is permitted to bolster the credibility of the witness during examination-in-chief.

2.11 PRIOR IDENTIFICATION

2.11.1 The law

If a witness makes an in-court identification of a criminal defendant, the party tendering the witness must generally prove that the witness identified the same person in a pre-trial procedure.[52] The prior identification is admitted as substantive evidence that the present identification is correct. However, it also enhances the witness's credibility by strengthening the inference that the witness is consistent. The preferred procedure is a formal identity parade conducted at a garda station at which the suspect lines up alongside seven or eight individuals of similar age, height, physical appearance and dress.[53] In exceptional circumstances, the courts will accept

52. *R v Christie* [1914] AC 545. Exceptionally, a court will permit a dock identification even where it was not preceded by a valid pre-trial identification. See eg *DPP v Cooney* [1998] 1 ILRM 321.

53. There are safeguards associated with a procedure of this kind such as supervision by a garda not directly involved in the investigation, prior notice for the suspect, the right to refuse to participate or to object to an aspect of the procedure, and the right to the presence of a legal representative. See *DPP v Marley* [1985] ILRM 17.

evidence of informal identifications that conform to the basic guarantee of fair procedures.[54] In a jury trial, the trial judge must caution the jury about the dangers associated with visual identification evidence.[55] The propriety of identification procedures and the proper use of identification evidence at trial turns in large measure on the terms in which the trial judge cautions the jury.[56]

2.11.2 Elements of the foundation

The elements of the foundation include the following:

1. The witness has already made an in-court identification of the person.
2. The witness had an opportunity to observe the person in advance of the trial.
3. The witness had an adequate opportunity to observe the person.
4. The pre-trial identification procedure was conducted in a fair manner.
5. During the pre-trial procedure, the witness identified the same person.

2.11.3 Sample foundation

The hypothetical fact scenario is a criminal prosecution for careless driving causing death. The prosecution calls a witness, Ms Catherine Cup, who is prepared to testify that the accused, Mr Sam Saucer, was the driver of the car that knocked down a pedestrian, Ms Jill Jug. She is also ready to testify that she identified the accused in a formal identification parade at the local garda station shortly after the accident. The witness has already described the accident which occurred at noon. The prosecution is the proponent.

P. What did the car do after it struck Ms Jug?

W. It stopped a short distance away.

---

54. See eg *DPP v Allen* (18 December 2003, unreported) CCA (photograph from video surveillance camera); *DPP v Cahill & Costello* [2001] 3 IR 494 (informal parade); *DPP v Rapple* [1999] 1 ILRM 113 (photograph); *DPP v O'Reilly* [1990] 2 IR 415 (informal parade).

55. *AG Casey (No 2)* [1963] IR 33.

56. See eg *DPP v Christo* [2005] IECCA 3 (31 January 2005); *DPP v O'Toole* (26 May 2003, unreported) CCA.

P. Who was driving that car? (1)
W. The defendant, Mr Saucer.
P. Where is he sitting? (1)
W. (*Pointing to the defendant)* Over there.
P. Judge, may the record reflect that the witness has identified the defendant, Sam Saucer? (1)
J. It will so reflect.
P. Ms Cup, how many times have you seen the defendant? (2)
W. Three times.
P. What were those occasions? (2)
W. Well, I saw him at the scene of the accident, today in court and on one other occasion.
P. What was that other occasion? (2)
W. It was at an identity parade, a line-up, at the garda station.
P. When did this identity parade occur? (2)
W. It was about 4:00 pm on the afternoon of the accident.
P. Where did the gardaí conduct this identity parade?
W. It was in a big room off the entrance to the station.
P. How was the lighting in the room? (3)
W. It was fine.
P. How close were you to the men participating in the identity parade? (3)
W. I was about ten feet away.
P. In what direction were you facing? (3)
W. I was facing straight ahead. I was looking at the men in the line-up.
P. How long did the gardaí permit you to observe the men? (3)
W. As long as I wanted. But I didn't need much time.
P. How many men were in the identity parade? (4)
W. There were six.
P. How were they dressed? (4)
W. They were all wearing dark clothes.
P. How tall were they? (4)
W. They were roughly the same height, about five feet ten inches.
P. What, if anything, did the gardaí say about the men in the parade? (4)

W. They didn't say anything. They just brought me into the room and asked me if I recognised anyone.

P. What did the men do while you were observing them? (4)

W. Nothing. They just stood there.

P. What happened after the identity parade? (5)

W. The police asked me if I recognised the driver of the car in the parade.

P. What did you say? (5)

W. I told them that I did.

P. Whom did you identify? (5)

W. *(Pointing)* The defendant, Sam Saucer, the same person I just pointed out, over there.

2.12 FRESH COMPLAINT

2.12.1 The law

Another exception to the norm against bolstering the credibility of a witness is the doctrine of fresh complaint, which applies in prosecutions for rape or sexual assault.[57] The underlying assumption is that the victim of this type of offence is likely to make a report or complaint about the offence as soon as is reasonably practical after the event.[58] The fact or existence of a fresh complaint tends to strengthen the inference that the complainant is being consistent and truthful at trial. Moreover, there is a particular need for evidence of credibility in prosecutions for sexual offences; there are rarely eyewitnesses to the event, and the trial often becomes a contest between the opposing evidence of the complainant and the accused.

The evidence admitted under this doctrine is not restricted to proof of the fact of the complaint, ie that the victim made a complaint about a certain type of offence and identified a certain person as the perpetrator. The particulars of the complaint may also be proved.[59] However, the proponent must treat the evidence solely as evidence going to credibility and not as substantive evidence that the accused committed the offence. The defence is entitled to have the trial judge instruct the jury to that effect; the judge tells

57. *DPP v Brophy* [1992] ILRM 709.

58. [1992] ILRM 709; *DPP v DR* [1998] 2 IR 106.

59. *DPP v Brophy* [1992] ILRM 709.

the jury that they may consider the evidence of the complaint solely for the limited purpose of determining the witness's consistency and, consequently, his or her credibility.[60]

2.12.2 Elements of the foundation

The foundation for the admission of the complaint would include the following elements:

1. The complainant made a complaint to the authorities or to a person whom he or she encountered after the event.
2. The complainant made the complaint as speedily as could reasonably be expected.
3. The complaint was voluntary.
4. The complaint stated that the complainant was the victim of an offence.
5. The complaint identified the alleged perpetrator of the offence.

2.12.3 Sample foundation

The fact scenario is a criminal prosecution for rape. The victim, Ms Sarah Salmon, is testifying for the prosecution and is on the stand during examination-in-chief. She has already testified that the accused, Mr Tommy Trout, drove her to a remote area, raped her, and then drove off leaving her on the side of the road.

P. What did you do after the accused drove off?

W. I started running down the road. I was afraid he'd come back and I wanted to get to safety.

P. What, if anything, happened while you were running down the road?

W. I ran into the path of a fellow driving a jeep.

P. Who was this person? (1)

W. He told me that his name was Bob Bream.

P. How long was it after the assault that you met Mr Bream? (2)

W. About 10 minutes. I hadn't run very far before I met him.

---

60. *DPP v Gavin* [2000] 4 IR 557; *DPP v MA* [2002] 2 IR 601.

P. What, if anything, happened after you met Mr Bream? (1), (2), (3)

W. I told him everything that had happened. Then he gave me a lift back to town and took me to the hospital.

P. Precisely what did you tell him? (3), (4)

W. I said that I had just been raped in a car just up the road.

P. Who did you say raped you? (5)

W. I said it was the accused, Tommy Trout.

2.13 CONTRADICTION BY ANOTHER WITNESS

2.13.1 The law

Opposing counsel may challenge the credibility of a witness by proving that any fact to which he or she testified is false. This is done by calling a second witness who will provide contradictory testimony. The effect of the second witness's testimony is indirect and inferential: if the second witness is correct, the first witness must be lying or mistaken. The extent to which the opponent can contradict a witness in this way is limited by the common law relating to collateral facts. Courts will generally only allow the contradictory evidence where it relates to a central aspect of the witness's account.

2.13.2 Sample foundation

Suppose that a traffic accident occurred in a rural area. During examination-in-chief, Witness No 1, who has been called by the plaintiff, testifies that he was walking near the junction where the accident occurred. He testifies that there is a large, red barn at the junction. During the presentation of the defendant's case, the defendant calls Witness No 2, a farmer who lives in the area. The farmer testifies that the fields near the junction are vacant and that the nearest red barn is two miles away at another junction. If Witness No 1 is mistaken about the barn, he may be testifying about another collision at another junction.

In the case of the farmer's testimony, the only required foundation would be first-hand knowledge of the vicinity. Assume, for instance, that all the junctions in question are located within the vicinity of a town called

Cherryville. The proponent (the defendant) might establish the farmer's personal familiarity with the area in the following manner:

P. Where do you live?

W. I live on a farm just outside Cherryville.

P. How long have you lived there?

W. All my life. I was brought up there.

P. How many years have you lived there?

W. Fifty-two years.

P. How familiar are you with the roads in the area?

W. Very familiar.

P. How well do you know the junction between Cherryville Road and Blackwater Road?

W. Very well. I live only about a mile from there. I drive through there practically every day.

P. How well do you know the junction between Cherryville Road and Coast Road?

W. I'd know it just as well.

At this point, counsel for the defendant would elicit the farmer's testimony contradicting the testimony of the earlier witness. One possible technique for highlighting the contradiction is to preface the questions to the farmer with references to the contradictory testimony of the earlier witness.

2.14 PROOF THAT THE WITNESS MADE A PRIOR INCONSISTENT STATEMENT

2.14.1 The law

In some instances, counsel can impeach the credibility of a witness either through cross-examination or by extrinsic evidence. One such example involves the presentation of proof that the witness made a prior statement that is inconsistent with his or her testimony at trial. The procedure for the introduction of such a statement is contained in ss 4 and 5 of the Criminal Procedure Act 1865 and is similar to the procedure for challenging the consistency of a hostile witness during examination-in-chief.[61] Counsel must lay a proper foundation for the introduction of the statement. Counsel

61. Section 3 of CPA 1865; *AG v Taylor* [1974] 1 IR 97.

should put to the witness that he or she had on another occasion made a statement which differed materially from or contradicted the one he or she was making on the stand; if the witness denies making the statement, the witness should be asked to step down and counsel should present alternative proof that the statement was made. The witness should then resume his or her testimony; counsel should put the statement to the witness and draw his or her attention to the alleged inconsistency or contradiction.[62] The statement is typically admitted only for the limited purpose of challenging the credibility of the witness and, where appropriate, a jury should be instructed that the statement is not probative of any fact stated therein.[63]

2.14.2 Elements of the foundation

The elements of the foundation include:

1. That the witness on an earlier occasion gave an account of the matter in question.
2. That this account differs in some respect from the account which the complainant is now offering.
3. That this difference or inconsistency casts doubt on the overall credibility of the complainant.

2.14.3 Sample foundation

The hypothetical case is a trial in the Central Criminal Court where the accused denies the charge of unlawfully killing the deceased contrary to common law. The prosecution's case is that the accused and the deceased had been fighting in a public park on the evening in question. The prosecution alleges that during the course of this fight, the accused produced a knife from his pocket and stabbed the deceased.

One of the prosecution witnesses is Barry Beige, who is an associate of the accused. Mr Beige had been drinking with the accused on the evening in question and claims to have witnessed the events leading up to the death of the deceased. Mr Beige is fully co-operative at trial. The evidence given by

---

62. *AG v Taylor* [1974] 1 IR 97.

63. Part III of the CJA 2006 provides for the admissibility as substantive evidence of previous witness statements in certain circumstances. See **6.09**.

Mr Beige at trial is generally consistent with what was said by him when he was first interviewed by the gardaí. However, an inconsistency arises in relation to the quantity of alcohol that the witness had consumed on the evening in question. Of course, any inconsistency will be fastened upon by counsel for the accused in cross-examination, with a view to impeaching the witness's credibility and overall reliability as a witness.

The cross-examination follows. The defendant is the proponent.

P. You told counsel for the State a few moments ago that on the evening in question you consumed a total of about six cans of lager, correct?

W. That's correct.

P. I have to suggest to you that when you first made a statement to the gardaí, your story in this regard was somewhat different. (1), (2)

W. I'm sure it was about six cans.

P. You made a statement in Main Street Garda Station the day after the deceased was stabbed, correct?(1)

W. Yes.

P. And in that statement you said to the gardaí that before you went out on the evening in question you had had a shot of vodka at home. Do you remember saying that? (2)

W. Yeah, I remember saying that.

P. Why didn't you mention that in your direct evidence a few moments ago? (2)

W. I just forgot about it. I accept now that I did have a vodka before I went out that night.

P. Yes, but there's another difficulty. You also said to the gardaí that in the park you had 'a good few cans'. When you were asked further about this by the gardaí you then said 'six or seven cans'. But a moment ago you told the jury that you had 'six cans'. Which is it? (2) (3)

W. I'm pretty sure it was around six cans.

P. You're pretty sure. We'll it doesn't appear that you are. I have to suggest to you that there's a clear difference between having six cans, on the one hand, and having vodka *and* six or seven cans, isn't there? (2), (3)

W. Yes.

P. And I have to put it to you that your recollection of an important feature of that evening – the quantity of alcohol that you yourself consumed – is inconsistent and unreliable. (3)

2.15 CHARACTER

The law of evidence starts from the premise that all relevant evidence is admissible. Evidence of an individual's character, ie his or her traits, qualities and characteristics, is generally not admissible in civil and criminal proceedings for the simple reason that the courts do not consider it to be relevant.[64] There is a limited range of circumstances in which character evidence does have a bearing on issues raised at trial. In these instances, the evidence is admitted on the basis that it is relevant to the merits of the case. Of course, the law's preoccupation with relevance is tempered by other concerns which are reflected in exclusionary rules. The reliability of the evidence presented by the parties is one such concern and, as we shall see, is the rationale for the rules excluding evidence of opinion[65] and hearsay.[66] In relation to character, the concern justifying the exclusion of relevant evidence is the danger of prejudice. The party seeking to present character evidence at trial must satisfy the court not only that the evidence is relevant but also that the probative value of the evidence is not outweighed by its prejudicial effect.

The term 'prejudice' refers to the tendency of an item of evidence to tempt the finder of fact into deciding the case on an improper, usually emotional, basis. For example, evidence of the prior misdeeds of a criminal defendant raises the spectre of prejudice; such evidence creates a risk that the jury will convict, not because they are convinced beyond a reasonable doubt that the accused committed the crime, but rather because they conclude that the accused is a bad person who should be punished. The admissibility of evidence of an accused's bad character or prior misconduct is governed by common law[67] and statutory[68] exclusionary rules. However, it is important to

64. *DPP v Ferris* (10 June 2002, unreported) CCA.

65. See **Chapter 4**.

66. See **Chapter 6**.

67. *DPP v BK* [2000] 2 IR 199.

68. Section 1(e) and (f) of CJ(E)A 1924.

recall that the constitutional guarantee of a trial in due course of law[69] protects the accused from this, and indeed any other, form of prejudicial evidence. Even where such evidence is not caught by an exclusionary rule, it may be excluded at the trial judge's discretion. As Geoghegan J explained in *DPP v Meleady (No 3):*

> A judge, as part of his inherent power, has an overriding duty in every case to ensure that the accused receives a fair trial and always has a discretion to exclude otherwise admissible prosecution evidence if, in his opinion, its prejudicial effect, in the minds of the jury outweighs its true probative value.[70]

2.16 AN ACCUSED'S GOOD CHARACTER

2.16.1 The law

In criminal proceedings, the accused may adduce evidence of his or her good character at any stage in the proceedings.[71] The accused may elect to take the stand and testify as to his or her own good character in examination-in-chief. However, in so doing, the accused will run the risk that he or she will be cross-examined by the prosecution as to his or her bad character or prior misconduct.[72] Where the defence calls a witness other than the accused to testify as to the accused's good character, the witness must limit his or her testimony to evidence of the accused's general reputation or standing within the community; the witness is not permitted to give his or *opinion* of the accused's character.[73] Generally, the trial judge would be expected to instruct the jury that this type of good character evidence, ie evidence of reputation, is relevant to the issue of guilt or innocence. If the accused takes the stand and testifies in his or her own defence, the evidence of reputation may serve the additional purpose of enhancing the accused's credibility.

2.16.2 Elements of the foundation

The foundation for evidence of reputation is as follows:

1. The witness is a member of the same community (residential, business or social) as the accused.

---

69. Article 38.1 of the Constitution. See also Art 6 of the European Convention on Human Rights.

70. [2001] 4 IR 16 at 31.

71. See generally McGrath, *Evidence* (Thomson Round Hall, 2005) at 465–69.

72. Section 1(f)(ii) of the CJ(E)A 1924.

73. *DPP v Ferris* (10 June 2002, unreported) CCA; *R v Rowton* (1865) 1 Le & Ca 520, 169 ER 1497.

2. The witness has resided there for a substantial period of time.
3. The accused has a reputation for general, law-abiding character.
4. The witness knows the reputation.
5. The witness states the reputation.

2.16.3 Sample foundation

Our fact situation is a prosecution for assault. Mr Freddy Fist has been charged with a violent assault. During its case-in-chief, the defence calls Mr Nathan Neighbour as a character witness. Mr Neighbour has already identified himself and also identified Mr Fist as a neighbour of his. The defence is the proponent.

P. Mr Neighbour, where does Mr Fist live? (1)
W. At 45 Little Avenue, here in town.
P. Where do you live? (1)
W. At 51 Little Avenue.
P. How close do you live to Mr Fist? (1)
W. Just down the street.
P. How long has Mr Fist lived in your neighbourhood? (2)
W. I'd say about seven years.
P. How long have you lived there? (2)
W. For the past twenty years.
P. Does Mr Fist have a reputation in your neighbourhood? (3)
W. Yes, I'd say he does.
P. Do you know that reputation? (4)
W. Yes.
P. What is that reputation? (5)
W. He is known as a decent, law-abiding person.

2.17 AN ACCUSED'S BAD CHARACTER OR MISCONDUCT

2.17.1 The law

As previously discussed,[74] evidence of an accused's prior misconduct is generally inadmissible on the basis that its relevance to issues at trial is outweighed by its prejudicial effect.[75] The admission of such evidence

[74] See para **2.15**.

[75] *DPP v BK* [2000] 2 IR 199; *B v DPP* [1997] 3 IR 140.

threatens certain fundamental principles inherent in the guarantee of a trial in due course of law under Article 38.1 of the Constitution and Article 6 of the European Convention on Human Rights, notably, the presumption of innocence[76] and the burden of proof.[77] Nevertheless, evidence of prior bad acts is admissible in an exceptional, narrow category of cases in which the evidence goes to show something other than the accused's propensity for misconduct.[78] As a practical matter, the courts are extremely wary of this type of evidence and it is relatively rare that it is admitted at trial.

2.17.2 Elements of the foundation and sample foundation

Section 1(f) of the Criminal Justice (Evidence) Act 1924 prescribes certain circumstances in which the prosecution may cross-examine an accused as to his or her bad character or prior misconduct. One such circumstance is where the accused has asserted his or her good character in examination-in-chief.

The accused is charged with making gain or causing loss by deception contrary to s 6 of the Criminal Justice (Theft and Fraud Offencces) Act 2001. The prosecution alleges that the accused made a fraudulent insurance claim by staging a burglary in his home. The accused pleads not guilty and insists that he was the victim of a genuine burglary. The accused takes the stand and testifies in his own defence. The accused states during examination-in-chief that he is a person of unimpeachable good character and has no previous convictions. It transpires that 10 years previously the accused was convicted of an almost identical offence. Counsel for the State seeks and receives the permission of the judge to cross-examine the accused in relation to this.

P. You have been accused of this type of offence before, isn't that correct?

W. Yes.

P. In fact, you stood trial in the Circuit Criminal Court in 1999 for fraudulently making an insurance claim in connection with a burglary at a warehouse owned by you, isn't that correct? (1) (2)

---

76. *See eg DPP v O'T* [2003] 4 IR 286; *Hussain v UK,* App No 8866/04, Judgment of 3 March 2006, TLR (5 April 2006).

77. *See eg O'Leary v AG* [1993] 1 IR 102; *Best v Wellcome Foundation Ltd* [1993] 3 IR 421; *Sheldrake v DPP & AG* [2005] 1 AC 264.

78. *Makin v AG for New South Wales* [1894] AC 57; *DPP v Boardman* [1975] AC 421; *DPP v BK* [2000] 2 IR 199.

W. Yes.

P. At that time, it was alleged that you had staged a break-in at your premises so as to ground a fraudulent claim for compensation that you subsequently made to an insurance company. Do you remember that? (1) (3)

W. Yes.

P. And do you remember if you were found guilty or not guilty? (2)

W. Guilty.

P. Yes, a jury of your peers found that you were guilty of staging a break-in and making a fraudulent insurance claim. And here we are again and you now stand trial for staging a break-in to your premises and making a bogus insurance claim, isn't that correct? (4)

W. That's the charge but it's a lie.

P. There's a striking similarity between the two sets of facts though, isn't there? Back then it was your warehouse, you stage a break-in and make a bogus claim on your insurance; now it's your house, and you're alleged to have staged a break-in so you could claim on your insurance.

2.18 A WITNESS'S CHARACTER

2.18.1 The law

In criminal proceedings, the parties may attempt to undermine the credibility of a witness testifying for another party by cross-examining the witness as to his or her bad character.[79] For example, an accused who has been charged with a violent crime may attempt to prove the violent character of the alleged victim. The logical relevance of the cross-examination is that if the alleged victim has a violent personality, that personality increases the probability that he or she was the aggressor and threw the first punch.[80] However, if the purpose of the questioning is purely to impugn the

79. *AG v O'Sullivan* [1930] IR 552. It should be noted that in proceedings for sexual assault, evidence of the sexual history of the complainant is generally inadmissible. Section 3(1) of the Criminal Law (Rape) Act 1981 as amended by s 13 of the Criminal Law (Rape) (Amendment) Act 1990.

80. A witness may be cross-examined about any previous convictions he or she may have. Section 6 of CPA 1865.

credibility of the witness, counsel conducting the cross-examination cannot call additional witnesses to contradict the answers given.[81] Where the credibility of the witness has been challenged by bad character evidence, the party that tendered the witness will be afforded an opportunity to adduce rebuttal, good character evidence by way of re-examination.[82]

2.18.2 Elements of the foundation

The defence are attempting to establish the alleged victim's violent character by cross-examination as to a specific instance of misconduct. The elements of the foundation are:

1. When the event occurred.
2. Where the event occurred.
3. Who was involved.
4. What happened – namely a violent act by the alleged victim.

2.18.3 Sample foundation

The accused, Mr Freddy Fist, has been charged with a violent assault on Mr Paddy Punch on 1 December 2007. The prosecution has called Mr Punch as a witness. Counsel for the defence has cross-examined Mr Punch as to the events of 1 December 2007. The cross-examination continues.

P. Mr Punch, where were you on the evening of 17 November 2007? (1)

W. I can't remember.

P. Mr Punch, isn't it the case that you were in the Dew Drop Inn on Beech Street on the evening of 17 November 2007, just two weeks before the alleged incident between yourself and my client? (1), (2)

W. I might have been.

P. Mr Punch, isn't it true that on the evening in question, at the Dew Drop Inn, you had a physical altercation with Mr Kevin Kick? (3)

W. I didn't start that fight.

P. Mr Punch, isn't it true that you punched Mr Kick? (4)

81. *Harris v Tippett* (1811) 2 Camp 637.

82. *AG v O'Sullivan* [1930] IR 552.

W. Only after he'd called me a liar.
P. And isn't it also true that you punched and kicked him repeatedly? (4)
W. He was the aggressor. I went home covered in bruises.
P. Mr Punch, isn't it the case that Mr Kick spent one week in hospital recovering from his injuries? (4)
W. I wouldn't know anything about that.
P. I have no further questions for this witness.

2.19 CORROBORATION

In criminal proceedings, traditionally the courts have been reluctant to rest convictions on the testimony of certain witnesses standing alone.[83] Historically, the courts insisted that testimony of this kind be corroborated by evidence from some independent source. The requirement of corroboration *per se* has since given way to the more flexible mechanism of cautionary corroboration warnings.[84] During the course of his or her summing up, the trial judge delivers a special instruction to the jury regarding the manner in which they should approach the particular item of uncorroborated evidence. Specifically, the judge draws the jury's attention to the evidence in question, underscores the absence of corroboration, informs the jury that they are entitled to rely on the uncorroborated evidence, but warns them of the known risks in so doing. A cautionary warning of this kind is mandatory in two instances: where the prosecution presents an uncorroborated confession[85] or the uncorroborated testimony of an accomplice.[86] The judge has a discretion whether or not to issue the warning

83. *DPP v Hester* [1973] AC 296.

84. There remain a few offences in relation to which statute or the common law requires corroboration, eg treason, procuration and perjury. The issue whether a court could convict on DNA evidence (or more broadly forensic evidence) standing alone is an open question. The Law Reform Commission has recommended that a trial judge should have a discretion to issue a cautionary warning in such an instance. See Law Reform Commission, *Report on the Establishment of a DNA Database* (LRC 78-2005) at p 101; Heffernan, *Scientific Evidence: Fingerprints and DNA* (First Law, 2006) at ch 9.

85. Section 10 of the CPA 1993; *DPP v Murphy* [2005] 2 IR 125; *DPP v Connolly* [2003] 2 IR 1.

86. *DPP v Gilligan* [2005] IESC 78 (23 November 2005); *DPP v Ward* (22 March 2002, unreported) CCA; *AG v Carney* [1955] IR 324; *AG v Linehan* [1929] IR 19.

in relation to two other forms of uncorroborated evidence: the testimony of a complainant in relation to a sexual offence[87] and the testimony of a child.[88]

An important threshold issue that the judge must determine is whether corroboration exists in the particular case. Clearly, if the prosecution can establish the presence of independent, corroborating evidence, then the need for a cautionary warning is dispensed with. There has been some judicial debate concerning the kind of evidence that is capable of constituting corroboration. The classic definition was offered by Reading LJ in *R v Baskerville:*

> We hold that evidence in corroboration must be independent testimony which affects the accused by connecting or tending to connect him with the crime. In other words, it must be evidence which implicates him, that is, which confirms in some material particular not only the evidence that the crime has been committed, but also that the prisoner committed it … The nature of the corroboration will necessarily vary according to the particular circumstances of the offence charged … The corroboration need not be direct evidence that the accused committed the crime; it is sufficient if it is merely circumstantial evidence of his connection with the crime …[89]

Where the defence establishes a *prima facie* case for a corroboration warning in relation to the testimony of a particular witness, the prosecution will need to show:

1. The evidence admitted in the case includes evidence independent of the testimony in question.
2. The independent testimony tends to show that the accused committed the offence for which he or she is charged.

The Court of Criminal Appeal addressed the issue in detail in the important case of *DPP v PC.*[90] In that case, the accused was tried in respect of various counts of indecent assault upon a female contrary to s 10 of the Criminal Law (Rape) Act 1981 and unlawful sexual intercourse with a female under the age of 15 years contrary to s 1(1) of the Criminal Law (Amendment) Act of 1935, on diverse dates. The accused was convicted of the offence contrary

87. Section 7 of the Criminal Law (Rape) (Amendment) Act 1990; *DPP v JEM* [2001] 4 IR 385; *DPP v C* [2001] 3 IR 345; *DPP v Gentleman* [2003] 4 IR 22.

88. Section 28 of the CEA 1992.

89. [1916] 2 KB 658. See also *DPP v PC* [2002] 2 IR 285; *DPP v Slavotic,* (18 November 2002, unreported) CCA.

90. [2002] 2 IR 285. The case is noted at (2002) (12) (4) ICLJ 33.

to s 1(1) of the 1935 Act,[91] was found not guilty by direction of the trial judge in respect of one count and the jury failed to agree on their verdict in respect of six other counts.

With regard to the count on which he was convicted, the evidence led at trial was that the defendant met with the complainant outside her school in his car. She got into the car and they drove to his house where sexual intercourse took place in what was stated to be his bedroom.

On appeal, it was argued on behalf of the defendant that the conviction should be quashed, since, *inter alia*, the trial judge erred in directing the jury that the evidence of the complainant in relation to the defendant's bedroom was capable of amounting to corroboration of her evidence. The complainant had given evidence of a number of details including which room in the house was the bedroom, the presence of a dressing table or wardrobe and slippers beside the bed. The prosecution relied on the fact that the window in the room was opposite the door and it had curtains, as being corroborating evidence. On appeal, it was argued that these details were so commonplace that they could not amount to independent evidence sufficient to constitute corroboration.

The appeal was upheld and the conviction quashed. The Court of Criminal Appeal accepted that in this case the feature in question – a window with curtains – was so 'commonplace and anodyne' that it was 'not of sufficient particularity' to amount to corroboration.[92] Although the independent testimony could refer to everyday features, it must be such that it is capable of identifying the layout of a particular room before it could be considered to amount to actual corroboration.

The Court of Criminal Appeal emphasised that corroboration was independent evidence which inculpated the defendant by connecting or linking him with the crime. In order to amount to corroboration, the evidence must confirm in some material particular not only the evidence that the crime had been committed but also that the defendant committed it. Evidence of a feature which was so commonplace that it was not of sufficient particularity, or of a sufficiently material nature independent of the complainant's version of events, was not corroboration.[93]

91. This provision was subsequently found to be unconstitutional by the Supreme Court in the case of *CC v Ireland* [2006] 4 IR 1.

92. [2002] 2 IR 285 at 302–03.

93. See also *DPP v Gilligan* [2005] IESC 78 (23 November 2005); *DPP v Gannon* (21 March 2003, unreported) CCA.

Chapter 3

DOCUMENTS

3.01 INTRODUCTION

The presentation of evidence in the form of *viva voce* testimony in court is a central feature of the Irish system of justice.[1] Our rules of evidence embody the traditional preference of the common law for oral evidence with its attendant safeguards of the oath or affirmation, the delivery of testimony directly before the finder of fact and the testing of the witness's credibility and account by cross-examination.[2] There are many instances, however, in which a party may be permitted to offer proof in documentary form.[3] It is important to note that the term 'documentary evidence' is broadly defined for evidentiary purposes to encompass a wide range of informational sources including written statements and reports, maps, graphs, drawings, photographs, film and audio recordings, and electronic data.[4]

The typical basis for admitting documentary evidence is that it constitutes the best available evidence in the circumstances. The cogency of this justification for the admission of a document will depend upon the nature of the case. For example, where the dispute between the parties centres on the document itself, such as a contract or a will, the document usually constitutes the best evidence of what the parties agreed or what the testator intended. Similarly, a dispute over a document, such as a record, an account or an electronic transmission, is best resolved by firsthand reference to the original source. In other instances, documentary evidence may play an important but less central role in the proceedings. For example, a letter written by a person shortly before his or her death, may shed some light on the person's state of mind. Similarly, a telephone record may permit the

1. See eg *Mapp v Gilhooley* [1991] 2 IR 253.
2. See eg *DPP v Kelly* [2006] 3 IR 115; *Donnelly v Ireland* [1998] 1 IR 321.
3. See generally McGrath, *Evidence* (Thomson Round Hall, 2005) ch 12.
4. Electronic Commerce Act 2000; s 2 of the CEA 1992; Documentary Evidence Act 1925; *Keane v An Bord Pleanála* [1997] 1 IR 184; *McCarthy v Flynn* [1979] IR 127.

court to draw inferences about the extent of communication between the parties to the proceedings or perhaps between one of the parties and a third party. This evidence may enable a party to prove a fact in issue; for example, it may assist a plaintiff in establishing an element of a cause of action or the prosecution in establishing an element of an offence.

A party presenting a document must authenticate the document, ie present proof that the document is what the party claims it is. If the party claims that a deceased person signed a letter, the party must prove that the document is a genuine letter signed by the deceased. If a party offers a photograph of a road traffic junction, the party must show that the photograph accurately depicts the junction. Thus, a party presenting documentary evidence may have to establish, for instance, the fact that the document is an original[5] or the fact that it was duly executed.[6] Consequently, the admission of documentary evidence is premised on accompanying testimony from a witness who can introduce and contextualise the evidence for the finder of fact.

Even where the law permits an offer of proof in documentary form, the evidence will not be admitted if it is caught by any of the exclusionary rules of evidence. Thus, a document that contains an out-of-court statement that is being offered in-court as proof of the matter stated may be excluded unless it comes within a recognised exception to the rule against hearsay.[7] Some such exceptions, notably the common law exception for public records and the statutory exception for business records in criminal proceedings, substantially undercut the application of the rule to documentary evidence.[8] A document that has been obtained in breach of constitutional rights will be excluded in the absence of extraordinary excusing circumstances; a document obtained through conduct which is unlawful but does not involve a breach of constitutional rights may be excluded at the discretion of the trial judge.[9] Documentary evidence is subject to the rule against opinion evidence and generally will be admissible only if the content is limited to assertions of fact. A notable exception is the opinion of an expert witness

5. *Primor plc v Stokes Kennedy Crowley* [1996] 2 IR 459.

6. See eg s 8 of the Criminal Procedure Act 1865.

7. See **Chapter 6**.

8. See ss 3–8 of CEA 1992. This statutory exception for business records applies only in criminal proceedings. See *Director of Corporate Enforcement v Bailey* [2007] IEHC (1 November 2007).

9. See **Chapter 7**.

which may be offered where the proceedings raise an issue of fact outside the ordinary experience of the finder of fact.[10] In addition, the various privileges may be invoked by a party to resist disclosure of documentary evidence whether during discovery or at trial.[11]

There are additional evidentiary purposes to which documents are put during the course of proceedings. For example, as we have seen, a written statement made by a witness on a previous occasion may be used to challenge the consistency of the witness's account of the material facts and, by extension, the witness's credibility.[12] A written complaint made by the victim of a rape or sexual assault may be used to bolster the credibility of the complainant at trial.[13] In both of these instances, the document is not offered as proof of its contents but rather for the secondary purpose of undermining or bolstering the credibility of the witness.[14] In exceptional circumstances, however, a previous witness statement may be admitted as proof of its contents.[15]

DISCOVERY

3.02 BACKGROUND

Discovery is the process whereby a party in civil proceedings may, in advance of the trial of the action, obtain documentation in the possession or control of another party, or occasionally from a non-party.[16] The rationale

---

10. See **Chapter 4**.
11. See **Chapter 5**.
12. See **Chapter 2**.
13. See **Chapter 2**.
14. In a jury trial, the trial judge would be expected to instrúct the jury accordingly. See **Chapter 2**.
15. See **6.09**.
16. A more definitive exposition of the law relating to discovery is beyond the scope of this text and readers are advised to consult specialist texts in this regard. See eg Abrahamson, Dwyer and Fitzpatrick, *Discovery and Disclosure* (Thomson Round Hall, 2007); Delany and McGrath, *Civil Procedure in the Superior Courts*, (2nd edn, Thomson Round Hall, 2005) at p 265 *et seq*. On disclosure in criminal proceedings, see eg Walsh, *Criminal Procedure* (Thomson Round Hall, 2002).

underpinning the discovery process was explained by Finlay CJ in the following terms:

> the basic purpose and reason for the procedure of discovery … is to ensure as far as possible that the full facts concerning any matter in dispute before the court are capable of being presented to the court by the parties concerned, so that justice on full information, rather than on a limited or partial revelation of the facts arising in a particular action, may be done.[17]

In the context of High Court and Supreme Court litigation, the process is governed by the Rules of the Superior Courts (Ord 31) and by a substantial body of case law that has now accumulated in relation to discovery.[18] In the context of Circuit Court litigation, regard should be had to the Circuit Court Rules. The principles underpinning discovery are the same, however, irrespective of the court in which discovery is sought. In the High Court, discovery applications are made before the Master of the High Court, by way of notice of motion grounded on affidavit. The Master's decision may be appealed to a High Court judge, and this in turn may be appealed to the Supreme Court.

Relevance and necessity are key touchstones as to whether discovery is required. Broadly speaking, the documentation sought on discovery should be likely to confer a litigious advantage on the party seeking discovery. If there is an obvious alternative way of obtaining the information sought, this may militate against an order for discovery being made, albeit that this is not absolute.[19]

Discovery will not be ordered if the application is in the form of what is frequently described as a 'fishing expedition'. That is, a party is not entitled to seek discovery on what is a purely speculative basis in the hope that this may work to his or her tactical advantage, or to the detriment of the other side. In all the circumstances, the documentation being sought must be necessary to ensure that the proceedings are fairly disposed of after each side has had the chance to fully and effectively make its case. Neither may discovery be used as a means of substantiating a plea which would otherwise

---

17. *Allied Irish Bank plc v Ernst & Whinney* [1993] 1 IR 375, 390.

18. Amongst the most important Supreme Court decisions are: *Taylor v Clonmel Healthcare Ltd* [2004] 1 IR 169; *Framus Ltd v CRH plc* [2004] 2 IR 20 and *Ryanair plc v Aer Rianta cpt* [2003] 4 IR 264.

19. See eg *Ryanair plc v Aer Rianta cpt* [2003] 4 IR 264.

be unstatable. For example, in a defamation action, a defendant may not plead justification where there is no evidence of the truthfulness of the allegations made against the plaintiff, and then seek to justify such a plea by obtaining documentation by way of discovery.[20]

3.03 AFFIDAVITS

3.03.1 Background

Evidence may be placed before a court either orally, or by affidavit. An affidavit is a statement made on oath, set out in a specific format, which is 'sworn' or signed by the witness (known as the deponent) in the presence of a solicitor or commissioner for oaths. Many applications that come before the courts must be accompanied by a supporting affidavit known as the 'grounding affidavit'. The Rules relating to affidavits are set out in Ord 40 of the Rules of the Superior Courts and Ord 25 of the Circuit Court Rules.

Affidavits may be sworn both by parties to the proceedings and by other persons who possess information relevant to the proceedings, such as expert witnesses, for example. The deponent must be at least 18 years of age in order to swear the affidavit. Since evidence is given on oath in an affidavit, it is as if the deponent on the affidavit was actually present in court and in the witness box, in terms of the solemnity of what is said. The obvious difference, of course, is that the witness is not present in court to be cross-examined on his or her evidence. The Rules of Court provide for the possibility that a deponent on an affidavit may be ordered to attend court to be cross-examined. This does happen, but is relatively rare. Far more common is the situation where a witness who is testifying at the trial of an action is cross-examined about evidence given on affidavit at an earlier stage in the proceedings.

Hearsay evidence will frequently be given on affidavit, but strictly speaking this is only to be done in interlocutory motions. This is provided for in the Rules of the Superior Courts and in the Circuit Court Rules. The general rule, however, is that no less than a witness who gives oral evidence in court, a deponent on an affidavit should only give evidence of matters which he or she can prove from within his or her own knowledge.

---

20. See eg *McDonagh v Sunday Newspapers* [2005] 4 IR 528.

3.03.2 Elements of an affidavit

In terms of format, a grounding affidavit should contain the following:

1. A heading and the title of the proceedings.
2. An oath by the deponent.
3. A so-called 'means of knowledge' clause indicating the deponent's involvement in the proceedings.
4. A reference to the proceedings in a separate paragraph.
5. A series of numbered paragraphs setting out the evidence.
6. A so-called 'prayer for relief' is the final paragraph.
7. The signature of the deponent and the date of signing.
8. The name and signature of the person before whom the affidavit is sworn.

3.03.3 Sample affidavit

The following is a sample affidavit, of a relatively straightforward nature. The fact scenario is a personal injuries claim arising out of a road traffic accident. The defendant brings a motion to compel the plaintiff to furnish to the defendant x-rays taken of the plaintiff. The deponent on the affidavit is the defendant's solicitor, Mr Oliver Orange.

THE HIGH COURT

Record No 2007/1234P

Between:

BENJAMIN BLUE

Plaintiff

-and-

WILLIAM WHITE

Defendant

AFFIDAVIT OF OLIVER ORANGE

I, Oliver Orange, Solicitor, of 1 Nowhere Street, Dublin 2, aged eighteen years and upwards, MAKE OATH, and say as follows:

1. I am the Solicitor on record for the Defendant herein, and I make this Affidavit for and on his behalf, and I do so from facts within

my own knowledge save where otherwise appears, and whereso appearing I believe the same to be true and accurate.

2. I beg to refer to the proceedings already had herein, when produced.
3. I say that by letter dated 1 January 2008, I wrote to the Plaintiff's Solicitors requesting them to make all x-rays taken of the Plaintiff available, and affording them a period of twenty-one days within which to do so. I say that on 1 March 2008 I wrote them a further letter again requesting them to make the x-rays available to my office. In this regard I beg to refer to copies of this correspondence which I have pinned together and upon which marked with the numbers and letters 'JO1' I have signed my name prior to the swearing hereof.
4. I say that in the report of the defendant's expert, Dr Gerard Green, dated 19 March 2008, he states that he had not seen the x-rays of the Plaintiff and he is at a loss to know why the Plaintiff's symptoms persist. In this regard, I beg to refer to a copy of the said report upon which marked with the numbers and letters 'JO2' I have signed my name prior to the swearing hereof.
5. I say and believe and have been so advised that it is necessary for the proper preparation of the Defendant's case that the Plaintiff makes the said x-rays available to Dr Green.
6. Accordingly, I respectfully pray this Honourable Court for an Order for Discovery in the terms of the Notice of Motion herein and for such further or other Order as this Honourable Court may deem appropriate.

SWORN by the said OLIVER ORANGE on the [Agent Please Insert] day of 2008
at [Agent Please Insert] In the city of [Agent Please Insert] before me a Commissioner for Oaths/Practising Solicitor and I know the Deponent.

The following affidavit is sworn in an action for breach of contract, whereby a claim for a liquidated sum of money has been originated by way of summary summons. The plaintiff company is a bakery supplier which is suing the defendant baker for failing to pay for equipment and products supplied by the plaintiff to the defendant pursuant to contract. The grounding affidavit is sworn by th plaintiff company's managing director.

Record No 2008/1234P

THE HIGH COURT

Between:

BAKE AND CAKE SUPPLIERS LTD

Plaintiff

-and-

THE BIG BAKERY LTD

Defendants

AFFIDAVIT OF BARRY BAKER

I, BARRY BAKER, Company Director, of 1 Suburban Street, Dublin, aged eighteen years and upwards, MAKE OATH and say as follows:

1. I am the Managing Director of the Plaintiff Company in this action and I make this affidavit for and on behalf of the Plaintiff and with its consent and authority. I do so from facts within my own knowledge save where otherwise appears, and where so otherwise appears I believe the same to be true and accurate.
2. I beg to refer to the proceedings already had herein, when produced, and in particular to the Special Indorsement of Claim on the Summary Summons issued and served herein.
3. I say and believe that on or about 1 January 2008 the Plaintiff and the Defendant entered into a contract pursuant to which the Plaintiff was to supply equipment and machinery to the Defendant. I beg to refer to the said contract, a copy of which I have attached and which I have endorsed my name with the letter 'A' prior to the swearing hereof.
4. I say that the Plaintiff's claim is for the sum of €40,000 which sum is due and owing by the Defendant to the Plaintiff on foot of goods sold and delivered within the last six years and/or on foot of an account stated and settled. The said €40,000 is made up of a total of three invoices raised by the Plaintiff in respect of goods supplied to the Defendant. The invoices are dated 25 January 2008, 2 February 2008 and 16 February 2008.

5. I say that the invoices were raised on foot of equipment and products for use in the baking process, which equipment and products were delivered by the Plaintiff to the Defendant on or about 21 January 2008. The said invoices are in the amounts of €25,000, €7,500 and €7,500 respectively. In this regard I beg to refer to a copies of the said invoices which I have pinned together and upon which marked with the numbers and letters 'BB1' I have signed my name prior to the swearing hereof.
6. I say that the Plaintiff has repeatedly called upon the Defendant to discharge the sum owing, yet despite the aforesaid demands, the Defendant has failed, neglected, and/or refused to pay the said sum or any part thereof. In this regard I beg to refer to copies of the letters of demand dated the 1 March 2008 and 22 March 2008 upon which marked with the numbers and letters 'BB2' I have signed my name prior to the swearing hereof.
7. I say and believe that the whole of the said sum of €40,000 is still justly due and owing by the Defendant to the Plaintiff.
8. I say and believe that the Appearance as entered to the said Summons on behalf of the Defendant was entered for the sole purpose of delay and that there is no Defence to the Plaintiff's claim either *bona fide* or at law.
9. I say and believe and am so advised that I have liberty to apply to this Honourable Court for interest pursuant to the Courts Act 1981, and that there are good reasons and justice why the Defendants should pay interest on the said amount. I say that the said debt is due as a result of the said contract and the Defendants by delaying the due payments of their liabilities are clearly depriving the Plaintiff of any use and value of the money concerned.
10. I therefore pray this Honourable Court for an Order in terms of the Notice of Motion herein granting the Plaintiff liberty to enter final judgment as against the Defendant in the amount of €40,000 together with interest and costs and such further or other order this Honourable Court shall deem appropriate.

SWORN by the said on the
[Agent Please Insert] day of
2008
at [Agent Please Insert] In the city of [Agent Please Insert] before me a Commissioner for Oaths/Practising Solicitor and I know the Deponent.

3.04 INTERROGATORIES

'Interrogatories' is the name given to the series of questions that a party can require an opposing party to answer on oath. This is done in advance of the trial of the action, and is designed to assist a party in establishing its case, or weakening the case of its opponent.[21] The basic purpose of interrogatories is to avoid injustice where one party has the knowledge and ability to prove facts which are important to the opposing party's case in circumstances where such opposing party does not have the knowledge or ability to prove these facts either at all or without undue difficulty.[22] So far as is possible, interrogatories should take the form of questions which are capable of being answered 'yes' or 'no'. Interrogatories must be answered by affidavit.

Order 31 of the Rules of the Superior Courts provides that where a party seeks to deliver interrogatories, the leave of the court shall be given 'as to such only of the interrogatories as shall be considered necessary either for disposing fairly of the cause or matter or for saving costs'.[23] In fact, the courts adopt an even stricter approach in practice. Interrogatories are permitted only in exceptional circumstances,[24] where there is a stringent necessity for same or where some clear litigious purpose is served at that particular juncture. This test may be met where the party exhibiting the interrogatories establishes that answers to them would save costs or promote the fair and efficient conduct of the action in question. Fair disposal of the case or saving costs is established once the purpose of an interrogatory is either to sustain the plaintiff's case or to destroy the defendant's case.[25]

Interrogatories must relate to matters in question in the proceedings and, accordingly, it will be necessary at the outset to carefully scrutinise the pleadings with a view to identifying the issues arising. Thus, the information being sought by the applicant must relate to facts which are in issue in the

21. For thorough analysis, see Delany and McGrath, *Civil Procedure in the Superior Courts,* (2nd edn, Thomson Round Hall, 2005) at p 331 *et seq.*

22. See *Bula Ltd (in receivership) v Tara Mines Ltd* [1995] 1 ILRM 401 (*per* Lynch J).

23. For detailed analysis, see O'Floinn, *Practice and Procedure in the Superior Courts* (2nd edn, Tottel Publishing, 2008) at p 283 *et seq.*

24. For discussion of the law on interrogatories, see the judgment of the Master of the High Court in *Kennedy v Killeen Corrugated Products Ltd* (4 November 2005, unreported).

25. See eg *Money Markets International Stock Brokers (in liquidation) v Fanning* [2001] 1 ILRM 1.

proceedings. The respondent cannot be asked anything other than whether the specified fact is true or false. He or she cannot be asked the source of knowledge for his or her answer. The plaintiff is entitled to interrogate the defendant as to facts that tend to support the plaintiff's case, or to impeach the defendant's case, but not as to facts that support the defendant's case.

A distinction should be drawn between interrogatories which relate to the facts in dispute on the one hand and, on the other, interrogatories which relate to evidence of the facts in dispute, with the established authorities allowing the former but not the latter. It has been judicially acknowledged that this can be a fine and difficult distinction to draw.[26] Where fraud is pleaded, it is not necessary to seek the permission of the court to deliver interrogatories. However, in all other cases, such permission is required.

The following hypothetical is based on a personal injuries action arising from an accident in the workplace. The plaintiff alleges that due to the negligence and breach of duty (including statutory duty) of the defendant, she suffered injury because a trap door was defective. The plaintiff has alleged that the defendants were on notice of the door being defective prior to the accident and failed to act on advice furnished that the door was defective.

The plaintiff brings a motion, grounded on affidavit, to have the following interrogatories delivered to the defendant:

THE HIGH COURT

Record No 2008/1212K

RUBY RED

Plaintiff

-and-

PURPLE PIPING COMPANY

Defendant

Interrogatories on behalf of the Plaintiff for the examination of the Defendant:

1. Did not the Defendant's Line Manager, Mr Yellow, expressly draw to the attention of the Defendant's Safety Officer,

26. *Mercantile Credit Co of Ireland v Heelan* [1994] 2 IR 105 at 112; [1994] 1 ILRM 406 at 411 (*per* Costello J).

Mr Green, that the trap door was defective prior to the accident complained of by the Plaintiff?

2. Did not other employees of the Defendant make complaints regarding the said trap door prior to the accident in question?
3. Did not other employees, prior to the Plaintiff's accident, report to the Defendant of having to expend excessive effort in opening the said trap door?

Given the reluctance of courts to order interrogatories, it must be conceded that a judge might or might not make the necessary order in a case such as this. It would depend on all the circumstances of the case, on the pleadings, on whether evidence could easily be led at trial in respect of the issues involved, or whether the plaintiff, if deprived of such answers in advance of the trial, would be seriously prejudiced etc.

3.05 EXPERT REPORTS

3.05.1 Background

The procedures governing the presentation of expert evidence are designed to facilitate its admission and at the same time to limit and control its role in the proceedings. The basic principles of fairness and reciprocity that underpin disclosure generally, apply with particular force in relation to experts. Where one side presents expert evidence, the other side is entitled to respond by testing that evidence and presenting its own expert opinion. Although orality remains the guiding principle for ordinary witnesses, expert evidence is initially furnished in documentary form.[27] In civil proceedings, expert reports are exchanged during discovery and typically exert considerable influence on settlement negotiations. Gradual reform has led to the streamlining and expedition of proceedings, particularly in actions for personal injuries and in proceedings before the Commercial Court.

SI 391 of 1998 governs the disclosure of expert reports in personal injuries actions and is designed in part to extend the scope of pre-trial disclosure and minimise the element of surprise at trial.[28] Its provisions were inserted into

---

27. There is an emerging trend in favour of admitting expert evidence at trial in documentary form. See eg s 19 of the Civil Liability and Courts Act 2004. But see *Curran v Finn* (20 May 1999, unreported) SC.

28. Rules of the Superior Courts (No 6) (Disclosure of Reports and Statements) 1998 (SI 391/1998).

Ord 39 of the Rules of the Superior Courts as rr 45–51. Rule 46(1) requires the parties to exchange schedules listing all reports from expert witnesses intended to be called and, subsequently, to exchange copies of the reports themselves.[29] The concept of 'expert report' is broadly defined and encompasses any statement or report containing the substance of the evidence to be adduced including maps, photographs, calculations and like matter.[30] Where an expert compiles two reports – a preliminary report and subsequently a final report – the obligation to disclose may extend to both reports. Kearns J stated in *Payne v Shovlin:*

> 'The relevant test, it seems to me, is whether or not the 'substance' of the evidence to be given, or part of it, is contained in the first report even if the views in that first report are later altered or modified or even given subject to qualification in such first report.'[31]

The extent of the obligation to disclose and, in particular, the issue of whether the rules require a party to disclose information unfavourable to his or her case is controversial. In *Galvin v Murray,* Murphy J stated: 'Clearly, the disclosure rules are designed to forewarn other parties of expert evidence with which they may be confronted. The rules have no role to play in investigating strengths or weaknesses of an opponent's case.'[32] However, in *Payne v Shovlin,* Kearns J took the view that 'the failure to produce an earlier report which contains a view different from that contained in the final report may produce exactly the kind of surprises' about which Murphy J warned.[33] Thus, the benchmark of ensuring that surprises do not occur either in examination-in-chief or during the cross-examination of an expert witness suggests an extensive obligation to disclose information in the form of expert reports.

29. The exchange of expert reports should be contemporaneous so as to prevent mischief or abuse of the procedure. *Kincaid v Aer Lingus Teoranta* [2003] 2 IR 314.

30. Rule 45(1)(e). See *Payne v Shovlin* [2006] 2 ILRM 1; *Doherty v North Western Health Board* [2005] IEHC 404 (1 December 2005). Expertise is cast in similarly broad terms. Rule 45(1)(e) refers to 'accountants, actuaries, architects, dentists, doctors, occupational therapists, psychologists, psychiatrists, scientists, or any other expert'. See *Galvin v Murray* [2001] 1 IR 331; *O'Sullivan v Kieran* [2004] IEHC (11 February 2004).

31. [2006] 2 ILRM 1 at 11.

32. [2001] 1 IR 331. See also *Kincaid v Aer Lingus Teoranta* [2003] 2 IR 314.

33. [2006] 2 ILRM 1 at 12.

3.05.2 Elements of the foundation

Where a party fails to discharge its obligation to disclose the report of an expert witness, the other side may apply to the court for an order of disclosure. The elements of the foundation might include:

1. The party has listed an expert witness in its schedule of witnesses.
2. The party has failed to hand over the report of its expert witness.
3. The deadline for exchange of expert reports has elapsed.
4. The party has failed to respond to further requests for disclosure issued after that date.

3.05.3 Sample foundation

The hypothetical scenario is a personal injuries action within the meaning of the disclosure rules. The plaintiff was injured in a road traffic accident which occurred on 1 March 2007. The plaintiff has sued the driver of the other car, but has also sued the local county council (the second-named defendant) on the basis that the section of the road where the accident took place was in a dangerous state of disrepair at the time of the collision.

The plaintiff is seeking disclosure of expert reports prepared by the second-named defendant's engineering experts regarding the state of the road on the day in question. The plaintiff's application will be made to the High Court by way of notice of motion grounded on affidavit. The said notice of motion seeks, *inter alia*, an order directing the second named defendant to disclose all reports prepared, pursuant to SI 391/1998.

The following is a specimen affidavit upon which the said notice of motion might be grounded:

THE HIGH COURT

Record No 2008/1111P

ANDREW AMBER

Plaintiff

-and-

BILLY BLUE and BROADSIDE COUNTY COUNCIL

Defendants

AFFIDAVIT OF SAMUEL SILVER

I, Samuel Silver, a Solicitor, of Main Street, Central Town, aged eighteen years and upwards MAKE OATH and say as follows:

1. I am a Solicitor in the firm of Silver & Company, Solicitors on record for the Plaintiff in the above entitled proceedings, and I make this affidavit for and on behalf of the Plaintiff and with his consent and authority. I make this affidavit from facts within my own knowledge, save where otherwise appearing, and where so appears I believe the same to be true and accurate.
2. I beg to refer to the proceedings already had herein, when produced.
3. I say that the Plaintiff's claim herein arises out of a road traffic accident that occurred on 1 March 2007 at Subsidiary Street, Central Town as a result of which the Plaintiff has suffered severe personal injuries, loss and damage. The first named Defendant was at all material times the driver of the vehicle with which the Plaintiff's vehicle came into collision. The second named Defendant is a local authority with responsibility for the said Street's maintenance and repair.
4. I say that the Plaintiff has alleged negligence and breach of duty (including statutory duty) against the first named Defendant, and negligence and breach of duty (including statutory duty) against the second named Defendant.
5. I say that the Notice of Trial in this matter was duly served on both of the defendants on 1 January 2008, and I beg to refer to a copy of the said Notice of Trial upon which I have marked with the numbers and letters 'AB1' prior to the swearing hereof.
6. I say and believe that the second named Defendant, despite repeated demands, has failed to comply with its obligations of disclosure pursuant to Statutory Instrument 391 of 1998. In this regard, I beg to refer to a bundle of letters which this firm sent to the solicitors for the second named Defendant and upon which, marked with the numbers and letters 'AB2' I have marked my name prior to the swearing hereof.
7. I say that, in particular, the second named Defendant has refused to make available expert reports carried out on its behalf of the locus of the accident in the immediate aftermath of the said accident in this case.
8. I say that, although one such report has been furnished by the second named Defendant, subsequent reports have not been

disclosed. I say and believe that the Plaintiff herein is entitled to disclosure of all reports prepared in relation to the locus of the accident in this case, and not simply the first or 'main' such report.

9. I say and believe that unless the second named Defendant makes disclosure of all such reports, there is a very real risk that the Plaintiff could be prejudiced at the trial of this action by virtue of being denied access to the said reports prior to the commencement of the trial. I say and believe that the said disclosure is necessary to avoid trial by ambush and to ensure that the issues are clarified by the exchange of reports prior to the trial of this action.
10. I say and believe that it is likely that the reports prepared which have not yet been disclosed contain information that may be of crucial importance to the Plaintiff in prosecuting his action against the second named Defendant.
11. I say and believe that there is no satisfactory explanation for the failure of the second named Defendant to make disclosure of the said report.
12. Accordingly, I pray this Honourable Court for an Order in the terms of the Notice of Motion herein, and for such further or other order as to this Honourable Court shall seem appropriate.

SWORN by the said on the day of 25th day of March 2008 at 1 River Street In the city of Dublin before me a Commissioner for Oaths/ Practising Solicitor and I know the Deponent.

DOCUMENTS ADMITTED INTO EVIDENCE

3.06 PROVING THE CONTENTS OF A DOCUMENT

3.06.1 Background

Irish law requires that a party seeking to rely on the contents of a document must adduce primary evidence of those contents.[34] Typically, this is achieved

34. *Primor plc v Stokes Kennedy Crowley* [1996] 2 IR 459.

by producing the original document in court.[35] In certain instances, primary evidence may be adduced in another form. For example, an admission by a party to the proceedings as to the contents of a document may constitute primary evidence thereof.[36]

The primary evidence rule is subject to a number of exceptions whereby the contents of a document may be proved by secondary evidence, such as a copy. For example, the parties to civil proceedings may agree to accept secondary evidence of a document. In addition, secondary evidence is admissible where the original document has been lost or destroyed or where production of the original is physically or legally impossible.[37] The best way to establish secondary evidence is to produce a copy of the document supported by the testimony of a witness that it is a true and accurate copy of the original. The contents of a document may also be proved by oral evidence in most instances.

3.06.2 Sample foundation

The following hypothetical is based on an action for breach of contract arising out of a franchise agreement. The plaintiff, Mr Freddy Franchisee, operated a pest control business using the franchise of the defendant, Pesky Pest Control Co Ltd. Freddy Franchisee asserts that it was a term of the contract that Pesky Pest Control would give him six months' notice if it decided to terminate the agreement. The contract was drawn up over 20 years ago, in the form of a somewhat rudimentary written agreement. No written copy of the contract can be located. Both parties accept that a contract existed, but Pesky Pest Control denies that it was required to give six months' notice (or any notice) to Freddy Franchisee prior to termination. Freddy Franchisee wants to prove that this notice requirement formed part of the contract, and calls Mr Walter Wise to give evidence. Mr Wise has worked closely with Freddy Franchisee as his business advisor for many

35. A duplicate document constitutes an original for this purpose. See McGrath, *Evidence* (Thomson Round Hall, 2005) at para 12.09 (citing cases).

36. *AG v Kyle* [1933] IR 15. In the case of an enrolled document (ie a document filed in a public registry), a copy produced by the public office will be accepted as primary evidence.

37. *Primor plc v Stokes Kennedy Crowley* [1996] 2 IR 459. Other exceptions are enshrined in statute. See eg s 30 of the CEA 1992.

years, and was present when the contract in question was entered into between the parties.

Mr Wise is being examined-in-chief by the counsel for the plaintiff. The plaintiff is the proponent.

P. Mr Wise, please state your occupation.

W. I'm a businessman, with an expertise in the area of franchising. I advise people on entering into a franchise business.

P. Is the plaintiff in this action known to you?

W. Yes, I have known him for over thirty years.

P. Have you worked with him?

W. I have acted as his business advisor since 1983, in return for an annual fee.

P. Were you acting in that capacity when the plaintiff and the defendant entered into the contract that is the subject matter of this action?

W. Yes, I was present when the contract was drawn up.

P. When was that?

W. I don't recall the exact date, but I'm quite certain that it was sometime in June 1986.

P. Where was the contract drawn up?

W. In a meeting in Brown's Hotel on Broad Street in Town. That hotel has since changed its name to Green's, I believe.

P. Did you see the contract?

W. Yes, I was advising Mr Franchisee in relation to it, and regarding terms that should be included.

P. Was it a long, detailed document?

W. Not at all. I would describe it as having been fairly rough and ready. It certainly wasn't like a contract that lawyers would draft. It was just written up there and then between the parties.

P. Do you recall the terms that were included in the contract?

W. Yes.

P. Mr Wise, was there a term in the contract relating to notice that would have to be given if either side purported to terminate the agreement.

W. Yes, the contract provided that a period of six months' notice would have to be given before either side terminated the agreement.

P. How can you be so sure of that?

W. I distinctly remember it because I was the one who advised Mr Franchisee to make sure that that was inserted. I've advised a number of franchisees down through the years who have been left high and dry after the franchisor terminated the agreement without notice. I've always advised my clients to have a six-month notice period included, to protect themselves.

P. Do you recall seeing such a term in the signed, final agreement between the parties in this case?

W. Yes, I do. It was the last term that was inserted, and once that was inserted I advised Mr Franchisee to sign the contract, which he did in my presence.

P. Thank you, Mr Wise.

3.07 PROVING A DOCUMENT WAS DULY EXECUTED

3.07.1 Background

A document is presumed to have been executed on the day and date it bears; where there is no date, or the wrong date, the correct date may be proved by oral evidence. The handwriting and signature on a document may be proved by calling the writer, or by calling a witness who saw the document signed, or by calling a witness who has acquired knowledge of the writing. Alternatively, it may be possible to prove a document by comparing it with another which has been proved to the satisfaction of the court to be genuine. If the party against whom a document is tendered admits its authenticity, this may be regarded as sufficient.

3.07.2 Testimony of a witness who observed the document's execution

One way in which a party can authenticate a document where due execution is disputed is by the direct evidence of a witness who observed the document's execution and recognises the document executed.

3.07.2.1 Elements of the foundation

The following are the elements of the foundation:

1. Where the witness observed the execution of the document.
2. When the witness observed the execution of the document.

3. Who was present.
4. The event that occurred, ie the execution of the document.
5. The witness recognises the document.
6. The means by which the witness recognises the document.

3.07.2.2 Sample foundation

Assume that one issue in a commercial dispute between a plaintiff distributor and a defendant retailer is whether the defendant signed a certain cheque. The witness, Mr Eddie Employee, works for the plaintiff, and testifies that he observed the defendant signing the cheque. The plaintiff is the proponent (ie is presenting evidence of the cheque).

P. Where were you on the afternoon of 4 February 2007? (1), (2)
W. I was in the defendant's shop.
P. Who was there? (3)
W. Just myself and the defendant.
P. What, if anything, happened while you were there? (4)
W. The defendant was signing some cheques to pay his monthly bills.
P. Mr Employee, I am now handing you plaintiff's exhibit number five for identification. What is it? (5)
W. It is a cheque the defendant signed that afternoon.
P. How do you recognise it? (6)
W. Well, the defendant handed it to me and asked me to take a look at it. I recognise the signature and other writing on it.
P. How long did you have to examine it? (6)
W. About a minute or so.
P. How carefully did you examine it? (6)
W. Closely enough to recognise it now.
P. What characteristics of the cheque are you relying on to recognise it?
W. I remember the payee on the cheque, who is my employer. I also remember the amount of the cheque and the defendant's signature, which is rather peculiar.
P. Thank you. I have no further questions for this witness.

3.07.3 Testimony of a witness familiar with the author's handwriting

Even if the party cannot locate a person who observed the document being executed, the party may be able to find someone familiar with the author's handwriting style. The admissibility of testimony on handwriting style may be admitted occasionally as an exception to the general prohibition on opinion evidence. The primary problem of proof for the party presenting the document is establishing that the witness is sufficiently familiar with the author's handwriting style to recognise that style. Ideally, the witness will have observed the author sign his or her name on several previous occasions. However, it may be sufficient that the witness has seen the author's signature under reliable circumstances. For example, the secretary of one company executive may have seen documents bearing the signature of another executive of the same company on hundreds of prior occasions. Even if the witness has never seen that second company executive sign a document, a court may take the view that the witness is sufficiently acquainted with the executive's handwriting style.

3.07.3.1 Elements of the foundation

The elements of the foundation are:

1. The witness recognised the author's handwriting on the document.
2. The witness is familiar with the author's handwriting style.
3. The witness has a sufficient basis for familiarity.

3.07.3.2 Sample foundation

The plaintiff is seeking to establish that the defendant wrote and signed a cheque and, with this in mind, calls Ms Francine French who is a friend and co-worker of the defendant. Although Ms French did not observe the defendant signing the cheque in question, she testifies that she is familiar with the defendant's handwriting style.

P. Ms French, I am now handing you plaintiff's exhibit number three for identification. What is it?

W. It is a cheque.

P. Who signed the cheque? (1)

W. I'd say that the defendant signed it.

P. Why do you say that? (2)
W. Well, I recognise the defendant's handwriting style on the cheque and his signature, which is very distinct. The defendant's name is also printed on the cheque.
P. How well do you know the defendant's handwriting style? (3)
W. Very well.
P. How did you become familiar with the defendant's handwriting style? (3)
W. We've been friends for years.
P. How many years? (3)
W. About ten.
P. How often have you seen the defendant sign his name? (3)
W. Oh, loads of times. We work for the same company and I've often been there when he's written a note or a memo and signed it.

3.07.4 Comparison of writings or signatures

Handwriting or a signature may also be proved by asking a witness to compare a disputed writing with another writing which is established to the satisfaction of the court as having been written or signed by the person in question.[38] Section 8 of CPA 1865 provides:

> Comparison of a disputed writing with any writing proved to the satisfaction of the judge to be genuine shall be permitted to be made by witnesses; and such writings, and the evidence of witnesses respecting the same, may be submitted to the court and jury as evidence of the genuineness of the writing in dispute.

The reference in the section to 'witnesses' suggests that the comparison may be undertaken by any witness. Nevertheless, in contemporary practice, this method of authentication might be more appropriately undertaken by an expert witness.

3.07.4.1 Elements of the foundation

The elements of the foundation are:

1. The witness qualifies as an expert.

---

38. *DPP v Malocco* (23 May 1996, unreported) CCA.

2. The witness has compared the disputed document and the comparison document.
3. On the basis of the comparison, the witness concludes that the same person wrote and/or signed the two documents.
4. The witness specifies the basis for his or her opinion, ie the similarities between the two documents.

3.07.4.2 Sample foundation

The plaintiff is seeking to establish that the defendant wrote and signed a cheque. Assume that the comparison document, a letter, has been accepted by the court as genuine, ie as a letter written by the defendant. The plaintiff calls Mr Eamon Expert, a questioned-document examiner. The examination-in-chief might unfold as follows:

P. What is your occupation? (1)
W. I am a technician at Forensics Co Ltd.
P. What kind of business does the company engage in? (1)
W. It's a private forensic laboratory. We do various kinds of scientific work for legal cases.
P. How long have you worked there? (1)
W. For about 12 years.
P. What are your duties there? (1)
W. I work mostly on questioned-document examination.
P. What does that involve? (1)
W. Among other things, we try to determine who wrote or signed documents.
P. What is your formal education? (1)
W. I have a Bachelor of Science from the Metropolitan University.
P. What other training, if any, have you had?
W. I've attended several short courses on questioned-document examination organised by forensic science institutes and associations.
P. How often have you testified as an expert questioned-document examiner? (1)
W. Numerous times. I'd say about thirty times.
P. Mr Expert, I'm now handing you plaintiff's exhibit two and plaintiff's exhibit three. What are they?

W. They're handwriting specimens.

P. Have you seen these documents before? (2)

W. Yes.

P. On what occasion did you see them? (2)

W. The plaintiff's solicitor gave me the documents and asked me to examine them for this case.

P. When was this?

W. It was six months ago, in May 2007.

P. What did you do with the documents?

W. Well, I examined them under an optical microscope to determine whether they had a common authorship. In other words, to see if they were written by the same person.

P. How long did you study the documents? (2)

W. I spent the better part of an afternoon, maybe three hours, working on the comparison.

P. How did you make the comparison? (2)

W. I made a detailed study of the documents under the microscope. I had some aspects of the documents blown up into enlarged photographs and I studied the enlargements as well.

P. You stated that you recognise these documents as the ones you previously examined. How can you be sure of this? (2)

W. On the basis of the peculiarities of the handwriting style. They are uniform throughout each document. They're quite distinctive.

P. Do you have an opinion on the question of whether the author of exhibit two also wrote exhibit three? (3)

W. Yes.

P. What is that opinion? (3)

W. In my view, the documents were written by the same author.

P. What is the basis for your opinion? (4)

W. In all, I detected five unique writing characteristics common to both documents. There was a common misspelling, a spacing peculiarity, a tail on each letter 'y', the pronounced loop on each letter 'o' and the rather unique way in which the letter 's' is written. These characteristics all point to common authorship.

P. Thank you, Mr Expert.

3.08 PROVING A COPY OF A DOCUMENT

3.08.1 Background

In circumstances where the original of a document cannot be produced, it is permissible to prove the document by means of a copy. Copies are a very common form of 'secondary evidence'. The traditional common law position is that where there are duplicate originals of a document, both are treated as originals, and thus as primary evidence.[39] However, our focus at this point is on a situation where a copy of a document has to be proven to be a true copy of the original. Generally, it will suffice if the witness is in a position to state categorically that the copy is a true and authentic copy of the original document.

3.08.2 Elements of the foundation

The elements of the foundation might include:

1. That the witness was present when the copy was made.
2. That the original cannot be produced for some particular reason.
3. That the witness recognises the copy as being a copy of the original document.

3.08.3 Sample foundation

In an action arising out of an alleged breach of a lease agreement, it transpires that the original lease agreement cannot be produced. However, the plaintiff's solicitor, Mr Brian Brown, is in a position to give evidence that the copy sought to be admitted into evidence is a true copy of the original. Mr Brown takes the stand and is examined by counsel for the plaintiff.

P. What is your occupation?

W. I am a Solicitor in the firm of Brown & Company Solicitors.

P. What is your relationship with the plaintiff in this action?

W. I have been the plaintiff's solicitor for many years.

P. Were you in any way involved in advising the plaintiff about the lease agreement that is currently a matter of dispute before this court? (1)

---

39. *Forbes v Samuel* [1913] 3 KB 706.

W. Yes, I spent considerable time advising the plaintiff about the proposed lease, and I was present when the agreement itself was drawn up.
P. When and where was that lease agreement drawn up?
W. The agreement was drawn up in a function room in Tiptop Hotel, Leafy Avenue, in the City Centre on 12 February 2007.
P. Please explain to the court whether the original copy of the agreement is to hand? (2)
W. The actual original copy is not to hand. I can only apologise to the court for that, and say that it was due to an error in my office that the original copy of the agreement has gone astray. I can say that in over thirty years in practice I have never before misplaced the original copy of a document in this manner.
P. Mr Brown, I am now handing you the plaintiff's exhibit number one. What is it? (3)
W. This is a copy of the original document. It's one of a number of copies that were made almost immediately after the original was signed by the parties and witnessed.
P. How and when were copies distributed, Mr Brown?
W. I personally gave three copies to the defendant and his solicitor on 12 February 2007.
P. Mr Brown, does the document I have handed you reflect a true and accurate copy of the lease agreement entered into between the parties in this case?
W. Yes, it does.
P. How sure are you of that Mr Brown?
W. I am quite certain of it.

BUSINESS RECORDS

3.09 THE LAW

The Criminal Evidence Act 1992 provides for the admissibility of business records as an exception to the rule against hearsay in criminal proceedings.[40] Far more limited provision exists in statute and at common law in relation to civil proceedings, although business records are frequently admitted on

40. CEA 1992, ss 3–8.

consent.[41] The rationale for reliance on business records is that they constitute the best available evidence of a disputed matter. If a business conducts hundreds or thousands of similar transactions during the course of any given year, it is doubtful whether any single employee will remember any particular transaction. Where the transaction has been recorded, the process whereby the record was created creates an inference of the reliability of the entry. It is the precise, routine manner in which the business compiles and maintains its records that safeguards their reliability.

3.10 CONVENTIONAL BUSINESS RECORDS

3.10.1 Background

In the case of ordinary or conventional business records, authentication is typically established by offering proof of proper custody. It is generally sufficient if the witness is familiar with the business's filing system, took the record from the correct file and recognises the exhibit as the record removed from the files.

3.10.2 Elements of the foundation

The elements of the foundation might include:

1. The witness has personal knowledge of the business's filing system.
2. The witness removed a record from a certain file.
3. It was the correct file.
4. The witness recognises the exhibit as the record he or she removed from the files.
5. The witness specifies the basis on which he or she recognises the exhibit.

3.10.3 Sample foundation

In an action for breach of contract, the plaintiff business, Collegiate Clothing Manufacturers, is seeking to authenticate a bill it prepared in June 2007. The plaintiff calls Ms Deirdre Digit as its witness.

---

41. See para **6.07**.

P. What is your occupation? (1)
W. I am a bookkeeper.
P. Where do you work? (1)
W. I work at the plaintiff's main office.
P. How long have you worked there? (1)
W. About seven years.
P. What are your duties? (1)
W. I ensure that we have proper records of all the money and goods flowing into and out of the company. I supervise the preparation of the records, the maintenance of the records and, where appropriate, their eventual destruction.
P. How well do you know the plaintiff's filing system? (1)
W. Extremely well. In fact, I helped design the system.
P. Ms Digit, I am now handing you plaintiff's exhibit number four. What is it? (4)
W. It is a bill from our file for June 2007. It's one of the bills that I removed from the file for use in these proceedings.
P. When did you remove it from the file? (2)
W. Two months ago. I gave the bill to the company's solicitor so it could be used at trial. But I photocopied the bill first and put the photocopy in the file so we would maintain a complete record.
P. How can you recognise the bill? (5)
W. I recognise the handwriting of the clerk, Noel Numbers. I've known Noel for years. Also, I can recall generally the contents of each of the bills I took out of the file and gave to the solicitor.

3.11 COMPUTER RECORDS

3.11.1 Background

Computer-generated evidence is a species of scientific evidence. The process of generating data by computer is beyond the knowledge of most laypersons. The presentation of scientific evidence usually requires proof of the validity of the underlying theory and the reliability of the instrument. However, computers are so widely used that a trial judge may take judicial notice of the validity of the theory underlying computers and the general reliability of computers. Where a judge is willing to accept a simple authentication of a computer record, it may be enough for the party to show that the business has successfully used the computer system in question and that the witness recognises the record as output from the computer. A more extensive foundation would require proof of the reliability of the particular computer used, the dependability of the business's input procedures for the computer, the use of proper procedures to obtain the document offered in court and the witness's recognition of that document as the printout from the computer. Furthermore, if the computer printout contains symbols and terminology beyond the understanding of the layperson, the party may need to call an expert to explain the document to the finder of fact.

3.11.2 Elements of the foundation

A sample foundation might include some (but not necessarily all) of the following elements:

1. The business uses a computer.
2. The computer is reliable.
3. The business has developed a procedure for inserting data into the computer.
4. The procedure has in-built safeguards to ensure accuracy and identify errors.
5. The business keeps the computer in a good state of repair.
6. The witness used the computer to print out certain data.
7. The witness used the proper procedures to obtain the printout.
8. The computer was in working order at the time the witness obtained the printout.
9. The witness recognises the exhibit as the printout.
10. The witness explains how he or she recognises the printout.

3.11.3 Sample foundation

Suppose that Alpha Company Limited has instituted proceedings against Beta Company Limited seeking damages for anti-competitive practices. Alpha is seeking to demonstrate a decline in its gross sales during the period 2000 to 2006. To this end, Alpha has presented the court with a computer printout to show its gross sales in each of those years. Alpha is the proponent and, as its witness, Alpha calls Mr Gamma.

P. Mr Gamma, what is your occupation?

W. I am an accountant at Alpha Company Limited.

P. How long have you worked for Alpha?

W. Just over ten years.

P. What are your duties at Alpha?

W. I work generally with our accounts but I specialise in the maintenance of our computer records.

P. How does Alpha maintain its business records? (1)

W. We maintain the overwhelming majority of our data on computer. We use a modern system of networked computers.

P. What is a system of networked computers? (1)

W. Well, you have individual computers at each workstation but they're networked or wired together. That means that an employee at a sales desk on the first floor can enter information about a sale directly into the central company sales database. It also means that in our accounting department on the third floor, I can use the computer at my desk to access the same information. It's a very efficient way of doing business.

P. Mr Gamma, please describe the network at your company. (1)

W. The three components of our network are the hardware, the software and the personnel.

P. Which hardware do you use?

W. We use Omega 45A computers. All the employees linked into the network have one at their desk. I have one sitting on my desk.

P. How long have you used that computer? (2)

W. For the last three years.

P. In your experience, how widely is that model used? (2)

W. Very widely. Because I'm the computer specialist in accounting, I regularly attend business technology conferences and trade shows. The technology develops so fast that it is no longer state of the art, but it's got a reputation for being popular and dependable.

P. What software do you use? (2)

W. All the computers have Delta business database. It is specially designed for businesses with networks.

P. How long have you used that software? (2)

W. For the same period – the last three years.

P. How widely is that software used by businesses? (2)

W. My impression is that it is one of the most popular not just in this country but worldwide. We buy upgrades to the software as well. The last upgrade was about two months ago.

P. Finally, what about the personnel? (3)

W. We give our employees training.

P. Which employees receive training? (3)

W. Any employee who might have occasion to make a sale and input sales data into the database. They receive a full day's training in the use of hardware and software. Since we purchase regular upgrades, they also receive periodic refresher training.

P. Who conducts the training? (3)

W. At first, we hired an outside information technology consultant. But within a year I was familiar enough with the system to be able to do the training. I've personally trained every new employee for the past two years.

P. What procedures does Alpha have for using these computers to create and maintain its records? (3)

W. As I've indicated, the employee who makes the sale actually inputs the data directly into the networked system. At the same time, the employee also prints out a paper copy of the transaction at his or her workstation.

P. What happens to the paper copies? (4)

W. They're sent to the Accounting Department at the end of each working day.

P. What does the Accounting Department do with them? (4)

W. At the end of each week, we randomly select a few paper copies from each workstation and double check them against the electronic data. That way we can ensure that the entries are correct.

P. How is the computer network maintained? (5)

W. We have a service contract with Omega. One of their service representatives visits our offices every two months to check the equipment and carry out preventative maintenance. Also, if any of our employees encounters a mechanical problem, he or she calls the accounting department and we in turn can call on an Omega service representative.

P. Mr Gamma, I am now handing you the plaintiff's exhibit number two. What is it? (6), (9)

W. It's a statement of the total sales figures for each of the years from 2000 to 2006. I printed it out and gave it to the company solicitor for use in these proceedings.

P. When did you print it out? (6)

W. Two months ago. I gave the bill to the company's solicitor so it could be used at trial. But I photocopied the bill first and put the photocopy in the file so we would maintain a complete record.

P. How did you obtain the printout? (7)

W. I went to the terminal, requested the sales figures and then clicked on the print command.

P. What was the condition of the computer at the time? (8)

W. It seemed to be grand. I had used it several times already that day and it was working as well as always.

P. How can you recognise the printout? (9), (10)

W. I put my initials and the date in the top lefthand corner. I recognise them.

3.12 FAXED DOCUMENTS

3.12.1 Background

Recent decades have witnessed a communications revolution. Much of the business correspondence that used to be conducted by post is instead transmitted by fax machine or e-mail. Even when the testimony is based on a relatively new technology, however, the principles governing authenticity remain the same, ie the party presenting the faxed document or e-mail may be required to demonstrate that the evidence is what the party claims. The following three hypothetical scenarios illustrate some of the different claims which a party might make.

First, suppose that the only issue is whether the recipient of a fax had notice of certain facts set out in the fax. The recipient, a company, calls an employee to testify that she received the fax. The source of the information is irrelevant for this purpose; regardless of who sent the fax, the employee can testify that she received it and that the fax itself gave the recipient notice of the information. The essential question is *whether the alleged recipient actually received a fax with certain contents.* The recipient's only claim is that the fax was produced on the recipient's facsimile machine and the employee's testimony suffices to establish that claim.

In the second scenario, the issue is whether a purported recipient, once again a company, received a fax setting out certain information transmitted by an alleged sender. The essential question is thus *whether a fax transmitted by a certain sender reached the alleged recipient.* In this variation of the hypothetical, the witness is an employee of the company that *sent* the fax rather than the company receiving the fax. The employee might give the following foundational testimony: the employee's company uses a fax machine; the machine is capable, when operating properly, of transmitting and receiving a fax; the machine was in proper working order on the occasion in question; before using the machine, the employee looked up the addressee company's fax number in a reliable directory or obtained the fax number from another reliable source; the employee dialled that number on the machine; the sheet of paper containing the facts passed through the machine; and the machine generated a transmission report listing the dialled number and indicating that transmission had occurred. The witness is shown an exhibit which the witness identifies as the sheet that passed through the originating fax machine.

In this second scenario, the proponent claims that: (1) the exhibit is the paper that the witness passed through the fax machine at the transmitting end, and (2) the paper is an accurate copy of the document that the other company received at its end. The foregoing foundation is adequate to establish that twofold claim. The witness is certainly competent to prove the first claim. With respect to the second claim, an adequate foundation is presented by evidence that the fax machine employed to send the fax is capable of transmitting an accurate reproduction when properly employed and that, in the particular case, the fax machine was properly employed. A trial judge could take judicial notice of the general reliability of fax machines.

In a third hypothetical situation, the issue is the identity of the sender of a fax. The essential question is *whether a fax which reached a certain recipient was transmitted by an alleged sender.* The addressee or recipient company is the plaintiff in a contract action alleging that the defendant company sent it an offer that the plaintiff accepted. The plaintiff is the proponent and the witness is one of the plaintiff's employees. The employee testifies that she received the fax in question and the proponent claims that the fax is an accurate copy of the offer transmitted by the defendant. This fact pattern differs from the preceding versions. In the first fact pattern, the source of the fax was irrelevant; here the source is critical – if the defendant company was not the source, the defendant is not contractually liable to the plaintiff. In the second fact pattern, the witness was an employee of the sending or transmitting entity; here the witness is an employee of the recipient.

The identity of the sender of the fax might be established in one of several ways. First, if the fax in question bore the sender's fax number automatically imprinted on each page and the imprinted digits are demonstrated to be the sender's fax number, an adequate foundation has arguably been presented. Second, the fax received might disclose information known only to the alleged sender. Third, if the recipient of the fax in question had earlier contacted the alleged sender by letter, phone or fax, the proponent might establish that the fax in question was obviously a response to the earlier correspondence.

3.12.2 Elements of the foundation

On the basis of the above, the foundation might contain the following elements:

1. The receiving business uses a facsimile machine.
2. The facsimile machine is standard equipment that can both send and receive documents by telephone. The trial judge could take judicial notice of this proposition.
3. The machine accurately transmits copies of original documents.
4. A procedure exists for checking for mechanical and human error.
5. The facsimile machine accurately and automatically records the time and date of transmittal.
6. A cover sheet, faxed with the document, displays the phone number of the originating fax machine and the name and fax number of the person to whom the document is directed.
7. Each fax page received is automatically imprinted with the fax number of the originating machine.
8. The fax number stated on the cover sheet and on the fax pages is the number of the alleged sender.
9. The witness identifies the exhibit as the cover sheet received on the addressee's fax machine.

3.12.3 Sample foundation

In the following hypothetical scenario, the plaintiff, Surefire Supply Co Ltd has instituted proceedings in contract against one of its customers,

Weatherproof Windows Co Ltd. The proceedings concern an order placed by Weatherproof Windows with Surefire Supply for the supply of 300 window frames. As part of its case, Surefire Supply is seeking to establish that one of its employees, Ms Ruth Reliable received a 'faxed' letter from Weatherproof Windows containing an order for 300 window frames. Counsel for Surefire Supply is the proponent and Ms Reliable is the witness.

P. Where do you work?

W. At Surefire Supply Co Ltd.

P. What is your position there?

W. I am executive secretary and assistant to the Managing Director, Bobby Boss.

P. As of 11 September 2007, the date in question here, did Surefire Supply own a facsimile machine? (1)

W. Yes.

P. As of that date, for how long had Surefire Supply had the facsimile machine?

W. Over four years.

P. How often, if ever, did you have occasion to use the facsimile machine?

W. Hundreds of times, both sending and receiving faxes.

P. What procedure did you use in September 2007 when you wished to fax a document to someone? (2), (3), (4), (5), (6), (7)

W. I would fill out a cover sheet indicating the person to whom the document was directed and that person's phone number. The cover sheet would also contain other information such as the total number of pages being transmitted, the date and time of the transmission and a statement that, in case of poor transmission, the party receiving the document should call me at the number written on the cover sheet so that I could fax the document again. I would then feed the cover sheet and the document to be transmitted into the fax machine. The machine would transmit them to the number I dialled. The machine also automatically recorded the time and date of transmittal on the documents being faxed and automatically imprinted our fax number on the top of each page.

P. What was the procedure in September 2007 for documents which you received by fax?

W. The same as I described but in reverse. We'd get the cover sheet that the person faxing the documents had filled out. If the sender used a fax machine like ours, the originating fax number was automatically imprinted somewhere on the page, either on the very top or the bottom.

P. Have you ever had occasion to compare original documents that you have sent by fax with the documents received by another fax machine? (4)

W. Yes. I handle the paperwork for Surefire Supply's contracts and I often see documents that I have faxed to some third party that are being returned to me in the post with some additional writing on them.

P. How closely do the faxed documents resemble the original documents? (4)

W. They're exact copies. The machine transmits precisely what appears on the original document.

P. To your knowledge, could you alter your fax machine to create a difference between a document being faxed and the document received? (3)

W. I don't know of any way that could be done.

P. Directing your attention to 11 September 2007, what, if any, fax transmissions did you receive that day?

W. I received a fax from Weatherproof Windows Co Ltd that day.

P. Ms Reliable, I am now handing you plaintiff's exhibit number four. Can you tell me what it is?

W. This is the four-page document and cover sheet that I received on our fax machine on 11 September 2007. The document indicated that it was sent from Weatherproof Windows. Our machine had been called and the document had been transmitted to it.

P. How, if at all, does the present condition of the document differ from its condition when you received it on 11 September 2007? (9)

W. It doesn't. As far as I can tell, it's in exactly the same condition.

P. What date, time and telephone number, if any, are imprinted on the document?

W. 11 September 2007, 10:15 am and (01) 7654321.

P. What is the significance of the date and time, 11 September 2007, 10:15 am? (3), (5), (6)

W. It's the date that I received the documents from Weatherproof Windows and, to the best of my recollection, it's the approximate time.

P. Where, if anywhere, does the fax number appear on those pages? (7)

W. Well, it's on the originating cover sheet. And it has also been imprinted on each page.

P. Whose telephone or fax number is (01) 7654321? (8)

W. It's the phone and fax number of Weatherproof Windows.

P. How do you know that? (8)

W. I've faxed documents back and forth to them numerous times. Sometimes, I pick up the phone and talk to someone in their office immediately after getting or sending a fax. I'm certain that it's their number.

3.13 E-MAIL

Like faxes, electronic mail ('e-mail') can pose evidentiary problems. To appreciate the potential difficulties that may accompany authentication of e-mail, we must first understand the technology. E-mail is more versatile than fax; it can be sent over a variety of network links, ranging from dial-up to fibre optic lines to wireless connections. E-mail is ordinary text but other formats can be sent, including graphic images.

The mechanics of a standard e-mail system are straightforward. To send e-mail, the person opens the e-mail application. The user next sees the e-mail screen consisting of two parts: the header and the body. The visible part of a typical header includes at least three lines. The first line is for the sender's e-mail address. That line has usually been filled in already but it is sometimes a simple matter for the sender to change the entry in that line. The second line is for the recipient's address. An Internet e-mail address consists of a local part and a host part: username@hostname. The local part includes the mailbox, login name or user ID of the intended recipient. The host name includes the networks serving the user. The third subject line is provided for a brief summary of the title of the message.

After completing the heading, the sender composes the body of the message. Once the sender completes the message, he or she ordinarily types 'send' or presses a 'send' button. Alternatively, the user might press a 'queue' button and send queued messages before signing off. The programme then sends the message through the computer networks connecting the source (the sender) and destination (the intended recipient). Service providers (servers) intervene between the sender and the recipient to transmit the message. After travelling through various servers and networks, the message reaches the recipient's inbox. When that person logs on and checks mail, he or she will be told, 'You have new mail'. At that point, the recipient opens the message and reads it. Most programmes have a reply feature. To use this feature, the recipient types 'reply' or clicks a 'reply' button. Depending on the programme, the recipient then types the reply immediately before or after the message received. The programme then automatically sends the reply to the original sender. The original sender receives a message including both the original message and the recipient's reply. A similar feature permits the recipient to 'forward' the message to one or more third parties.

One fundamental difference between e-mail systems and fax is that it is usually easier to change the e-mail address of the sender than to change the sending number on a fax. In some e-mail systems when the sender is completing the heading, it is a simple matter to enter a fictitious name or someone else's name. Some fax machines automatically imprint the sending number on the pages printed out at the recipient's end. Although a sophisticated user of the fax might be able to either disable that function or change the number, doing so requires a level of expertise above and beyond the elementary knowledge needed to send a fax message. Thus, it is less justifiable to accept an e-mail message at face value than to presume the authenticity of a fax. Consequently, there is an even greater need to lay an adequate foundation establishing the authenticity of the message.

The Electronic Commerce Act 2000 sets out, *inter alia*, the framework for the legal recognition of electronic signatures and contracts. The Act provides that information is not to be denied legal effect, validity or enforceability solely on the basis that it is wholly or partly in electronic form, whether as an electronic communication or otherwise. The Act provides that where a signature to a document is required to be witnessed, that requirement is taken to have been met if the signatory and the witness use advanced electronic signatures and the other party so consents.[42] It

42. Section 14 of the Electronic Commerce Act 2000.

should be noted that the Act does not extend to the law governing wills, trusts, an enduring power of attorney and the swearing of an affidavit or other sworn declaration.[43]

Although e-mail is a relatively new technology, in some instances a party may be able to authenticate an e-mail message by adapting a traditional evidentiary principle. For example, a circumstantial inference of authenticity may be established by demonstrating that the e-mail is a reply to earlier correspondence. The proponent makes a foundational showing that he or she obtained an e-mail address from a reliable source (such as an online directory), sent an e-mail message to the address obtained from such source and in due course received a message responding to the earlier message. In the context of e-mail, 'due course' will ordinarily be a shorter period of time than in the case of conventional correspondence or even faxed correspondence.

A second traditional means of authentication centres on the content of the message. If the recipient used the reply feature to respond, the new message will include the sender's original message. If the sender dispatched that message to only one person, its inclusion in the new message indicates that the new message originated with the original recipient. Alternatively, the proponent may be able to show that only the purported author was likely to know the information reflected in the message.

A third potential method of authentication is proof of action consistent with the message. Suppose that after the recipient of the message, the purported sender takes action consistent with the content of the message. In a business context, the action might be the delivery of merchandise mentioned in the message. The common law recognised action consistent with the message as sufficient to establish a circumstantial inference of authenticity and, arguably, the method has continuing resonance in the e-mail setting.

There are other more *avant-garde* techniques for authenticating e-mail above and beyond the three traditional techniques mentioned in the preceding paragraphs. For example, a party might provide the court with information about cutting-edge technologies such as cryptography and digital or electronic signatures. Laying a foundation for the admission of e-mails in this fashion would necessitate calling one or more expert witnesses. The proponent might then call a lay witness, such as a company employee, to explain how the technology was used in the instant case.

---

43. For a more thorough discussion, see McDermott, *Contract Law* (Tottel Publishing, 2001) at p 256 *et seq*.

3.14 INFORMATION POSTED AT A BUSINESS'S WEBSITE

3.14.1 Background

E-commerce has become one of the most important types of business activity. In order to participate in e-commerce, many businesses have established websites that customers can visit. The information posted at these sites can become relevant as evidence in litigation. Where a party seeks to use assertions posted at a web site as evidence, the party will need to lay a foundation for an exception to the rule against hearsay or, alternatively, lay a foundation for the admission of the assertion for a non-hearsay purpose (ie for a purpose other than as substantive evidence of the matter stated). For example, in proceedings for breach of warranty, the plaintiff customer might want to prove that in purchasing the defendant manufacturer's goods, the customer relied on an assurance posted on the defendant's website. In that situation, the assurance is admissible for the original or non-hearsay purpose of establishing the existence of the warranty. Similarly, in proceedings for libel, an allegedly defamatory assertion posted on the defendant's website would be admissible. Clearly, the plaintiff would be adducing the assertion simply to establish the fact that it was made; the last thing the plaintiff would want to prove is the truth of the assertion, truth being a defence to the action in tort.

Whatever the hearsay status of the proposed testimony about the information posted on the website, other issues may arise regarding the authentication of the information. Views about the reliability of testimony concerning website data may vary. A federal trial judge in the United States put some of the relevant concerns thus:

> While some look to the Internet as an innovative vehicle for communication, the Court continues to warily … view it largely as one catalyst for rumor, innuendo, and misinformation … Anyone can put anything on the Internet. No web-site is monitored for accuracy and nothing contained therein is under oath or even subject to independent verification absent underlying documentation. Moreover, the Court holds no illusions that hackers can adulterate the content of any web-site from any location at any time.[44]

---

44. *St Clair v Johnny's Oyster & Shrimp Inc* 76 F Supp 2d 773, 774-5 (SD Tex 1999).

On the other hand, s 22 of the Electronic Commerce Act 2000 provides that the probative value of writing shall not be undermined simply because the writing is in electronic form.[45]

3.14.2 Elements of the foundation

To authenticate testimony describing information allegedly posted at a website, Professor Imwinkelried suggests the following foundation based on experience in the United States.[46]

1. The Internet exists and is an effective medium for electronic communication.
2. On the Internet, a person or entity can establish a web site that other persons can visit.

Propositions 1 and 2 are sufficiently well known that a trial judge may take judicial notice of them.

3. A certain person or entity operates a web site with a particular universal resource locator (URL) address, usually prefaced with 'www'.[47]
4. At a certain time, someone visited the website.
5. When they visited the site, they found certain information posted there.[48]

---

45. The terms 'electronic' and 'information' are broadly defined in s 2 of the Act and include writing, text, images, computer programs, software and databases conveyed *inter alia* by digital technology.

46. *Evidentiary Foundations* (6th edn, LexisNexis, 2005) at 4.03[5].

47. If extrinsic proof of the identity of the operator of the site is required and the alleged operator is a party to the proceedings, an out-of-court admission may suffice. Otherwise, a party might rely on circumstantial evidence. If that person or entity alone is likely to possess the information posted at the site, that fact can establish the identity of the site's operator. Or if persons have visited the site, ordered merchandise from a particular company and later received merchandise from that company, that course of conduct identifies the operator of the site.

48. There are several potential methods of proving that the information was posted there. To begin with, the proponent could call the webmaster responsible for maintaining the site. If the witness recalled the posting of the information, he or she could testify from personal knowledge. Alternatively, if the webmaster maintained records of postings, the records would qualify as business records. (contd \...)

6. The information in question is attributable to the business.[49]

3.14.3 Sample foundation

The hypothetical scenario is an action for breach of warranty. Ace Cars Co Ltd claims that it purchased tyres from SnugFit Co Ltd and that, in so doing, it relied on a representation about the quality of the tyres posted on the SnugFit website. It claims further that the tyres delivered by SnugFit did not live up to the representation. The witness has identified himself as Mr Bill Buyer, the head of Ace Cars' Purchasing Department.

P. What are your duties at Ace Cars?
W. I'm in charge of the Purchasing Department. I'm responsible for ordering all our supplies from manufacturers and wholesalers.
P. What contact, if any, have you had with SnugFit Co Ltd?
W. They're one of our regular suppliers.
P. What do they supply you with?
W. Mostly tyres.
P. When you want to contact SnugFit, what means of communication do you use?
W. I used to phone them. But they've maintained a website for the past couple of years. So now I usually deal with them by visiting their website.
P. What is the address of their website? (3)
W. It's 'www.snugfit.com'.
P. How do you know that? (3)
W. I've been dealing with them through their website for the past couple of years. I've ordered goods from that website on

48. (contd) The person who visited the site could also testify from firsthand knowledge if he or she remembered the contents of the posting the person found at the site. Better still, if the person printed out the information, he or she could authenticate the printout as an accurate copy of the data he or she read at the site at that time.

49. In large measure, the attribution depends on the part of the website where the information was posted. Some websites feature chat rooms which third parties can visit and in which they can post messages. Without a manifestation of adoption by the business, a chat room posting cannot be imputed to the business. However, if the information appears in a part of the site purportedly maintained by the business itself, the information can potentially be attributed to the business.

numerous occasions and subsequently received both the goods and the bills for the goods.

P. How do you know that the goods were SnugFit goods? (3)

W. The tyres arrive in boxes with SnugFit labels and the tyres themselves bear the SnugFit inscription.

P. What contact, if any, did you have with SnugFit on 19 July 2007? (4)

W. My boss, Ms Mary Manager, asked me to place an order for 500 tyres for medium-sized trucks and I decided to order the tyres from SnugFit. So I visited the SnugFit website.

P. How did you do that? (4)

W. In the usual way. I logged on to my computer, accessed the Internet and typed in the address of the SnugFit website.

P. What happened after you did that? (4)

W. I got straight on to the website in a matter of seconds.

P. What did you do after you reached the website? (5)

W. I went to their product list and searched for tyres suitable for medium-sized trucks.

P. How can you as a customer post anything there? (6)

W. You can't. All you can do is read the information SnugFit has posted and print out what's posted.

P. So what did you do? (5)

W. I found a description of a tyre that was suitable for use by medium-sized trucks. I read it carefully to make sure that the specifications would meet our needs. Then I printed it out. The particular model was a little more expensive that the other models so I wanted to show Ms Manager the printout so she could make the final decision whether to order that model.

P. Mr Buyer, I am now handing you plaintiff's exhibit number three. What is it? (5)

W. It's the printout of the description of that tyre.

P. How can you recognise it? (5)

W. I remember the contents for a start. Also, immediately after printing it out and before showing it to Ms Manager, I placed my initials and the date in the top, right-hand corner. They're still there.

P. Mr Buyer, would you read the second full paragraph of the printout to the court please?

W. Certainly.

MISCELLANEOUS

3.15 PHOTOGRAPHS

Like other articles, still photographs must be authenticated or verified. Traditionally, some courts insisted that the photographer appear to provide the necessary testimony. However, the prevailing view today is that any person familiar with the scene or object depicted may verify the photograph.

3.15.1 Elements of the foundation

The elements of the foundation are:

1. The witness is familiar with the object or scene.
2. The witness explains the basis for his or her familiarity with the object or scene.
3. The witness recognises the object or scene in the photograph.
4. The photograph is a fair and accurate depiction of the object or scene at the relevant time.

3.15.2 Sample foundation

The following hypothetical scenario involves proceedings in tort arising out of a road traffic accident. The collision occurred at the junction of Blue Street and Green Avenue. The plaintiff calls a witness to verify the photograph of the junction. The witness has already identified herself as Ms Brenda Banker. The accident occurred in 2006.

P. Where do you work? (2)

W. I a manager at a bank on Green Avenue.

P. Where is the bank located on Green Avenue? (2)

W. The address is 20–24 Green Avenue.

P. How long have you worked there? (2)

W. About seven years.

P. Ms Banker, I am now handing you plaintiff's exhibit number three. What is it? (3)

W. It's a photograph of the junction where Blue Street intersects with Green Avenue.

P. How do you recognise it? (2)

W. Well, as I said, I've worked around the corner from the junction for years now.

P. How often have you passed the junction? (2)

W. I couldn't say exactly. Hundreds of times.

P. What perspective or viewpoint does this photograph show? (3)

W. Let's see. Blue Street runs from the north to the south and Green Avenue runs from the east to the west.

P. Which corner are you on? (3)

W. You're on the southwest corner.

P. In which direction are you facing? (3)

W. You're facing north; you're looking up Blue Street.

P. How accurate is this photograph? (4)

W. Very. It's a good, true depiction as far as I can tell.

P. How accurately does it show the junction as it was in 2006? (4)

W. I'd say it's a good photograph for that purpose. I worked in the area at that time and I think it shows roughly how the junction looked then.

P. How has the junction changed, if at all, since 2006? (4)

W. Some of the businesses have changed so some of the signs are different. But the junction itself hasn't changed at all. It's the same size, the traffic flows the same way and the street markings are the same.

3.16 EXHIBITS

There are few legal rules governing the handling, marking and formal introduction of exhibits. Although relatively simple to accomplish, the inability to mark an exhibit, lay the foundation and introduce it into evidence effectively and efficiently is frustrating and detracts from the persuasiveness of the evidence. Despite the lack of hard and fast rules, a number of general principles may be followed, unless the court instructs counsel otherwise. The following discussion focuses on the mechanics of laying evidentiary foundations for tangible exhibits. The process is not merely one of form; it also serves the practical function of explaining to the participants in the proceedings the nature of the exhibit and what it represents.

3.16.1 Handling exhibits

The first step in the process of admitting exhibits comprises three elements: marking the exhibit, calling the exhibit to the attention of opposing counsel and presenting the exhibit to the witness. Marking involves organising exhibits in a numbered or lettered system and is ordinarily done before the commencement of the trial. If it has not been possible to mark an exhibit in advance, counsel should ask the permission of the court to mark it as the next exhibit. For example, counsel may hand the exhibit to the clerk and state: 'Judge, I'd ask that this exhibit be marked by Ms Ryan [the registrar].' Ideally, related exhibits should be marked at the same time, especially if counsel intends to show them as a group to the witness. Once an exhibit is marked, it takes on the identity of that number or letter. Thereafter, counsel should refer to the exhibit by its number or letter but may supplement that reference with a brief description of the exhibit to communicate to the court what item or document is at issue. For example, counsel might say to the witness: 'Mr Joyce, let me show you plaintiff's exhibit number five, a letter dated 8 April 2003.'

Calling exhibits to the attention of opposing counsel can be accomplished in two basic ways. First, the traditional practice is for the proponent of the evidence to take the exhibit to opposing counsel and either show it to the opposing counsel or provide opposing counsel with a copy. Typically, this action is accompanied by language to the effect: 'Judge, I am showing (or giving a copy of) exhibit number three to my colleague.' This announcement, directed to the judge, makes clear on the record what is happening to the exhibit in question. A second, more informal practice, involves the exchange of exhibits in advance of trial, which obviates the need for counsel to satisfy this element at the trial itself.

Showing the exhibit to opposing counsel has the benefit of conveying an image of fairness – the proponent is not trying to sneak anything past opposing counsel. In addition, although an objection to the exhibit would generally be premature, many judges will agree that opposing counsel should be given an opportunity at least to see the evidence at this stage. By presenting the document to opposing counsel, counsel may prevent opposing counsel interrupting the process of laying an evidentiary foundation with a request to examine the exhibit.

Assuming that the opponent offers no objection at the point of being shown the exhibit, the proponent should next take the exhibit and show it to the witness. The proponent should avoid leading the witness by telling him or her about the contents of the exhibit; instead, counsel should hand the exhibit to the witness and ask him or her to describe the exhibit generically. In a jury trial, it is important to note that an exhibit should not be displayed to the jury before it is received into evidence.

3.16.2 Laying the foundation or predicate for admissibility

The terms 'foundation' and 'predicate' refer to the testimony the proponent must elicit from the witness in order to admit the exhibit into evidence. The information required of the witness will depend on the nature of the evidence. When questioning the witness, counsel should make sure to refer to the exhibit by its assigned number or letter and by the witness's characterisation of the exhibit so as to avoid confusion and maintain the accuracy of the record. The need for accuracy and consistency is particularly important where counsel is asking the witness about several exhibits.

3.16.3 Formally offering the exhibit into evidence

After laying the necessary foundation, counsel should formally offer the exhibit into evidence, for example, by stating: 'Judge, I'm now asking that exhibit No 4 be admitted into evidence.' The offer should be short, to the point and confident in tone. It should serve as a clear signal to opposing counsel to make any appropriate objections in order to avoid the risk of waiver and, likewise, it should alert the trial judge to the need for a ruling. If the judge defers a ruling on the exhibit, the proponent should later remind the court of the deferral and, if necessary, request a ruling. Before concluding, counsel must make sure that the judge has ruled on all the exhibits that counsel offered into evidence. Ideally, counsel should keep a checklist of all exhibits, noting the point in the proceedings at which each exhibit was offered into evidence and indicating whether the exhibit in question was admitted or excluded.

3.16.4 Showing or reading the exhibit to the jury

In a jury trial, if the trial judge admits the exhibit into evidence, the proponent must ensure that the jury sees or hears the exhibit, either immediately or later in the trial. This process is sometimes referred to as 'publishing' the exhibit. Although the term is rarely used, it serves as a reminder that the jury is entitled to examine exhibits admitted into evidence. When the exhibit is an item of physical evidence, such as a knife, counsel might state: 'Judge, I request permission to show Exhibit No 1 to the jurors for their inspection.' When the exhibit is a document, counsel might say: 'I request permission to read [the pertinent portions of] Exhibit No 2 to the jury, Judge.' Occasionally, opposing counsel will object on the basis that the document speaks for itself. However, the manner in which the document is placed before the jury – such as having counsel or the witness read from the document or circulating the document among the jurors – is a matter for the trial judge. When counsel has completed his or her use of an exhibit, it should be handed to the registrar.

Chapter 4

OPINION EVIDENCE

4.01 INTRODUCTION

Generally, witnesses must limit their testimony to facts within their personal knowledge or perception. They are permitted neither to express opinions nor to draw inferences from the facts which form the basis of their testimony. The prohibition on opinion evidence is designed to protect the finder of fact from the potentially undue influence of a witness. The common law has doubts about the relevance, subjectivity and trustworthiness of opinions and for this reason prefers that witnesses restrict their testimony to statements of observed fact. The witness states the primary, sensory information, and the finder of fact, whether judge or jury, then draws the inferences or conclusions from the underlying information.[1]

The prohibition on opinion evidence is a general norm rather than an absolute, categorical rule. There are two situations in which the law sanctions testimony in the form of opinion. In the first situation, a lay witness may express an opinion if he or she cannot put in words all the underlying information and communicate that information to the jury. For example, a witness cannot articulate all the sensory impressions that led the witness to the conclusion that a car was travelling at 100 kilometres an hour rather than 60 kilometres an hour. The lay witness's inability to express the underlying information necessitates permitting the lay witness to voice an opinion.

In the second situation, the finder of fact lacks the knowledge or skill to draw the proper inferences from the underlying data. If the subject matter is technical or scientific, the judge or jury may lack the necessary expertise to evaluate the hard data; lacking the expert knowledge and skill, they cannot draw reliable inferences or opinions from the facts. In this situation as well, the law sanctions opinion evidence but here the testimony is that of an expert witness as opposed to a lay witness.

---

1. *AG v Kenny* (1960) 94 ILTR 185; *Hollington v Hewthorn & Co Ltd* [1943] KB 587; *Folks v Chadd* (1782) 3 Doug. KB 157.

4.02 LAY OPINION TESTIMONY

A non-expert or lay witness is permitted to express an opinion in a limited but diverse range of circumstances. There is a miscellany of situations in which the line between fact and opinion is sufficiently blurred that it is difficult to discern whether the witness is testifying as to the former or the latter. Lay opinion that is intertwined with fact may be admitted as a matter of practical necessity where it constitutes the best available evidence on point. Testimony of this kind is sometimes referred to as 'collective fact opinion.'

A classic example is identification evidence because it involves not merely the recitation of facts but also the mental comparison by the witness of information gleaned from the respective sightings of the accused, first at the crime scene and later in court.[2] The law permits the witness to provide the court with a factual description of the person he or she observed at the crime scene and, in addition, to offer his or her opinion that the person in question was the accused. Another example is the description by a witness of the apparent condition of a person or object. The rationale here is partly that the information is too vague or extensive to be susceptible to precise summation[3] and partly that the testimony necessarily involves an element of subjective assessment.[4] Other matters on which courts have accepted lay opinion include the value of a material object,[5] and a person's apparent age,[6] sanity[7] or drunkenness.[8] Aside from these common law examples, various statutes permit the admission of opinion in specified circumstances.[9]

2. *DPP v Cahill & Costello* [2001] 3 IR 494; *DPP v Cooney* [1998] 1 ILRM 321; *R v Turnbull* [1977] QB 224; *AG v Casey (No 2)* [1963] IR 165.

3. *Sherrard v Jacob* [1965] NI 151.

4. *AG v Kenny* (1960) 94 ILTR 185.

5. *R v Beckett* (1913) 8 Cr App R 204.

6. *R v Cox* [1898] 1 QB 179.

7. *Wright Doe d'Tatham* (1837) 7 Ad & E 313; *Glynn v Glynn* [1990] 2 IR 326.

8. *AG v Kenny* (1960) 94 ILTR 185; *Sherrard v Jacob* [1965] NI 151.

9. Eg opinion of certain members of An Garda Síochána under s 8 of the Proceeds of Crime Act 1996 or s 3(2) of the Offences Against the State (Amendment) Act 1972.

4.03 COLLECTIVE FACT OPINION

4.03.1 The law and elements of the foundation

The elements of the doctrine are these: (1) the witness's opinion is based on perceived facts; (2) the opinion is a style of inference that lay persons commonly and reliably draw; and, most importantly, (3) the lay witness cannot articulate all the underlying sensory data supporting the opinion. This doctrine sanctions opinions on such subjects as height, distance, speed, colour and identity. The second and third elements are questions of law; the judge asks himself or herself whether lay persons commonly draw this type of inference and whether it would be practical for the lay witness to articulate all the underlying factual data. The first element (the witness's opinion is based on perceived facts) is a question of fact and the foundation for this element includes proof that:

1. The witness was in a position to observe.
2. The witness in fact observed.
3. The witness observed enough data to form a reliable opinion.
4. The witness states the opinion.

4.03.2 Sample foundation

The following situation is an action in tort arising from a road traffic accident. The plaintiff, Ms Ruby Red, alleges that the defendant, Mr Bernard Blue, caused the accident by speeding. The accident occurred on 17 November 2006 at the junction between Primary Road and Secondary Avenue in the town centre. The plaintiff calls Mr Sam Silver as a witness. Mr Silver has already identified himself. The plaintiff is the proponent.

P. Where were you on the morning of 17 November 2006, at approximately 10 o'clock? (1)

W. I was standing at the junction between Primary Road and Secondary Avenue in the centre of town.

P. In which direction were you facing? (1)

W. I was about to cross Primary Road so I was facing the junction itself.

P. What, if anything, did you see while you were standing there? (2)

W. I saw a blue car on Secondary Avenue approaching the junction.

P. What else did you see? (2)

W. There was a red car approaching the junction on Primary Road.

P. Mr Silver, I'd like to focus for a moment on the blue car. How far was the blue car from the junction when you first saw it? (3)

W. A couple of hundred feet away, at most.

P. How much time did you have to observe the blue car before it reached the junction? (3)

W. Several seconds. I had a fairly good opportunity to see it.

P. Do you have an opinion of the blue car's speed? (4)

W. Yes.

P. In your opinion, how fast was the blue car travelling? (4)

W. I'd say 60 kilometres an hour. It was travelling fairly fast.

P. What happened when the blue car reached the junction?

W. It hit the red car.

P. Who was the driver of the blue car?

W. (*Pointing at the defendant*) Bernard Blue, the fellow sitting over there.

P. How can you recognise him?

W. After the two cars collided, he got out of the blue car, and I walked over to see what had happened.

P. How long did you stay at the scene of the accident?

W. About an hour. I talked to the drivers and later to the garda officers who were called to the scene.

P. How close were you standing to the defendant, Mr Blue?

W. When I was talking to him, he was no more than a foot or two away from me.

P. What were the lighting conditions?

W. It was broad daylight.

P. Was it raining?

W. No.

P. How well could you see him?

W. Very well.

P. Who was the driver of the red car?

W. (*Pointing at the plaintiff*) Ruby Red, that lady over there.

P. How can you recognise her?

W. She was also at the scene of the accident. I saw her step out of the red car. I went over to her and talked to her.

4.04 SKILLED LAY OBSERVER TESTIMONY

4.04.1 The law

The judge will assume that the witness has enough ordinary, human experience to estimate distance, time or height. The judge's assumption explains why the foundation for collective fact opinions is so minimal. However, there is a second type of lay opinion, sometimes referred to as 'skilled lay observer testimony', that requires a more extensive foundation. This category includes opinions about a person's voice or handwriting style.[10] A lay witness cannot express an opinion identifying someone's voice unless the witness has had repeated opportunities to hear that voice. Similarly, a lay witness cannot identify a person's handwriting style unless the witness is familiar with the person. In each of these situations, if the witness has had repeated, prior opportunities for observation, the witness may qualify as a skilled lay observer.

4.04.2 Elements of the foundation

The foundation for skilled lay observer testimony includes these elements:

1. The witness is familiar with the person or his or her voice or handwriting style.
2. The witness explains how he or she became familiar.
3. The witness states his or her opinion.

4.04.3 Sample foundation

Assume that one issue in a commercial case is whether the defendant signed a certain cheque. The witness did not observe the cheque's execution, but he is familiar with the author's handwriting style.

P. Judge, I request that this be marked plaintiff's exhibit number 7 for identification.

J. It will be so marked.

P. I am now showing the exhibit to my colleague.

10. *R v Silverlock* [1894] 2 QB 766. Voice identification and handwriting analysis may also be the subject of expert opinion. See eg *R v Robb* (1991) 93 Cr App R 161.

P. (*To the witness*) I now hand you the plaintiff's exhibit number 7 for identification. What is it?
W. It seems to be a cheque.
P. Do you have an opinion as to who signed the cheque? (3)
W. Yes.
P. In your opinion, who signed the cheque? (3)
W. I'd say that the defendant signed it.
P. Why do you say that? (1)
W. I recognise his handwriting style on the cheque.
P. How well do you know the defendant's handwriting style? (1)
W. Very well.
P. How did you become familiar with his handwriting style? (2)
W. We've been business partners and friends for years. (2)
P. How many years?
W. About thirteen.
P. How often have you seen the defendant sign his name? (2)
W. Tens, maybe hundreds, of times.

4.05 EXPERT OPINION TESTIMONY

The principal exception to the rule against opinion evidence pertains to the testimony of expert witnesses. The courts now routinely admit evidence of the opinions of person who are acknowledged experts in scientific, technical or other fields.[11] The rationale is the need on the part of the finder of fact for expert assistance in relation to matters calling for special knowledge.[12] The expert places the relevant facts in a meaningful context from which the finder of fact then draws the necessary inferences to determine the case.

A party wishing to tender an expert opinion must satisfy two admissibility requirements. First, the party must demonstrate a genuine need on the part of the court for expert knowledge in relation to a matter at issue in the proceedings. This requirement is essentially a manifestation of the basic

11. See generally Kelleher, 'Expert Evidence in Ireland' (1996) 14 ITL 42; O'Flaherty, 'The Expert Witness and the Courts' (1997) 3 MLJI 3; McDermott, 'Expert Evidence in Criminal Trials' (2002) 12 ICLJ 16; Heffernan, *Scientific Evidence: Fingerprints and DNA* (FirstLaw, 2006) chs 1 and 2.

12. *AG v Kenny* (1960) 94 ILTR 185; *Davie v Edinburgh Magistrates* [1935] SC 34.

concept of relevance in the law of evidence. Before allowing a witness to testify or admitting testimony in documentary form, the court must be satisfied that the evidence is relevant to some matter in dispute. Lawton LJ stated the principle in *R v Turner:*

> An expert's opinion is admissible to furnish the court with scientific information which is likely to be outside the experience and knowledge of a judge or jury. If on the proven facts a judge or jury can form their own conclusions without help, then the opinion of an expert is unnecessary. The fact that an expert witness has impressive scientific qualifications does not by that fact alone make his opinion on matters of human nature and behaviour within the limits of normality any more helpful than that of the jurors themselves; but there is a danger that they may think it does.[13]

In *Turner,* the defence sought to admit the expert opinion of a psychologist that the accused had been provoked into killing the victim. The Court of Appeal held that whereas a jury might need the assistance of psychiatric opinion to adjudicate on a defence of insanity, there was no corresponding need for expertise on the subject of provocation. As Lord Lawton put it: 'Jurors do not need psychiatrists to tell them how ordinary folk who are not suffering from any mental illness are likely to react to the stresses and strains of life.'[14] In certain kinds of proceedings, such as proceedings for medical negligence, expert evidence is so common that the basic need for expertise is invariably conceded. Even here, however, disputes may arise regarding the type of specialist medical opinion that is required and the number of expert witnesses.

The second requirement that the proponent must meet is to demonstrate that the witness is qualified by virtue of training or experience to testify in relation to the disputed matter. The courts have defined the term 'expert witness' liberally. As Murphy J stated in *Galvin v Murray:* 'In general terms, an expert may be defined as a person whose qualifications or expertise give an added authority to opinions or statements given or made by him within the area of his expertise.'[15] Witnesses who are tendered as

---

13. [1975] QB 834.

14. *Id.* See also *DPP v Kehoe* [1992] ILRM 481.

15. [2001] 1 IR 331. Section 2 of the Civil Liability and Courts Act 2004 defines expert evidence as 'evidence of fact or opinion given by a person who would not be competent to give such evidence unless he or she had a special skill or expertise.'

experts usually possess formal qualifications from respected educational institutions and professional bodies.[16] However, the law recognises that expert knowledge may be gleaned through less conventional education or training.[17] Similarly, certain fields of expertise have evolved such that they are no longer the exclusive preserve of particular kinds of experts.[18]

The proponent may use an expert witness in a number of different ways. First, the expert may appear in the proceedings purely as a fact witness. Suppose that the accused is being prosecuted for sexual assault. The complainant testifies that during the assault he or she scratched the assailant's face and drew blood. It happened that the accused visited their doctor the day after the alleged rape. The accused could call his or her doctor as a witness and elicit the doctor's testimony that there were no scratches on the accused's face. The witness certainly would not have to be an expert to observe the accused's face, but it is equally clear that the witness is not incompetent to testify as to *facts* solely because he or she is an expert.

The second possibility is to have the expert witness testify to a lay opinion about the significance of the facts in the case. As we have seen, lay witnesses may opine on the subject of the speed of a motor vehicle. Suppose that a garda, who is a certified radar operator, observes a passing car. The officer could not only testify to the speedometer reading assuming the proponent laid a proper foundation for that evidence, but because the officer personally saw the car, the officer could also testify to his or her lay opinion of the car's speed. Just as a witness who happens to be an expert

16. See eg *Egan v Midland Health Board* [2006] IEHC 227 (7 July 2006) (*per* Johnson J): 'In regard to the disagreement between the parties two experts of great eminence and experience were called, each of whose curriculum vitae is such as to demonstrate that they are each leaders in the field of orthopaedic surgery and in particular the field of hip replacement.'

17. *R v Dallagher* [2003] 1 Cr App R 195 (ear print experts); *R v Silverlock* [1894] 2 QB (handwriting expert).

18. Eg the courts have recognised that expert opinion relating to allegations of child sexual abuse is not limited to medical opinion but may extend to the opinion of suitably qualified social workers. *Southern Health Board v CH* [1996] 1 IR 219. Similarly, a DNA analyst can offer an opinion not only as to the existence of a DNA match but also as to the statistical likelihood of the match occurring in the population at large. *R v Doheny and Adams* [1997] 1 Cr App R 369.

may relate facts any lay person could observe, the witness may express any opinions to which a layperson could testify.[19]

The third use of expert evidence is as a means of educating the finder of fact about the scientific or technical principles they need to evaluate the facts. The expert witness explains the principles without applying them to the specific facts of the case; the finder of fact, whether judge or jury, applies the principles to the facts. Frequently, the reliability of the science on which the evidence is based is itself the subject of controversy. For example, there are sharp differences of opinion over the reliability of sound spectrography (voiceprint) evidence. If the prosecution wishes to introduce sound spectrography evidence in criminal proceedings, the prosecution must persuade the jury to believe the evidence. The prosecution might call one or more speech scientists to testify solely about the validity of the underlying theories of interspeaker variability and invariant speech; the witness or witnesses might not even refer to the voiceprint examination being offered as evidence in the proceedings. The sole function of the testimony would be to educate the jury about the general scientific theories and convince them of the validity of those theories.

The most common function of expert evidence is to present the court with an expert evaluation of the facts in the case. When the proponent employs an expert in this manner, the expert usually relies on a general theory or principles to evaluate the facts of the case. After stating his or her qualifications, the expert's testimony follows a syllogistic structure. The expert describes a general explanatory theory (the major premise), states the case-specific facts to be evaluated (the minor premise), and derives an opinion (the conclusion) by applying the major premise to the minor premise.

4.06 THE EXPERT'S QUALIFICATIONS TO FORM THE OPINION

4.06.1 The law

The law permits expert opinion testimony because the expert can draw inferences beyond the capability of judges and jurors. The expert can do so because the expert has knowledge or skill that the finder of fact lacks. The expert can acquire the knowledge or skill by education, experience or a

19. *AG v Kenny* (1960) 94 ILTR 185.

combination of both. The expert's background usually includes academic and professional education and practical experience. As noted above, the courts tend to be fairly liberal in assessing the qualifications of witnesses tendered as experts.

4.06.2 Elements of the foundation

The foundation for the expert's qualifications might include the following elements:

1. The witness has acquired degrees from educational institutions.
2. The witness has had other specialised training in this field of expertise.
3. The witness has been admitted to professional practice in the field.
4. The witness has practiced in the field for a substantial period of time.
5. The witness has taught in the field.
6. The witness has published in the field.
7. The witness belongs to professional organisations in the field.
8. The witness has previously testified as an expert on this subject.

4.06.3 Sample foundation

Our fact situation is a civil action for personal injuries. The plaintiff, Mr Richard Rose, alleges that the defendant, Ms Brid Buttercup, negligently caused the accident in which Mr Rose was injured. The statement of claim alleges that the plaintiff has suffered severe brain injury as a result of the accident. The plaintiff calls Dr Helen Hawthorn. The plaintiff is the proponent. Dr Hawthorn has already identified herself.

P. What is your formal education? (1)

W. I have an undergraduate medical degree and a postgraduate degree in neurology.

P. Which undergraduate medical school did you attend? (1)

W. The National Medical School.

P. What degree did you obtain there? (1)

W. A Bachelor of Medical Science.

P. Which postgraduate school did you attend?

W. The International Medical School.

P. What was your specialty?
W. Neurology, brain problems.
P. What degrees did you obtain from The International Medical School? (1)
W. A Masters in Medical Science and a Doctorate in Medical Science.
P. Did your formal education include practical experience? (2)
W. Yes. Both my undergraduate and postgraduate studies included residencies at hospitals where I had opportunities to specialise in various fields and gain practical experience.
P. But your postgraduate studies were devoted almost exclusively to neurology? (2)
W. Yes.
P. What did you do after graduating from The International Medical School?
W. I returned to this country and began my medical practice.
P. What did you have to do to practice in this country? (3)
W. I had to be admitted to practice by The Medical Council.
P. What is your current position?
W. I am the Chief Consultant in Neurology at The National Hospital.
P. How long have you held that position? (4)
W. Since 1995.
P. How many clients with neurological problems have you treated? (4)
W. I can't name the exact number. I've probably treated hundreds.
P. How much of your time do you devote to the practice of medicine?
W. About 80% of my working time.
P. What else do you spend your professional time on? (5)
W. For one thing, I lecture at The National Medical School.
P. How long have you lectured there?
W. For four years now.
P. What courses do you lecture?
W. I lecture two courses in the field of neurology.
P. What else do you spend your professional time doing? (6)
W. I try to publish with some frequency.
P. What journals have published your articles? (6)

W. Some of the leading medical and neurological journals, including *The Medical Times*.

P. How many articles have you published? (6)

W. Ten.

P. What topics did you cover in these articles? (6)

W. All of the articles relate to neurology.

P. What professional organisations do you belong to? (7)

W. Several, including The Board of Neurology and The International Association of Neurologists.

P. How often have you testified in court? (8)

W. I'd say at least ten times.

P. How many times were you permitted by the judge to give expert testimony? (8)

W. Each time.

P. What subjects did you testify on? (8)

W. I testified on neurology.

In the above foundation, the expert had formal academic degrees as well as practical experience. In some cases, formal degrees are unnecessary; practical experience, standing alone, is sufficient for the witness to qualify as an expert. For example, a farmer might be permitted to testify as an expert on agricultural practices and a garda officer as an expert on the *modus operandi* for various crimes.

4.07 THE GENERAL THEORY OR PRINCIPLE ON WHICH THE EXPERT RELIES

4.07.1 The law

After the expert witness has been questioned as to his or her credentials, the proponent presents the witness's substantive evidence. The expert may begin by stating the general scientific theory or principle that he or she proposes to rely on (the major premise). If the witness is a psychiatrist, the witness may testify that there is a recognised symptomology for a particular mental disease or disorder. To be a permissible premise for expert testimony, the theory or principle must assist the finder of fact. If the subject is a matter of common knowledge, there is no need for expert testimony. Relying on his or her personal experience, the judge decides whether there is a sufficient need for expert testimony on the subject. The judge typically finds a sufficient need when he or she concludes either that the subject is altogether beyond a layperson's ken or that an expert can draw a substantially more reliable conclusion on this subject than a layperson.

Even assuming that there is a demonstrated need for expert testimony in the case and that the witness is a qualified expert, the proponent will also want to establish the reliability of the principle or theory on which the testimony is based. In Ireland, the reliability of expert evidence is not a question of admissibility but rather a matter going to the weight of the evidence. Perhaps the most common method of establishing reliable expert knowledge is to demonstrate that the theory or principle in question is generally accepted within the relevant scientific community.[20] Other means include showing that there has been adequate empirical verification of the validity of the theory or technique.[21]

4.07.2 Elements of the foundation

The proponent might seek to establish the following:

1. The expert used a particular theory to evaluate the facts in the case.
2. The theory in question has been experimentally verified.
3. The theory is generally accepted by the majority of experts in the pertinent scientific specialty.

4.07.3 Sample foundation

The following hypothetical situation is an adaptation of a sample foundation contained in Professor Imwinkelried's *Evidentiary Foundations.*[22] It

20. See eg *Byrne v Ryan* [2007] IEHC 206 (20 June 2007); *Shuit v Mylotte* [2006] IEHC 89 (2 March 2006).

21. But see *Best v Wellcome Foundation Ltd* [1993] 3 IR 421 (*per* Finlay CJ): 'I am satisfied that it is not possible either for a judge of trial or for an appellate court to take upon itself the role of a determining scientific authority resolving disputes between distinguished scientists in any particular line of technical expertise. The function which a court can and must perform in the trial of a case in order to achieve a just result is to apply common sense and a careful understanding of the logic and likelihood of events to conflicting opinions and conflicting theories concerning a matter of this kind.' See also *Quinn v Mid Western Health Board* [2005] 4 IR 1; *News Datacom Ltd v Lyons* [1994] 1 ILRM 450.

22. (6th edn, LexisNexis, 2005) at 9.03[3].

concerns a prosecution for rape and draws on the historical use in American courts of expert testimony about rape trauma syndrome (RTS). The prosecution alleges that on 15 October 2007, the accused, Mr Paddy Pine, raped the complainant, Ms Olive Oak. During her examination-in-chief, Ms Oak described the rape and identified the accused as the rapist. During cross-examination, she admitted that, although on the day in question she reported the alleged rape to the authorities, the next day in a conversation with her mother, Ms Oak refused to confirm or deny that there had been a rape. As their next witness, the prosecution calls Dr Adam Ash, a psychiatrist. The prosecution proposes to elicit Dr Ash's testimony about RTS to rehabilitate Ms Oak's credibility.[23] After stating his credentials, Dr Ash testifies to establish the empirical validity as well as the general acceptance of RTS:

P. Doctor, what is your specialty? (1)

W. For the past few years, I've concentrated my practice and research in the area of rape trauma syndrome.

P. What is rape trauma syndrome? (1)

W. The theory holds that in most cases after a rape victims cope with that traumatic event in a manner that is predictable.

P. What is that manner? (1)

W. Their reaction usually progresses through two phases. The initial stage is the acute phase. They try to come to terms with the physical trauma and the immediate psychological impact. They experience disorganisation in their lives. They become confused.

P. What do you mean by confused? (1)

W. They're indecisive. Even if someone asks them point blank about the rape, out of shame or a sense of morality, they are often reluctant to discuss it. Again, that's the acute phase. That's followed by the long-term phase.

P. What happens during that phase? (1)

W. They begin reorganising their lives. They may move, change their telephone number and visit family and friends much more frequently to gain moral support. They often develop phobias. They may have a fear of being alone.

P. What research, if any, have you done on rape trauma syndrome? (2)

23. *People v Bledscoe,* 36 Cal 3d 236, 681 P 2d 291, 203 Cal Rptr 450 (1984); *People v Roscoe,* 168 Cal App 3d 1093, 215 Cal Rptr 45 (1985).

W. I was fortunate enough to participate in original research done on the subject in Boston. That's where Burgess and Homstrom did the first intensive study of this subject.

P. When and where did they conduct that study? (2)

W. Between July 1972 and July 1973, they interviewed all the rape victims admitted to the emergency ward of Boston City Hospital.

P. How many persons did they study? (2)

W. About 150 women were included in the database.

P. What were the backgrounds of the women included in the study? (2)

W. All sorts – they were all races. About 70% were adult and the rest were minors. In fact, there were three male children included in the study.

P. How did the researchers conduct the study? (2)

W. They initially interviewed these people, and they then followed up by studying the changes in the life patterns after the traumatic incident.

P. What findings did the researchers make? (2)

W. In the overwhelming majority of cases, there was a clear pattern.

P. What do you mean by 'the overwhelming majority'? (2)

W. I mean about 85 to 90% of the cases.

P. What was the pattern? (2)

W. It was the two stages, the acute and long-term phases, that I described a few moments ago.

P. What other research, if any, has been done on rape trauma syndrome? (2)

W. There have been several other studies, including Sutherland and Scherl.

P. What were the findings in those studies? (2)

W. About the same. You can quibble with percentages, but the virtually uniform finding is that in most cases, there is a definite pattern of coping behaviour after a rape. Moreover, this body of research demonstrates that these symptoms appear much more frequently among rape victims than they do among the baseline or general population.

P. Doctor, how well accepted is rape trauma syndrome? (3)

W. It's very well accepted in my field.

P. What evidence is there that the syndrome is well accepted? (3)

W. The latest editions of the leading, authoritative treatises on psychiatry all mention the syndrome. Also, the leading professional organisations refer to it in their standard publications, such as diagnostic manuals.

4.08 EXPERT OPINION BASED ON FACTS PERSONALLY KNOWN

4.08.1 The law

During the course of his or her testimony, the expert typically states the factual, case-specific information to which the relevant scientific theory will be applied (the minor premise). The facts or data on which the expert relies may be perceived by or made known to the expert during or in advance of the proceedings. If the information is of a type reasonably relied upon by experts in the particular field in forming opinions or drawing inferences on the subject, the facts need not be admissible in order for the opinion or inference to be admitted. In other words, the expert may rely on hearsay in formulating his or her opinion.[24]

4.08.2 Elements of the foundation

An expert may base his or her opinion on facts of which the expert has first-hand knowledge. For example, doctors usually base their opinions in part on conditions and symptoms they personally observed during an examination of the patient.[25] The foundation for this basis ordinarily includes the following elements:

1. Where the witness observed the fact.
2. When the witness observed the fact.
3. Who was present.
4. How the witness observed the fact.
5. A description of the fact(s) observed.

---

24. *Southern Health Board v CH* [1996] 1 IR 219; *State (D & D) v Groarke* [1990] 1 IR 305.

25. *H v St Vincent's Hospital* [2006] IEHC 443 (20 December 2006).

4.08.3 Sample foundation

We shall continue with our hypothetical examination of the expert neurologist, Dr Helen Hawthorn, which began at **4.06.3** above.

P. Where were you on the afternoon of 17 November 2007? (1), (2)

W. In my office.

P. What, if anything, happened that afternoon? (3)

W. I conducted an examination of the plaintiff, Mr Richard Rose.

P. Who is Mr Rose? (3)

W. (*Pointing at the plaintiff*) He's the plaintiff, the gentleman sitting over there.

P. Who was present during this examination? (3)

W. Just Mr Rose, myself and my nurse, Ms Linda Lilly.

P. What happened during the examination? (4)

W. I personally examined the plaintiff for any symptoms of brain damage.

P. How did you conduct the examination? (4)

W. I conducted a manual inspection of his cranium and then administered a battery of standard eye and co-ordination tests.

P. How long did this examination take? (4)

W. About three hours. I conducted a very thorough examination.

P. What, if anything, did you observe during the examination?

W. I saw some symptoms and signs of brain damage.

P. What were the symptoms? (5)

W. For one thing, there was a deep scar on the front, right side of Mr Rose's head.

P. How deep? (5)

W. Almost 1/8 of an inch into the surface – easily deep enough to cause some damage.

P. What else did you observe? (5)

W. There was a sort of vacancy in the plaintiff's eyes, again possibly indicating brain problems. Finally, the plaintiff exhibited significant difficulty in the eye-to-hand co-ordination tests.

4.09 EXPERT OPINION BASED ON HEARSAY

4.09.1 The law

In some instances, the expert may rely on statements or reports from third parties such as other experts even if the reports do not fall within any hearsay exception.[26] For example, if it is customary in a specialty to consider a particular type of data, the judge may allow the witness to use that type of information as part of the basis for the opinion. The evidence of the report is not admitted as substantive proof of the report's truth; the report is admitted for the limited purpose of showing the basis for the expert's opinion. The fact that the expert has heard and considered the report is some evidence that the opinion is well grounded.

4.09.2 Elements of the foundation

The foundation for this basis includes the following elements:

1. The source of the third-party report.
2. The content or tenor of the report.
3. It is customary within the specialty to consider that type of report.

4.09.3 Sample foundation

Our scenario continues:

P. Dr Hawthorn, in addition to the symptoms you personally observed during your examination of Mr Rose, what else have you considered? (1)

W. For one thing, I talked to Mr Rose's general practitioner, Dr Donal Daisy.

P. Who is Dr Daisy? (1)

W. Dr Daisy is a general practitioner based in Mr Rose's neighbourhood.

P. How long has he been in practice? (1)

W. I think about 15 years. He is a well-respected member of the local medical community.

26. *In re Family Law Act 1995, FP v SP* [2002] 4 IR 280.

P. When did you talk to him? (1)
W. The day after I examined the plaintiff.
P. Why did you talk to him? (3)
W. I had to get Mr Rose's medical history. Specifically, I wanted to know whether he had that scar or displayed the vacant stare or lack of co-ordination before his car accident.
P. What is the importance of the medical history? (3)
W. You just can't make an intelligent diagnosis without it.
P. What is the customary medical practice concerning the use of medical history? (3)
W. It is the custom here. It would be unprofessional not to gather the history and consider it in evaluating one's diagnosis. Use of the history is good, accepted practice.
P. What did Dr Daisy tell you about the plaintiff's medical history? (2)
W. He said that prior to the accident, there was no scar on the plaintiff's cranium. Further, prior to the collision, the plaintiff had not exhibited the symptoms of either vacancy of stare or lack of co-ordination.
P. Judge, I am not suggesting that this evidence be taken as proof that before the accident the plaintiff had no scar or vacant stare or lack of co-ordination. Rather, Judge, its sole function is in demonstrating one factor or element that Dr Hawthorn considered in arriving at her opinion.

4.10 EXPERT OPINION BASED ON ASSUMED FACTS

4.10.1 The law

Sometimes the testifying expert has neither examined the party nor even talked with an expert who has personally examined the party. The testifying expert may still express an opinion in response to a hypothetical question. In the hypothesis, counsel representing the proponent specifies the facts he or she wants the expert witness to assume. The expert then relies on his or her knowledge and skill to draw a proper inference from the facts in the hypothesis.

There are two limitations on hypothetical questions. The first is the theoretical limitation that the proponent must have already introduced evidence to support a finding that the assumed facts exist. In practice, trial judges generally permit the proponent to vary the order of proof and introduce proof of the assumed facts later. The second limitation is that the hypothesis must include all the undisputed, material facts. The reason for this limitation is obvious: if the hypothesis is incomplete and omits critical facts, the expert opinion may be misleading rather than helpful.

4.10.2 Sample foundation

Hypothetical questions can take two forms. In the first form, the proponent specifies the historical facts that he or she wants the expert to assume. For example, the proponent could say:

P. Dr Hawthorn, please assume the following facts as true:

First, that the plaintiff sustained a cut three inches in length and 1/8 inch in depth on the right, front part of his head.

Second, that the plaintiff bled profusely from that cut.

Third, that immediately after the accident, the plaintiff began experiencing sharp, painful headaches in the right, front part of his head.

In the second form, the proponent asks the witness to assume the truth of the testimony of another witness or witnesses. Assume, for instance, that the ambulance attendant, Mr Oran Orchid, has already testified. During his testimony, Mr Orchid stated that he observed the cut on the plaintiff's head, noted the bleeding and heard the plaintiff complain about a headache. The plaintiff now calls Dr Hawthorn.

P. Dr Hawthorn, where were you this morning?

W. Here in the courtroom.

P. What were you doing?

W. Listening to the evidence.

P. Whose evidence did you listen to?

W. Mr Orchid, the ambulance attendant, was on the stand most of the morning.

P. How well could you hear his evidence?

W. Very well. I had no difficulty hearing what he was saying.

P. Specifically, where were you sitting?

W. In that row behind you there.

P. How often did you leave the courtroom during Mr Orchid's evidence?

W. I didn't leave; I remained in the courtroom for the duration of his testimony.

P. Dr Hawthorn, please assume the truth of Mr Orchid's testimony about Mr Rose's condition immediately after the accident.

4.11 THE STATEMENT OF THE EXPERT OPINION

4.11.1 Background

In examination-in-chief, the objective of counsel is to elicit the witness's expert opinion. The expert will generally be asked not only to state his or her opinion but, furthermore, to vouch that the opinion is reasonably probable or certain. The witness may be willing to testify that he or she has formed the opinion to a reasonable medical or scientific certainty or probability.

4.11.2 Elements of the foundation

The foundation for the opinion might include the following elements:

1. The witness has formed an opinion.
2. The witness believes that the opinion is a reasonable medical or scientific certainty or probability.
3. The witness states the opinion.

4.11.3 Sample foundation

The hypothetical situation continues.

P. Dr Hawthorn, do you have an opinion on whether Mr Rose suffered brain damage as a result of the accident? (1)

W. Yes.

P. How positive are you of your opinion? (2)

W. I'm fairly confident of it. I think that any competent neurologist would reach the same conclusion.

P. What is the degree of your certainty? (2)

W. You can't treat this sort of conclusion as absolute, but I'm reasonably certain of my conclusion.

P. What is that conclusion? (3)

W. In my opinion, Mr Rose has suffered permanent brain damage, located in the right, front part of his cranium, as a direct result of the accident.

In the above foundation, the expert opines on the question of causation. That question falls squarely within the witness's medical expertise and is consequently a proper subject for an opinion by this witness. This reflects the erosion of the common law rule forbidding an expert from expressing an opinion on an ultimate issue to be decided by the finder of fact.

4.12 THE EXPLANATION OF THE EXPERT OPINION

4.12.1 The law

It is a matter of common sense that the finder of fact will not be persuaded by the expert unless he or she explains the opinion.[27] The proponent cannot expect a judge or jury to make a blind act of faith in the expert. As a practical matter, the finder of fact is unlikely to attach much weight to the opinion unless the expert explains his or her process of reasoning in plausible, common sense terms. Consequently, the customary practice is for the proponent to invite the expert to explain the opinion. The expert should explain the opinion in general terms and specifically relate the opinion to the bases the expert previously recited. The opinion will be most persuasive if the expert can demonstrate to the court that the opinion is firmly grounded in the facts to which the opinion relates.

4.12.2 Elements of the foundation

The foundation consists of two elements:

1. The expert explains the opinion in general terms.
2. The expert explains how each basis contributes to and supports the opinion.

---

27. *State (D & D) v Groarke* [1990] 1 IR 305.

4.12.3 Sample foundation

The scenario finally concludes:

P. Dr Hawthorn, why did you reach that conclusion? (1)

W. The symptoms show evidence of the existence of brain damage, and the medical history discloses only one possible cause.

P. What symptoms are you referring to? (2)

W. Well, the scar, the vacancy of the gaze and the lack of eye-to-hand co-ordination.

P. What is the significance of these symptoms? (2)

W. The scar is deep enough to indicate a wound that probably would have applied damaging pressure to the brain. The part of the brain located under the scar is the part that controls vision and eye-to-hand co-ordination. The other symptoms of vacant stare and lack of manual co-ordination confirm that pressure was applied in fact with resulting damage.

P. What medical history are you relying on? (2)

W. My consultation with Dr Daisy and the plaintiff's hospital records.

P. What is the significance of the medical history? (2)

W. It establishes the causation. The scar was apparently inflicted in the accident. Not only did the other symptoms not exist before the accident, they arose immediately after the accident. The timing is almost conclusive in my mind.

Chapter 5

PRIVILEGE

5.01 INTRODUCTION

In previous chapters, we have examined rules of law that exclude relevant evidence for policy reasons related to the way in which trials should be conducted. These rules reflect concerns that the finder of fact, in particular a jury, will misinterpret an item of evidence, overestimate the probative value of the evidence or lose sight of the merits of the case. This chapter is devoted to another type of doctrine, namely 'privilege', which also results in the exclusion of relevant evidence for policy reasons. In the case of privilege, however, the exclusion of the evidence promotes an extrinsic social policy, ie a policy related to conduct outside the courtroom.[1]

The privilege that protects the lawyer-client relationship epitomises this type of rule. Suppose that a party makes damaging admissions in a letter to his or her solicitor. The party had firsthand, personal knowledge of the facts admitted; the admissions are not only relevant, they are also reliable given that firsthand knowledge. However, a trial judge will exclude such a letter on the ground that it is a privileged communication. The privilege gives clients the assurance that they can disclose all the facts to their lawyers without fear that the facts will be divulged to others.[2] With fuller disclosure from their clients, lawyers can render more effective service. The law embodies the belief that the policy is important enough to warrant excluding even relevant, reliable evidence.

Similar reasoning underlies public interest privilege.[3] Modern government needs a vast amount of information to perform its various tasks, especially

---

1. On the Irish law relating to privilege, see generally McGrath, *Evidence* (Thomson Round Hall, 2005) ch 11; Fennell, *Law of Evidence in Ireland* (2nd edn, Tottel Publishing, 2003) ch 8; and Healy, *Irish Laws of Evidence* (Thomson Round Hall, 2004) ch 13.

2. *Smurfit Parisbas Bank Ltd v AAB Export Finance Ltd* [1990] 1 IR 469; *Three Rivers District Council v Governor and Company of the Bank of England (No 6)* [2005] 1 AC 610.

3. *Murphy v Dublin Corporation* [1972] IR 215; *Ambiorix Ltd v Minister for the Environment (No1)* [1992] 1 IR 277.

its regulatory functions, and sometimes the government cannot obtain information from particular sources without assuring confidentiality. The government's interest may be even more compelling if the information bears on national security. If the government invokes privilege, the court must weigh the purported public interest in the suppression of the information against the general public interest in the disclosure of all relevant evidence at trial. The court may conclude that the interest in maintaining the information's secrecy justifies the exclusion even of highly relevant and trustworthy evidence.

5.02 PRIVILEGES FOR CONFIDENTIAL RELATIONSHIPS

The Irish courts recognise privileges for certain types of confidential relationships. The most prominent is the privilege that applies to the lawyer-client relationship. Legal professional privilege comprises two distinct but interrelated strands. First, legal advice privilege protects confidential communications between the client and lawyer in the context of a professional legal relationship for the purpose of giving or receiving legal advice.[4] Second, litigation privilege protects information prepared or gathered by the lawyer in preparation for litigation.[5]

Other types of confidential relationship are also the subject of evidentiary privileges. Sacerdotal privilege safeguards from disclosure communications made in confidence by a parishioner to a parish priest in a private consultation.[6] The privilege may not be waived by the parishioner without the consent of the priest.[7] Sacerdotal privilege is unique to the priest-penitent relationship and does not apply by analogy to other counselling contexts.[8] There may be a broader privilege in modern times that applies to other forms of counselling, particularly marriage counselling, but any such privilege would be capable of waiver unilaterally by the persons being

4. *Smurfit Parisbas Bank Ltd v AAB Export Finance Ltd* [1990] 1 IR 469; *Miley v Flood* [2001] 2 IR 50.
5. *Gallagher v Stanley* [1998] 2 IR 267; *Re Proceeds of Crime Act 1996: MFM v PW* [2001] 3 IR 462.
6. *Cook v Carroll* [1945] IR 515.
7. *Cook v Carroll* [1945] IR 515.
8. *Johnston v Church of Scientology* (30 April 1999, unreported) HC (Geoghegan J).

counselled.[9] For example, a minister of religion may resist disclosing confidential communications received in his or her capacity as a marriage counsellor.[10]

There is a dearth of Irish case law on other confidential relationships that arguably are worthy of protection by means of comparable privileges. In other common law jurisdictions, statutes and case law recognise privileges for relationships such as doctor-patient, psychotherapist-patient, accountant-client and social worker-client. Some jurisdictions also protect from disclosure confidential communications between spouses and confidential communications between parents and children. The protection afforded to the institution of marriage by Article 41.3.1° of the Irish Constitution arguably includes a privilege in respect of confidential spousal communications. However, the contours of such a privilege have not as yet been drawn by the courts.[11]

What is privileged information? Simply stated, privileged information is a confidential communication between properly related parties made during the course of the relationship. The term 'communication' is broadly defined for purposes of privilege and extends to matters conveyed orally and in a variety of written forms. Confidentiality entails two elements: physical privacy and an intention on the part of the holder of the privilege to maintain secrecy. The presence of third parties generally destroys confidentiality,[12] although for practical business reasons this does not apply to support staff such as secretaries and clerks. Even if the communication is conveyed in private, privilege will not attach if the holder intended the subsequent disclosure of the communication outside the circle of confidence.[13] The requirement that the communication be made during the course of the relationship necessitates an examination of the purpose of the communication. For example, legal advice privilege applies only where the confidential communication is made in the context of a professional legal

9. *Id.*

10. *ER v JR* [1981] ILRM 125.

11. See s 26 of CEA 1992.

12. *Fyffes Plc v DCC Plc* [2005] 1 IR 59.

13. *Bord na gCon v Murphy* [1970] IR 301. For example, suppose that a client gave his or her lawyer information for the specific purpose of including it in a press release. The common sense inference would be that the client never intended that the information remain confidential.

relationship and for the purpose of giving or receiving legal advice.[14] The court must be satisfied that the lawyer was acting *as a* lawyer and not in some other capacity.[15]

If a holder of a privilege satisfies the court that the conditions pertaining to that privilege have been met, there is a *prima facie* case for privilege. However, an opposing party may defeat the assertion by showing that the holder has waived the privilege. Waiver may be express or implied and it may be intentional or inadvertent.[16] It may occur during pre-trial correspondence and negotiations between the parties or later during the course of the trial itself. Alternatively, a party may waive privilege by disclosing the privileged communication outside the courtroom to a third party.[17] Not every disclosure to a third party will effect a waiver, however. For example, disclosure to a third party for a limited, unrelated purpose and on condition of confidentiality will not result in loss of privilege.[18]

An assertion of privilege may also be defeated where an opposing party satisfies the court that a recognised exception to the particular privilege applies. Thus, a court will not recognise a claim of legal professional privilege where it can be shown that the privilege was used to further crime of fraud[19] or that the privileged information would exonerate an accused[20] or resolve a dispute over a will.[21] Similarly, in proceedings relating to the welfare of a child, exceptionally privilege may have to yield to disclosure where the judge is satisfied that this will enable the court to adjudicate in the best interests of the child.[22]

---

14. *Smurfit Parisbas Bank Ltd v AAB Expert Finance Ltd* [1990] 1 IR 469; *Three Rivers District Council v Governor and Company of the Bank of England (No 6)* [2005] 1 AC 610.
15. *Buckley v Incorporated Law Society* [1994] 2 IR 44; *Somatra v Sinclair Roche and Temperley* [2001] 1 WLR 2453.
16. *Guinness Peat Properties Ltd v Fitzroy Robinson* [1987] 1 WLR 1027.
17. *Fyffes Plc v DCC Plc* [2005] 1 IR 59.
18. *Id.*
19. *Murphy v Kirwan* [1993] 3 IR 501; *Bula Ltd v Crowley (No 2)* [1994] 2 IR 54.
20. *Ward v Special Criminal Court* [1998] 2 IR 225; *DPP v Kelly* [2006] 3 IR 115.
21. *Crawford v Treacy* [1999] 2 IR 171.
22. *L(T) v L(V)* [1996] IFLR 126.

5.03 LEGAL ADVICE PRIVILEGE

5.03.1 Elements of the foundation

Legal advice privilege protects confidential communications made during the course of the lawyer-client relationship. The underlying principle was stated by Jessel MR in *Anderson v The Bank of British Columbia:*

> The object and meaning of the rule is this: that as, by reason of the complexity and difficulty of our law, litigation can only be properly be conducted by professional men, it is absolutely necessary that a man in order to prosecute his rights or to defend himself from an improper claim, should have recourse to the assistance of professional lawyers, and it being so absolutely necessary, it is equally necessary, to use a vulgar phrase, that he should be able to make a clean breast of it to the gentleman whom he consults with a view to the prosecution of his claim, or the substantiating of his defence against the claim of others; that he should be able to place unrestricted and unbounded confidence in the professional agent and that the communications he so makes to him should be kept secret unless with his consent (for it is his privilege and not the privilege of the confidential agent) that he should be enabled properly to conduct his litigation. That is the meaning of the rule.[23]

The party asserting the privilege has the burden of satisfying the court that the conditions for the privilege have been met.[24] The information or document sought to be withheld must consist of a confidential communication[25] made in the course of a professional legal relationship[26] for the purpose of giving or receiving legal advice.[27]

The foundation includes the following elements:

1. The party is the proper holder of the privilege.
2. The privilege entitles the party to refuse to disclose information.

---

23. (1876) 2 Ch D 644, quoted with approval by Finlay CJ in *Smurfit Paribas Bank Ltd v AAB Export Finance Ltd* [1990] 1 IR 469, [1990] ILRM 588.

24. *Smurfit Paribas Bank Ltd v AAB Export Finance Ltd* [1990] 1 IR 469, [1990] ILRM 588; *Three Rivers District Council v Governor and Company of the Bank of England (No 6)* [2005] 1 AC 610.

25. *Geraghty v Minister for Local Government* [1975] IR 300; *Bord na gCon v Murphy* [1970] IR 301.

26. *Buckley v Incorporated Law Society* [1994] 2 IR 44.

27. *Smurfit Paribas Bank Ltd v AAB Export Finance Ltd* [1990] 1 IR 469, [1990] ILRM 588.

3. The information the party is seeking to suppress is privileged information.
   a. It was a communication.
   b. It was confidential.
   c. It occurred between lawyer and client during the course of a professional legal relationship.
   d. The purpose of the communication was the giving or receiving of legal advice.

5.03.2 Sample foundation

Our hypothetical scenario is an action in tort arising out of a road traffic accident. The plaintiff, Ms Polly Primrose, alleges that the defendant, Mr Frank Fern, caused the accident by speeding. Mr Fern takes the stand to testify on his own behalf. During examination-in-chief, he testifies that he was travelling at 50 kilometres an hour, 10 kilometres under the speed limit. He is then cross-examined by counsel for the plaintiff. At issue is the admissibility of a communication between the defendant/witness and his friend and solicitor, Mr Liam Lavender. Counsel for the plaintiff is seeking to elicit the information and, as such, is the proponent; counsel for the defendant is attempting to bar disclosure by asserting privilege.

P. Mr Fern, isn't it true that during examination-in-chief you testified that you were travelling at only 50 kilometres an hour before the collision?

W. Yes.

P. Isn't it true, Mr Fern, that when you spoke with your friend, Mr Liam Lavender, you told him that you were travelling at 70 kilometres an hour?

O. Judge, I object to that question. Mr Lavender is my client's solicitor and any supposed conversation between them is protected by legal professional privilege. (2)

P. Judge, Mr Lavender is a solicitor but he is also a long-standing friend of the defendant. The conversation to which I refer was between friends and not between a solicitor and his client.

O. Judge, may I question the witness to demonstrate that the conditions for privilege are met?

J. You may.

O. Mr Fern, who is this Mr Liam Lavender?

W. He is a friend of mine and has been for years. (4c)

O. What is his occupation? (4c)
W. He is a solicitor.
O. How do you know he is a solicitor? (4c)
W. He has his own firm, Lavender Solicitors, on Main Street and he has done legal work for me in the past.
O. Where and when did you talk to Mr Lavender about this case?
W. A couple of days after the accident. We met in his office.
O. What happened during that meeting? (4a)
W. I told him about the accident.
O. Precisely how did you give him information about the accident? (4a)
W. I told him about it. We had a conversation.
O. How many people were present when you had this conversation with Mr Lavender? (4b)
W. Just the two of us.
O. How many doors are there to his office? (4b)
W. Just one.
O. Was the door open or closed while you talked to him? (4b)
W. It was closed.
O. After you told him about the accident, to whom did you authorise him to give the information? (4b)
W. No-one.
O. What did you want him to do with the information? (4b)
W. Keep it to himself, of course. He is my solicitor.
O. Why did you talk to him that day? (4d)
W. I thought I might need legal help. Even at the scene of the accident, the plaintiff said something about suing me.
O. In what capacity did you consult Mr Lavender? (4d) (2)
W. I was talking to him as a solicitor, as more than just a friend. (4c)
P. Judge, I have no further questions. In my respectful submission these communications between the defendant and his solicitor are privileged. (2)
J. I agree.

5.04 WAIVER

By its nature, legal professional privilege is effective only if the holder actively asserts the privilege before the court. Even if confident that he or she is entitled to resist disclosure, the holder may decide to waive the privilege for strategic or other reasons. However, waiver may also occur inadvertently by virtue simply of the holder's failure to assert it whether through ignorance or mistake. The privilege may be waived expressly, for example, while testifying on the stand or in written correspondence to the other parties to the proceedings. As noted, waiver will be implied where the holder fails to assert it. For example, even where the privilege has been invoked successfully, it may be subsequently waived or lost where the holder discloses the protected communication to a third party, including a party to the proceedings.[28] It is immaterial whether the disclosure to the third party was deliberate or unintentional; once the information has been disclosed, the confidence which the privilege seeks to protect has been destroyed.[29]

5.04.1 In court

The holder of a privilege who testifies at trial may waive the privilege by referring to the privileged communication during the course of examination-in-chief. If the party opposing the assertion of privilege intends to argue that the privilege has been waived, that party must be prepared to identify the aspect of the witness's testimony that constituted the waiver. The following is a continuation of the last hypothetical scenario involving the action in tort arising out of a road traffic accident. The plaintiff is the proponent.

P. Mr Fern, isn't it true that when you first spoke with your solicitor, Mr Lavender, you told him that you were travelling at 70 kilometres an hour?

O. Judge, I object to that question on the ground that it calls for information protected by legal professional privilege.

P. Judge, I concede that this communication would ordinarily be privileged. However, I contend that the defendant has already waived the privilege. My notes show that during examination-in-chief the defendant was asked the question: 'What was your speed just before the collision?' The defendant answered: 'I was going at a safe rate of speed. That's what I told my solicitor when I first discussed the accident with him, and it's the same story I'm telling today. That's the truth.' This shows that during examination-in-chief, the defendant expressly referred to his

28. *McMullen v Carty* (27 January 1998, unreported) SC.

29. *Guinness Peat Properties Ltd v Fitzroy Robinson* [1987] 1 WLR 1027. But see *Fyffes plc v DCC plc* [2005] 1 IR 59.

previous conversation with his solicitor about the accident. That reference waives the privilege.

J. I agree. The privilege is waived. You may proceed.

P. Mr Fern, let me repeat the question. Isn't it true that you told your solicitor that you were travelling at 70 kilometres an hour?

It must be conceded that in practice it would be unusual for counsel to establish waiver in the fashion outlined above. The ability of counsel to identify the aspect of the witness's testimony in which the privilege was waived is hampered by the fact that stenographers are not generally used in civil proceedings of the common or garden variety such as these hypothetical proceedings arising out of a road traffic accident. Where a stenographer is present in the courtroom – for example in a complex and costly commercial dispute – the position is more straightforward. Counsel may ask the trial judge to direct the stenographer to read aloud the portion of the witness's testimony in which the witness waived the privilege.

5.04.2 Out of court

The privilege may have been waived outside the courtroom, whether orally or in writing. The party opposing the privilege on grounds of waiver might lay the following foundation:

1. Where the out-of-court disclosure was made.
2. When the out-of-court disclosure was made.
3. To whom the disclosure was made.
4. The holder knew the addressee was outside the circle of confidence.
5. The holder disclosed the information to the addressee.
6. The disclosure was voluntary.

We continue the hypothetical scenario. Now the proponent will attempt to show that the holder waived the privilege by an out-of-court disclosure.

P. Mr Fern, isn't it a fact that when you first spoke with your solicitor, Mr Lavender, you told him that you were travelling at 70 kilometres an hour?

O. Judge, I object to that question on the ground that it calls for privileged information protected by legal professional privilege.

P. Judge, in my respectful submission the witness waived privilege on a previous occasion. I would ask permission to question the witness on this point.

J. You may proceed so to question the witness.

P. Mr Fern, isn't it true that on 19 January of this year, you had dinner with your cousin, Mr Harry Heather? (1), (2), (3)

W. Yes.

P. Isn't it correct that during this dinner, you discussed your accident with your cousin? (3), (5)

W. Yes.

P. Isn't it true that at the time, you knew your cousin wasn't working for your solicitor in this case? (4)

W. Yes.

P. Isn't it true that you told your cousin what you had told your solicitor about the accident, namely that you had been travelling at 70 kilometers an hour? (5)

W. Yes.

P. And no-one forced you to give that account to your cousin, did they? (6)

W. No.

P. I have no further questions on this point.

J. I have come to the view that any privilege was waived. You may proceed.

P. Mr Fern, let me repeat the question. Isn't it correct that you told your solicitor that you were travelling at 70 kilometres an hour?

W. Yes.

5.05 EXCEPTION FOR CRIME OR FRAUD OR CONDUCT INJURIOUS TO THE ADMINISTRATION OF JUSTICE

As noted above, the courts will not recognise a claim of privilege where it is shown that the client sought to use the privileged communication to further the commission of a crime or fraud or conduct injurious to the administration of justice.[30]

The foundation for the exception might contain the following elements:

1. At the time of the communication, the client knew that the contemplated course of conduct was illegal or fraudulent or contrary to the administration of justice.

---

30. *Murphy v Kirwan* [1993] 3 IR 501; *Bula Ltd v Crowley (No 2)* [1994] 2 IR 54.

2. The purpose of the communication was to obtain information or advice to facilitate the contemplated course of conduct.

Because of the difficulty of proving the client's state of mind, the courts will recognise the exception provided that it is reasonable to draw an inference of improper intent. The allegations of impropriety must be viable and plausible.[31] Suppose that Irish law requires the purchaser of commercial goods to pay a tax on the goods unless the goods are intended for export. If the goods are intended for export, the purchaser obtains a tax exemption form from the seller and submits it to the Revenue Commissioners. The prosecution alleges that in August 2006, the accused, Mr Paddy Plum, purchased goods for resale on the Irish market and wilfully evaded the tax. The goods were 230 DVD players.

The prosecution calls Ms Amy Apple as a witness. The prosecution is the proponent. Ms Apple has already identified herself and stated that she is a solicitor.

P. Ms Apple, where were you on the morning of 20 July 2006?

W. I was in my office.

P. Where is your office?

W. In Mountainside, on River Street.

P. What happened that morning?

W. I had a visit from a client.

P. Who was that client?

W. It was the accused, Mr Paddy Plum.

P. Where is Mr Plum now?

W. He is here in court.

P. Specifically, where in the court is he?

W. (*Pointing at the defendant*) He is sitting right there.

P. What happened when the accused came to your office that morning?

W. He asked for some advice.

P. What advice?

O. Judge, I object to that question. It calls for information protected by legal professional privilege?

P. Judge, I concede that Ms Apple is a solicitor and that the accused consulted her in that capacity. However, Ms Apple will give evidence that the defendant asked Ms Apple how he could

31. *Murphy v Kirwan* [1993] 3 IR 501.

evade paying a tax or filing a form in relation to the DVD players. She will further testify that she advised him that there was no way to avoid paying or filing. This conversation occurred in July, well before the delivery of the DVD players in August. She will also say that the accused told her that she obviously misunderstood his question and that he wanted her advice as to the best way to evade the law without getting caught. Since the accused had already entered into a contract to sell the goods, the inference is that the accused sought Ms Apple's advice to facilitate a future crime.

J. I think there is a sufficient basis to invoke the exception. I'll allow this line of questioning.

P. Ms Apple, what advice did the accused ask for?

W. He asked how he could get around paying a tax or filing a form.

P. What did you tell him?

W. I said that he couldn't; he had to do one or the other. If the goods were destined for sale on the Irish market, he had to pay the tax. If the goods were destined for export, he was not required to pay the tax but he was required to file a form with the Revenue. It was one or the other.

P. What did the accused say then?

W. He told me that I had obviously misunderstood his question. He said that he had already entered into a contract to sell the goods to a local company and that he wanted to know how he could avoid paying the tax.

In a variation of the scenario, the accused gives evidence and testifies on his own behalf. During examination-in-chief, the accused admits that he purchased the DVD players and neither paid the tax nor filed the exemption form. However, he also testifies that he did not understand the procedures for filing the form and claiming the exemption. The following occurs on cross-examination. The proponent is the prosecution.

P. Mr Plum, isn't it true that in June 2006, you spoke to Mr Gregory Grape of the Revenue Commissioners?

W. Yes. He had visited my office to inspect the books.

P. Isn't it true that during this conversation, you asked him whether you had to pay a tax on purchases for resale on the Irish market? (1)

W. Yes.

P. And didn't Mr Grape tell you that you had to do so? (1)

W. Yes.
P. Isn't it correct that on 3 July 2006 you entered into a contract for the sale of DVD players to a company called Electronics Ltd? (2)
W. Yes.
P. Isn't it true that you promised to deliver the DVD players to their offices in September 2006?
W. Yes.
P. Isn't it true that the number of DVD players you promised to sell then was 230? (2)
W. Yes.
P. And isn't that the exact number of DVD players that you bought on 1 August 2006? (2)
W. Yes.

5.06 LITIGATION PRIVILEGE

5.06.1 Background

Legal professional privilege is divided into two distinct but related strands. As we have seen, legal advice privilege protects confidential communications between lawyer and client made for the purposes of giving or receiving legal advice. Consequently, it may not protect such material as lawyers' notes, witness statements or expert reports. The notion that lawyers should have to disclose their pre-trial preparations is at odds with our adversarial system of litigation. It would strike many as unfair if one 'adversary' could reap the benefit of another lawyer's investigation of the facts and legal research. Thus, the courts have long recognised that a lawyer's preparations for trial, sometimes referred to as his or her 'work product', are privileged from disclosure both during and in advance of trial. Given the potentially broad application of this privilege, the courts have attached two important conditions, both of which relate to the relationship between the litigation and the item of evidence over which privilege is asserted. First, the proceedings must have commenced, or if not actually commenced then reasonably apprehended, at the time the evidence was created or procured.[32] Second, preparation for litigation must have been the dominant purpose for which the evidence was created or procured.[33]

32. *Silver Hill Duckling Ltd v Minister for Agriculture* [1987] IR 289.

33. *Gallagher v Stanley* [1998] 2 IR 267; *Bord na Móna v Sisk* [1990] 1 IR 85.

5.06.2 Elements of the foundation

The party invoking litigation privilege must establish the following:

1. The party is asserting the personal right to refuse to disclose the material during discovery or at trial.
2. The party claiming the privilege is the proper holder. The privilege is generally asserted by the lawyer although the client may also have standing to assert it.
3. The information the party is seeking to suppress is derivative rather than primary material. Primary material is material directly connected to the case such as the actual brake from the car involved in an accident. An example of derivative material would be a model of the brake. The lawyer's effort and imagination play a role in the very creation of derivative material.
4. The information constitutes the lawyer's work product. It is not necessary to show that the lawyer personally prepared the material. The privilege extends to information gathered or collected by or on behalf of the lawyer.
5. The material was prepared in anticipation of litigation. Proceedings must have been commenced or reasonably apprehended and must have been the dominant purpose for preparing or gathering the material.

5.06.3 Sample foundation

The issue of litigation privilege ordinarily arises during discovery; one party seeks discovery of a document and the opposing party resists discovery by claiming the privilege. Given this context, the lawyers usually present their supporting facts in affidavits rather than eliciting live testimony. To illustrate the doctrine, we shall present first the affidavit of the party claiming privilege and then the affidavit of the party opposing privilege. In our hypothetical scenario, the defendant, Mr Ryan River, is seeking discovery of an accident reconstruction report compiled by the plaintiff's expert, Professor Larry Lake. The plaintiff, Ms Sarah Stream, is resisting discovery.

THE HIGH COURT

Record No 2006/1111P

SARAH STREAM

Plaintiff

-and-

RYAN RIVER

Defendant

AFFIDAVIT OF WALTER WEIR

I, Walter Weir, Solicitor, of Broad Street, Narrowville, aged eighteen years and upwards MAKE OATH and say as follows:

1. I am a Solicitor in the firm of Weir and Associates, Broad Street, Narrowville, Solicitors on record for the Plaintiff in the above entitled action, and I make this affidavit for and on her behalf and with her authority and consent. I make this affidavit from facts within my own knowledge, save where otherwise appearing, and where so appearing I believe the same to be true and accurate.
2. I beg to refer to the pleadings already had herein, when produced.
3. I say that the Defendant has sought the production of a report submitted to me by Professor Larry Lake. I say and believe that the said report is protected by litigation privilege and on this basis the Plaintiff is refusing to furnish Professor Lake's report to the Defendant. (1), (2)
4. I say that on or about 14 February 2005, I decided that I needed an expert evaluation of the physical evidence left at the scene of the collision between the Defendant's van and the Plaintiff's car on 11 February 2005. (5) I say that in the Statement of Claim, the Plaintiff has alleged that the Defendant's car drifted into her lane and that the point of impact was in her lane. I say that the Defence filed in this case denies these allegations.
5. I say that I lack the expertise in physics and the laws of motion to evaluate the physical evidence left at the accident scene. I say that, consequently, on or about 15 February 2005, I telephoned Professor Larry Lake who teaches in the Physics Department at The Metropolitan University. I say that I have used him in several prior cases as an accident reconstruction expert. I say that I told Professor Lake that I needed an expert evaluation for the accident scene as part of my pre-trial preparation, and that I asked him for a

confidential report on the subject. He agreed to prepare the report and submit it to me. (4)

6. I say that on or about 16 February 2005, Professor Lake and I visited the accident scene and, on 20 February 2005, he submitted his personal report to me. (3) The report recites his findings and conclusions as to the manner in which the collision occurred. I say that I have maintained the report's confidentiality; the only persons who have reviewed the report are Professor Lake, the Plaintiff and myself. I say that, at the present time, I have not decided whether to call Professor Lake as a witness at trial.
7. Accordingly, I say and believe that the said report is privileged and, accordingly, I pray this Honourable Court for an Order refusing the relief sought in the Notice of Motion herein.

SWORN by the said WALTER WEIR ON
of 2008
Before me a practising solicitor/ Commissioner for oaths, and I know the deponent.

The following is the format for an affidavit by the party seeking discovery:

THE HIGH COURT

Record No 2006/1111P

SARAH STREAM

Plaintiff

-and-

RYAN RIVER

Defendant

AFFIDAVIT OF CAROL CANAL

I, Carol Canal, Solicitor, of Long Street, Short Town, aged eighteen years and upwards, MAKE OATH and say as follows:

1. I am a Solicitor in the firm of Canal & Co, Solicitors, Long Street, Short Town, on record for the Defendant in the above-entitled action, and I make this affidavit on the Defendant's behalf and with his authority and consent. I make this affidavit from facts within

my own knowledge save where otherwise appears, and where so otherwise appearing I believe the same to be true and accurate.

2. I beg to refer to the pleadings already had herein, when produced.
3. I say that in the within application, the Defendant is seeking the production of a report submitted by Professor Larry Lake to the Plaintiff's solicitor, Mr Walter Weir. I say that the subject of the report is an expert evaluation of the physical evidence left at the scene of the collision between the Plaintiff's car and the Defendant's van. I say and believe that the report is logically relevant to the material facts in this case.
4. I say that at paragraph 7 of the Plaintiff's statement of claim, it is alleged that the Defendant's van drifted into her traffic lane and the point of impact was in her lane. I say that at paragraph 4 of the defence, the Defendant denies those allegations. I say and believe that it thus follows that the point of impact is a material fact or consequence in this case, and Professor Lake's accident reconstruction report undoubtedly discusses point of impact. (6)
5. I say and believe that the information contained in Professor Lake's report is essential to the effective pre-trial preparation of this case. I say and believe that if the trial judge finds as a matter of fact that the Defendant's van drifted into the Plaintiff's lane, that fact alone may persuade the court to conclude that the Defendant was negligent. However, if the court finds as a matter of fact that the point of impact was in the Defendant's lane, again that fact alone may convince the court that the Plaintiff's own carelessness caused the accident. (7)
6. I say and believe that there is no reasonably available, alternative source for this information. I say and believe that, in the first place, Professor Lake is widely regarded as the country's leading accident reconstruction expert. His report would be more authoritative than any other local expert's report. Secondly, Professor Lake's report may contain a more detailed description of the physical evidence at the accident than any other report.
7. I beg to refer to the Garda Accident Report, dated 12 February 2005, which is exhibited to this affidavit, and which I marked with the numbers and letters 'JB1' prior to the swearing hereof. The said report states, at paragraph 4, that there was 'a good deal of debris' but neither the report itself nor the diagram attached to the report indicates the nature or specific location of the debris.

8. I say that this firm did not come on record for the Defendant until 13 March 2005. I say that this firm immediately hired an accident reconstruction expert but she was unable to visit the accident scene until 16 March 2005, several weeks after the accident. I say that I accompanied her to the scene, but that on arrival we could not locate any skidmarks, gouge marks or debris clearly attributable to the accident. In contrast, Professor Lake visited the scene only a few days after the collision. Accordingly, I say and believe that Professor Lake's report may be the only source for critical information about the scene of the accident.
9. Accordingly, I pray this Honourable Court for an Order in the terms of the Notice of Motion herein.

SWORN by the said Carol Canal
on of 2008
Before me a practising solicitor/ Commissioner for oaths, and I know the deponent.

5.07 WITHOUT PREJUDICE NEGOTIATIONS

5.07.1 Background

The courts have long favoured the out-of-court settlement of legal claims. This is reflected in a well established privilege granted in respect of communications in furtherance of settlement. The simple rationale is the likelihood that parties would be discouraged from settling their disputes if anything that was said in the course of settlement negotiations could be used against them subsequently at trial.[34] The privilege allows the parties the freedom to negotiate safe in the knowledge that any concession or offer to compromise will be inadmissible in the event that the negotiations break down. The privilege is supported by the convention that parties engage in settlement negotiations on a 'without prejudice' basis, ie on the understanding that the content of the negotiations will be not be used to the prejudice of either party.[35]

---

34. *Ryan v Connolly* [2001] 2 ILRM 174; *Greencore Group plc v Murphy* [1995] 3 IR 520; *Rush & Tompkins v Greater London Council* [1989] AC 1280.
35. McGrath, *Evidence* (Thomson Round Hall, 2005) p 574 *et seq*.

There are certain conditions for a valid assertion of without prejudice privilege. The party asserting the privilege must satisfy the court that the communication which is sought to be disclosed was made in a genuine attempt to settle a dispute between the parties[36] which was the subject of actual or contemplated litigation.[37] The communication must have been made with the intention that it remain confidential in the event that the dispute was not resolved by settlement.[38] The use of the term 'without prejudice' is *prima facie* evidence rather than conclusive evidence of such an intention; the courts will base their conclusion as to the parties' intentions on all of the circumstances.

5.07.2 Elements of the foundation

The party attempting to *exclude the evidence* should lay the following foundation:

1. The communication is protected by privilege.
2. The party is the proper holder of the privilege.
3. At the time the communication was made, there was a dispute between the parties in respect of which legal proceedings had commenced or were contemplated.
4. The communication was made in a genuine attempt to settle the dispute.
5. The communication was made with the intention that it would not be disclosed subsequently.

5.07.3 Sample foundation

The first scenario is an action in tort for personal injuries arising out of a road traffic accident. The plaintiff, Mr Samuel Storm, is suing the defendant, Ms Therese Thunder. The plaintiff alleges that the defendant caused a collision and that in that collision, the plaintiff suffered injuries in the amount of €150,000. The plaintiff takes the witness stand to testify in

36. *Unilever plc v Proctor and Gamble Co* [2001] 1 All ER 783; *WH Smith Ltd v Colman* [2001] FSR 91.

37. *O'Flanagan v Ray-Ger Ltd* (28 April 1983, unreported) HC.

38. *Ryan v Connolly* [2001] 2 ILRM 174; *Dixons Stores Group Ltd v Thames Television plc* [1993] 1 All ER 349.

his own behalf. During cross-examination, the following occurs. The proponent is the defendant.

P. Mr Storm, isn't it true that in your statement of claim in this case, you claim that you have suffered €150,000 in damages?

W. Yes.

P. Isn't it a fact that on 17 February 2006, you attended a consultation here in the Court Building?

W. Yes.

P. Isn't it correct that while you were there, you offered to settle your whole claim for a lesser sum?

O. Judge, I object to that question on the ground that it calls for an inadmissible without prejudice statement. May I examine the witness on the point?

J. You may.

O. Mr Storm, why did you attend the consultation on 17 February? (1), (2)

W. I went there to discuss my claim against the defendant.

O. What was your claim? (3)

W. I took the position that Ms Thunder was at fault in the accident and caused my injuries.

O. What was your belief about the validity of this claim? (3)

W. I thought I was in the right. From my memory of the accident, I had the green light.

O. What did the defendant say about your claim? (3)

W. She denied that she was at fault.

O. What was the purpose of the meeting on 17 February? (4)

W. We wanted to see if we could settle without going to trial.

O. Why did you want to settle if you thought that your claim was valid? (4)

W. I was advised by my solicitor and by yourself that trials are unpredictable and that sometimes it is better to be conservative and accept less money than you ask for in your Statement of Claim. I still thought I had a good claim but that's why I was willing to talk about settling.

O. Were you not concerned that any offer you made might prejudice your claim if the case subsequently went to trial? (5)

W. No.

O. Why not? (5)

W. You told me that anything that I said in the meeting would remain confidential. Also, at the start of the meeting, Ms Thunder's barrister said that anything that was said on behalf of either party would not be used to the prejudice of either party. Everyone nodded in agreement.

O. Judge, I have no further questions. The witness's testimony shows that there was a dispute over his claim's validity and that he made his offer in a *bona fide* effort to compromise. The question to which I am objecting calls for the settlement offer itself which is protected by privilege.

J. The objection is well founded. The proposed line of questioning is impermissible.

The party attempting to *introduce the evidence* must be ready to make an offer of proof. In that regard, the party should state the following:

1. What the witness will testify to if the judge permits the party to pursue the line of questioning.
2. The evidence is relevant to some issue other than the general question of the claim's validity.
3. The issue the evidence relates to is a genuinely disputed question in the case.

Our hypothetical fact scenario is a claim for breach of contract. The plaintiff, Mr Lloyd Linen, is suing the defendant, Cotton Construction Co Ltd. The defendant filed a Defence and Counterclaim in response to the plaintiff's Statement of Claim. In its Counterclaim, the defendant alleges that the plaintiff did not reasonably mitigate damages; it alleges that after the defendant's breach, the plaintiff delayed three months before looking for another builder. The plaintiff gives evidence on his own behalf. The plaintiff has already testified to the contract's formation and the defendant's breach. The plaintiff is the proponent.

P. What happened after the defendant's work crew walked off the building site?

W. The next day I contacted Mr Stephen Silk, the defendant's Managing Director.

P. What happened when you contacted him?

W. We discussed how we might settle my claim against his company.

O. Judge, I respectfully request that that last answer be disregarded. The answer refers to inadmissible without prejudice negotiations.

P. Judge, the witness will testify that the parties began settlement negotiations that day and that the negotiations continued for over two months. (6) The testimony is relevant to explain the plaintiff's delay in hiring another builder. (7) In its Counterclaim the defendant alleged that the plaintiff did not properly mitigate damages. (8) The evidence is admissible for the limited purpose of rebutting the defendant's allegation.

J. I do not consider the objection to be well founded.

P. Mr Linen, let me repeat the question. What happened when you contacted Mr Silk?

W. We discussed settling my claim against his company.

P. How long did these discussions last?

W. On and off for over two months. I kept trying to get them back on the project. I wanted them to finish the job.

5.08 PUBLIC INTEREST PRIVILEGE

5.08.1 Introduction

Exceptionally, the State or one of its agents may refuse to surrender information sought in litigation on the ground that disclosure would be contrary to the public interest. 'Executive' or 'Crown' privilege was absolute at common law; the courts would accept at face value the State's assertion that disclosure would be prejudicial to the public interest. In the landmark case of *Murphy v Dublin Corporation,* the Supreme Court declared that the power to compel the attendance of witnesses and the production of documents is entrusted exclusively to the courts under the Constitution. As Walsh J stated:

> Power to compel the attendance of witnesses and the production of evidence is an inherent part of the judicial power of government of the State and is the ultimate safeguard of justice in the State. The proper exercise of the functions of the three powers of government set up under the Constitution, namely, the legislative, the executive and the judicial, is in the public interest. There may

> be occasions when the different aspects of the public interest 'pull in contrary directions' … If the conflict arises during the exercise of the judicial power then, in my view, it is the judicial power which will decide which public interest shall prevail.[39]

Like any other holder of privilege, the State has the burden of asserting the privilege and of persuading the court that it should be upheld in the given case.[40] Where the State asserts the privilege, the courts must weigh the competing public interests, ie the general interest in disclosure against the particular interest in confidentiality on which the State relies. There is no preference for disclosure over other public interests, such as national security,[41] foreign relations,[42] the prevention and detection of crime[43] or the proper functioning of the public service.[44] The courts must balance the competing interests on a case-by-case basis.[45] Moreover, there is no class or category of documents that is automatically exempt from production by virtue either of the rank of the person creating them or the status of the individual or body intended to use them.[46]

5.08.2 Elements of the foundation

To establish a *prima facie* case for invoking public interest privilege, generally the party opposing discovery must establish the following:

1. The party asserting the privilege is the holder.
2. The party is asserting the appropriate kind of privilege, ie the entitlement to withold the information and to prevent a third party from making disclosure.
3. The information is privileged.

---

39. [1972] IR 215 at 233.
40. Similarly, public interest privilege may be waived. *McDonald v RTÉ* [2001] 1 IR 355.
41. See eg *Gormley v Ireland* [1993] 2 IR 75.
42. See eg *Walker v Ireland* [1997] 1 ILRM 363.
43. See eg *Breathnach v Ireland (No 3)* [1993] 2 IR 458; *McDonald v RTÉ* [2001] 1 IR 355.
44. See eg *Cully v Northern Bank Finance Corp.* [1984] ILRM 683.
45. *Ambiorix v Minister for the Environment (No 1)* [1992] 1 IR 277.
46. [1992] 1 IR 277. On cabinet confidentiality, see *AG v Hamilton (No 1)* [1993] 2 IR 250; *O'Brien v Ireland* [1995] 1 ILRM 22; *Irish Press Publications Ltd v Minister for Enterprise* [2002] 4 IR 110.

To defeat the privilege, the party seeking discovery generally must show the following:

4. The information is relevant to the material facts of consequence in the case. Ideally, the party should argue that the information relates to the central or one of the pivotal issues in the case.
5. There is no reasonably available, alternative source for the information.

5.08.3 Sample foundation

The issue can arise during discovery or at trial. The first illustration is an affidavit claiming privilege in an action for product liability. The plaintiff, Ms Tina Tonic, is suing Medic Co Ltd. The Statement of Claim alleges that the defendant negligently manufactured a 'Cold and Flu' medicine and that when the plaintiff consumed some of the medicine, she sustained serious internal injuries. The plaintiff has served a subpoena on the Minister for Health. Three years ago, the Department of Health conducted a national survey of pharmacies to determine the level of complaints about certain medicines. One of the medicines was the 'Cold and Flu' product the plaintiff purchased. The plaintiff seeks the Department of Health's report evaluating the survey. The Minister for Health has brought a motion to quash the subpoena. The following is the affidavit supporting the Minister's motion.

AFFIDAVIT OF SALLY SYRUP

I, Sally Syrup, Civil Servant, of Range Road, Pasturetown, aged eighteen years and upwards, MAKE OATH and say as follows:

1. I am a senior civil servant in the Department of Health (1) and my office is located in the Department of Health, Government Row, City Centre.
2. I beg to refer to the pleadings already had herein, when produced.
3. I say that the Plaintiff in the above-entitled proceedings has served a subpoena *duces tecum* upon me. I say that the subpoena directs me to produce for inspection and copying a survey entitled 'Complaints to Pharmacists About Medicines' completed by the Department of Health in 2004. That information is within the jurisdiction of the Department. (2) On that ground, I refuse to surrender the report and respectfully request that this Honourable Court quash the subpoena served upon me. (2)

4. I say that the Department of Health began this survey in 2002 with a view to deciding whether we should remove any of the identified medicines from the market. The said report was finished in early 2004. I say that the report summarises the survey and discusses medical problems possibly caused by the various medicines. I say that the report states conclusions and recommendations with respect to each medicine studied.
5. I say and believe that it would be contrary to the public interest to relate this report for public inspection. I say that the Department of Health assured the pharmacists responding to the survey that we would maintain the confidentiality of their responses; many expressed fear of reprisal from the manufacturers which were their suppliers. I say that, in addition, this sort of decision-making process requires candour among public officials, and we can achieve that candour only if the decision-making process is confidential.
6. I say that, subsequently, in 2004, the Department formally published an order, removing certain medicines from the market. However, this report was completed before the issuance of the order and was part of the deliberative process which culminated in the issuance of that order. The report itself has never been released to any private person. Indeed, the report has been released only to government agencies directly concerned with medicine and health care, and we instructed them to maintain the confidentiality of the report. (3)
7. Accordingly, in the premises I pray this Honourable Court for an Order in terms of the Notice of Motion herein.

SWORN by the said SALLY SYRUP ON
of 2008

Before me a practising solicitor/ Commissioner for Oaths, and I know the deponent.

5.09 INFORMER PRIVILEGE

5.09.1 Background

Historically, the common law protected the identity of police and prison informers from disclosure at trial. This privilege was supported by a twofold justification: the need to protect the lives and safety of informers and the need to safeguard their valued contribution to the prevention and detection of crime. Indeed, the evolution of the privilege has involved its gradual extension from police and prison informers to informers of other public officeholders and entities engaged in law enforcement.[47] The Irish courts have applied protection of privilege to informers to the Director of Consumer Affairs[48] and the Police Complaints Board.[49] Traditionally, the Irish courts have been reluctant to extend the privilege to journalists' sources,[50] in the absence of a threat to life or limb.[51] However, the European Court of Human Rights has characterised the protection of journalists' sources as a basic condition for press freedom under Article 10 of the Convention,[52] and in a recent case the High Court recognised the privilege in principle.[53]

Informer privilege is subject to an innocence-at-stake exception. The court may order the disclosure of the informant's identity if disclosure would tend to exonerate an accused.[54] This common law exception arguably enjoys a contemporary constitutional and human rights dimension in so far as Article 38.1 of the Constitution and Article 6 of the Convention guarantee the

47. For example, in England, the privilege was recognised in relation to informers to the National Society for the Prevention of Cruelty to Children: *D v NSPCC* [1978] AC 1.

48. *Director of Consumer Affairs v Sugar Distributors Ltd* [1991] 1 IR 225.

49. *Skeffington v Rooney* [1997] 1 IR 22.

50. See eg *Re Kevin O'Kelly* (1974) 109 ILTR 97. But see *DPP v Nevin* [2003] 3 IR 321.

51. *Burke v Central Independent Television plc* [1994] 2 IR 61, [1994] 2 ILRM 161.

52. *Goodwin v United Kingdom* (1996) 22 EHRR 123.

53. *Mahon v Keena and Kennedy* [2007] IEHC 348 (10 October 2007).

54. *Marks v Beyfus* (1890) 25 QBD 494; *Director of Consumer Affairs v Sugar Distributors Ltd* [1991] 2 IR 225; *Ward v Special Criminal Court* [1998] 2 ILRM 493.

accused the right to introduce exculpatory evidence. However, the Supreme Court rejected this contention in a relatively recent case[55] concerning the belief evidence of a garda chief superintendent under s 3(2) of the Offences Against the State (Amendment) Act 1972.

5.09.2 Elements of the foundation

The foundation for informer privilege includes the following:

1. The privilege applies in this type of proceeding. Most of the cases recognising informer privilege are criminal prosecutions. However, the issue can arise in enforcement proceedings brought by statutory bodies and in civil proceedings, such as actions for defamation or proceedings concerning child protection.
2. The party claiming the privilege is a proper holder. The courts generally permit individuals representing the State, such as garda officers and prosecuting barristers, to invoke the privilege on the government's behalf.
3. The holder is asserting the appropriate kind of privilege.
4. The information is privileged.

5.09.3 Sample foundation

Our hypothetical scenario is a prosecution for drugs offences. The prosecution alleges that the accused, Mr Gustav Green, unlawfully sold cocaine to a Mr Bob Blue. The prosecution calls Garda William White as a witness. Garda White testifies that he was hiding in the house where the alleged sale occurred and observed the sale. The following occurs during cross-examination. Counsel for the defence is the proponent.

P. Garda White, isn't it true that someone else was with you when you observed the alleged cocaine sale?

W. Yes.

P. Who was that other person?

O. Judge, I object to that question on the ground that it calls for privileged information. On behalf of the State, I claim the privilege for the identity of an informer. (2), (3) I request permission to conduct a *voir dire* examination of the witness.

J. Very well.

---

55. *DPP v Kelly* [2006] 3 IR 115.

O. When did you first meet the person who was with you in the house?
W. About two months before.
O. What happened when you met this person? (4)
W. He told me that he thought a drug sale was going to occur in the neighbourhood within the next few months.
O. Where did he make this report? (4)
W. At the local garda station.
O. Whom did he report it to? (4)
W. To me.
O. How were you dressed at the time? (4)
W. I was wearing my regular garda uniform.
O. Who else was present when he made this report? (4)
W. No-one else. Just the two of us.
O. Where did this conversation occur? (4)
W. In a room at the station.
O. How many doors did the room have? (4)
W. Only one.
O. What position was the door in when you met this person? (4)
W. It was closed.
O. What, if any, assurances did you give the informer when he made this report to you? (4)
W. I told him that I wouldn't disclose his identity to anyone.
O. To whom have you revealed his identity? (4)
W. No-one. I've worked with him directly. I'm the informer's only contact.
O. Judge, I have no further questions. In my respectful submission, the conditions for informer privilege are met and the privilege should be applied.

5.10 SUBSEQUENT REPAIRS

5.10.1 Background

This section introduces an evidentiary doctrine similar to the privileges for confidential relations; it excludes logically relevant evidence to promote an extrinsic social policy. Sometimes referred to as the 'subsequent repair' doctrine, it operates to exclude evidence of subsequent precautionary measures by defendants in torts cases. The primary rationale for the doctrine is that admitting the evidence would discourage desirable safety improvements. A further justification is that, the relevance that evidence of subsequent events may have to the question of whether the defendant was negligent at a particular point in time is debatable. In some common law jurisdictions, evidence of subsequent repairs is the subject of a strict exclusionary rule. Nevertheless, it is by no means an absolute rule nor is it uniformly applied. Its application in the Irish courts is an open question; the following hypothetical situation proceeds on the premise that a court may exclude such evidence as a matter of policy or practice rather than strictly as a matter of law.

5.10.2 Elements of the foundation and sample foundation

The party attempting to exclude the repair evidence might lay the following foundation:

1. The defendant took certain action.
2. The defendant took the action as a safety measure.
3. The defendant took the action after the accident that gave rise to the proceedings.

Our hypothetical scenario is a negligence action arising from a slip-and-fall on the entrance to a department store. The plaintiff, Mr Cormac Copper, alleges that the defendant, Steel Stores Ltd, had a dangerous and unsafe slope at its entrance. Counsel for the defendant calls Ms Imelda Iron as a witness. Ms Iron identifies herself and states that she was the manager of the shop on the day of the accident. She describes the day, including her conversation with the plaintiff after the slip and fall. During cross-examination, the following occurs. The proponent is the plaintiff.

P. Ms Iron, isn't it true that one week after the plaintiff's accident, you hired a builder to reduce the slope at the entrance?

O. Judge, I object to that question on the ground that it calls for evidence of a subsequent repair, which evidence is inadmissible.

J. I agree. I do not see how that can be logically relevant to assessing whether on the day in question the defendant breached its duty of care to the plaintiff.

If there is any doubt about whether this evidence will be ruled inadmissible, the opponent should request permission to examine the witness in order to lay a complete foundation for the objection.

O. Ms Iron, what did you hire this builder to do? (1)

W. I employed Mr Billy Brass to reduce the angle of the slope leading to the entrance.

O. Why did you do that? (2)

W. We did it as a safety measure. We wanted to ensure that there wouldn't be a recurrence of the accident. We're concerned about the safety of our customers.

O. When did you employ Mr Brass? (3)

W. In late February 2006.

O. When did the plaintiff's accident occur? (3)

W. In the middle of February. I think it was the 12th of February.

O. Judge, I have no further questions for this witness. I reiterate my respectful suggestion that no weight should be attached to the evidence of this later reduction in the angle of the slope.

J. That submission is well-founded.

The rule against evidence of subsequent repairs applies only when the purpose for which the evidence is offered is to show that the defendant was negligent or culpable. The rule does not require the exclusion of evidence of subsequent measures when offered for another purpose, such as proving ownership or control.

The party who is seeking to establish that evidence of subsequent repairs is relevant other than as proof of the defendant's negligence or fault should offer to prove the following:

4. The evidence the witness will present if the judge permits the proponent to pursue this line of inquiry.
5. That the evidence is logically relevant to some issue other than the general question of negligence or fault.
6. That the issue the evidence relates to is disputed in the case.

Our second hypothetical scenario involves an action against a railway company. The plaintiff, Guaranteed Goods Co Ltd, is suing Trusty Train Co Ltd. The plaintiff alleges that the defendant's train derailed near the plaintiff's factory and caused extensive property damage. In its Defence, the defendant alleges that the cause of the derailment was the defective condition of the track and that under the railway company's contract with the adjacent landowner, the landowner was responsible for maintaining the track. The plaintiff calls one of its employees, Mr Michael Manager, as a witness. Mr Manager identifies himself and states that he is one of the plaintiff's employees. He is prepared to testify that on 3 December 2006, the day after the accident, one of the defendant's work crews repaired the track. The proponent is the plaintiff.

P. Mr Manager, where were you on 3 December 2006?

W. I was at work at our factory in Green Meadow.

P. What happened that day?

W. I was working outside, trying to repair some of the damage caused by the derailment the day before.

P. What, if anything, did you see while you were outside?

W. I saw some of the defendant's employees arrive.

P. How do you know that they were the defendant's employees?

W. They were all wearing grey overalls with the defendant's name and logo on them. They drove to the site in a truck with the defendant's name and logo on the side.

P. What were the defendant's employees doing?

O. Judge, I object to that question. I suspect that the plaintiff is attempting to elicit inadmissible evidence of subsequent repairs to the track.

J. Is that your intention?

P. Judge, the witness will testify that he saw the defendant's employees repair the track. (4) The evidence is relevant to prove that the defendant had control of the track and thus a duty to keep the track in a state of good repair. (5) In its Defence, the defendant specifically denied that it had control of the track or a duty to repair. (6) The evidence should be admitted for the limited purpose of proving the defendant's control of the track.

J. I agree. You may continue.

P. Mr Manager, let me repeat the question. What were the defendant's employees doing?

W. They were repairing the track.

Chapter 6

HEARSAY

6.01 OVERVIEW

The rule against hearsay precludes the admission into evidence of an out-of-court statement when offered as proof of the matter stated. The rule is grounded in fears about the reliability of in-court testimony relating to out-of-court statements when the proponent is attempting to use the statements as evidence in the case. In *R v Blastland*, Lord Bridge explained the underlying rationale in the following terms:

> Hearsay evidence is not excluded because it has no logically probative value. Given that the subject matter of the hearsay is relevant to some issue in the trial, it may clearly be potentially probative. The rationale of excluding it as inadmissible, rooted as it is in the system of trial by jury, is a recognition of the great difficulty, even more acute for a juror than for a trained judicial mind, of assessing what, if any, weight can properly be given to a statement by a person whom the jury have not seen or heard and who has not been subject to any test of reliability by cross-examination ... The danger against which this fundamental rule provides a safeguard is that untested hearsay evidence will be treated as having a probative force which it does not deserve.[1]

The common law prefers that the third party (the declarant) appear in court and subject himself or herself to cross-examination. It assumes that evidence will be more trustworthy if the declarant testifies under oath, in plain view of the finder of fact and subject to cross-examination.[2] The opponent may

1. [1986] AC 41, [1985] 2 All ER 1095. See also *Teper v R* [1952] AC 480 *per* Lord Normand: '[Hearsay] is not the best evidence and it is not delivered on oath. The truthfulness and accuracy of the person whose words are spoken by another witness cannot be tested by cross-examination, and the light which his demeanour would throw on his testimony is lost.'
2. See *Director of Corporate Enforcement v Bailey* [2007] IEHC 365 (1 November 2007) (*per* Irvine J): 'This is a rule which is operated to potentially exclude statements in circumstances where the maker of that statement will not testify, cannot have their demeanour observed and cannot have their credibility tested on cross examination. The rule is stated to demonstrate the confidence that can be reposed in the power of cross examination.'

use cross-examination to expose any errors of perception, memory, narration or sincerity. The rule against hearsay thus safeguards the fairness of proceedings by ensuring that a party has a reasonable opportunity to test the accuracy and veracity of a statement offered by the other party and the credibility of the maker of the statement.[3] It protects the integrity of the trial process from the distortive influence of secondhand information as well as the more sinister threat of invented or fabricated evidence.[4]

Lay persons commonly assume that the rule against hearsay applies to any out-of-court statement. Actually, the rule has a relatively narrow scope. As Kingsmill Moore J explained in *Cullen v Clarke:*

> [I]t is necessary to emphasise that there is no general rule of evidence to the effect that a witness may not testify as to the words spoken by a person who is not produced as a witness. There is a general rule subject to many exceptions that evidence of the speaking of such words is inadmissible to prove the truth of the facts which they assert; the reasons being that the truth of the words cannot be tested by cross-examination and has not the sanctity of an oath. This is known as the rule against hearsay.[5]

Evidence constitutes hearsay only if it is: (1) an assertive statement; (2) made by an out-of-court declarant; and (3) offered in court to prove the truth of the assertion. This third requirement significantly limits the scope of the rule because an out-of-court statement offered for a probative purpose other than to prove the truth of its contents is not excluded. Lord Wilberforce stated in *Ratten v R*:

> The mere fact that evidence of a witness includes evidence as to words spoken by another person who is not called, is no objection to its admissibility. Words spoken are facts just as much as any other action by a human being. If the speaking of the words is a relevant fact, a witness may give evidence that they were spoken. A question of hearsay only arises when the words spoken are relied on 'testimonially', ie, as establishing some fact narrated by the words.[6]

---

3. *Eastern Health Board v MK* [1999] 2 IR 99, [1999] 2 ILRM 321 (*per* Denham J); *Kiely v Minister for Social Welfare (No 2)* [1977] IR 267. On evidentiary rights including the right to cross-examine, see *In re Haughey* [1971] IR 217; *O'Callaghan v Mahon* [2006] 2 IR 32; *DPP v Kelly* [2006] 3 IR 115.
4. *R v Blastland* [1986] AC 41.
5. [1963] IR 368 at 378.
6. [1972] AC 378, [1971] 3 All ER 801.

As this quote implies, a typical alternative purpose for which an out-of-court statement may be admitted is to prove the fact that the statement was made.[7] Other such purposes include establishing the state of mind of the recipient of the statement,[8] explaining the nature of a transaction that the words accompanied[9] and proving a pre-trial identification of an accused in a criminal proceeding.[10] Out-of-court statements are often used for the limited purpose of impugning the credibility of the witness.[11]

The rationale for the rule explains its limited scope. We are interested in the declarant's credibility only when the out-of-court statement is being used to prove the truth of the assertion. In that circumstance, the value of the evidence depends on the credibility of the out-of-court declarant. Let us suppose that an in-court witness testifies that an out-of-court declarant said that the defendant's car was driven through a red light. The plaintiff wants to offer the testimony for the purpose of showing that the defendant's car was in fact driven through the red light. For that purpose, the value of the testimony depends upon the perception and memory of the out-of-court declarant. The opponent thus needs to cross-examine the out-of-court declarant in order to test the evidence.

Director of Corporate Enforcement v Bailey provides a recent case law illustration. The applicant served notice of his intention to institute proceedings against the respondent directors of a company seeking to disqualify them as directors. The respondents moved to curtail certain evidence put forward by the applicant in grounding affidavits: extracts from a report of a tribunal of inquiry, documentation from the Revenue Commissioners and material compiled by a firm of chartered accountants. Irvine J held that the evidence constituted hearsay and that only one of documents in question was admissible under an exception to the rule. This conclusion depended upon the threshold determination that the out-of-court statements were being offered for the truth of the matter stated:

> The affidavits … make it clear that the applicant invites the Court to consider the documentation exhibited in the grounding affidavits as evidence of wrongdoing for the purposes of deciding whether or not the respondents ought

7. *Subramaniam v Public Prosecutor* [1956] 1 WLR 965 at 970.
8. *Cullen v Clarke* [1963] IR 368.
9. *Hayslep v Gymer* (1834) 1 Al & El 162.
10. *R v Christie* [1914] AC 545 at 551.
11. *DPP v MA* [2002] 2 IR 601; *AG v Taylor* [1974] 1 IR 97.

> to be disqualified as directors pursuant to s 160(2) of the Companies Act, 1990 and also to influence the court as to the sanction to be imposed in the event of such disqualification.[12]

On the other hand, if the proponent does not offer the out-of-court statement for its truth, the opponent does not need to cross-examine the declarant. If the statement is logically relevant on some other theory, the value of the evidence usually depends on the credibility of the in-court witness. Suppose that the plaintiff has sued the defendant for slander. The plaintiff alleges that the defendant repeated the slanderous statement to X. The plaintiff calls X, the in-court witness, to testify that the defendant made an out-of-court statement that the plaintiff bribed a public official. The plaintiff does not want to offer the statement for its truth; quite to the contrary, if the defendant can show that the statement is true, the defendant has a complete defence to the plaintiff's action. The plaintiff wants to show only that at a particular time and place, the defendant made the slanderous statement. The value of X's testimony depends on X's credibility. Did X hear the statement correctly? Does X remember the statement correctly? If X testifies in court, the defendant can test the value of the evidence. Hence, the limitation on the scope of the rule against hearsay is a corollary of the rule's rationale: the rule is limited to statements offered to prove their truth because then and only then does the opponent need to cross-examine the out-of-court declarant.

Even if a statement falls within the definition of hearsay (ie even if it is an assertive statement, made by an out-of-court declarant and offered in court to prove the truth of the assertion), the statement may be admissible. A second significant restriction on the scope and application of the rule against hearsay are the numerous common law and statutory exceptions to the rule. The justifications for relaxing the rule that are said to underpin these various exceptions are, first, the need for reliance on hearsay evidence and, second, a circumstantial guarantee that the evidence is trustworthy. In reality, the exceptions are not only numerous but also specific and diverse. As Keane CJ observed in *Eastern Health Board v MK:*

> [O]ver a long period of time, both the courts and the legislature have sought to avoid the injustice and inconvenience which would flow from an unyielding adherence to the rule by allowing exceptions which, in turn, are subjected to

12. [2007] IEHC 365 (1 November 2007). See also in the same judgment at p 21: 'The Court is therefore being asked to accept as truth the content of the prejudicial material set out in those documents.'

refinements and qualifications. The result has been generally acknowledged to be a body of law which is confusing, complex and not entirely logical ...[13]

Some of the prominent exceptions to the rule against hearsay are now governed by legislation. For example, ss 3–8 of the Criminal Evidence Act 1992 permit the admission of business records and ss 15–20 of the Criminal Justice Act 2006 render admissible the previous statements of unco-operative witnesses. There is no equivalent statutory basis for the admission of business records or previous witness statements in civil proceedings.[14] The Bankers' Book Evidence Act 1879, as amended, makes limited provision for the admission of bank records[15] and the Companies Act 1963, as amended, relaxes the rule against hearsay in certain specific circumstances.[16] Under ss 23–25 of the Children Act 1997, an out-of-court statement by a child is admissible in proceedings concerning the welfare of the child where the court considers that the child is unable to testify by reason of age or that 'the giving of oral evidence would not be in the interest of the welfare of the child.' The Act makes equivalent provision for the admission of an out-of-court statement of a person with a mental illness.[17] The statute books are sprinkled with other seemingly minor exceptions that are often significant in practice.[18]

Statute has not eclipsed the numerous common law exceptions that restrict the application of the rule.[19] The courts will accept into evidence the out-of-

13. [1999] 2 IR 99, [1999] 2 ILRM 321. On reform of the rule against hearsay, see *Balance in the Criminal Law Review Group, Final Report* (March 2007) p 228 *et seq.*; Law Reform Commission, *Report on the Rule Against Hearsay in Civil Cases* (LRC 25-1988); McGrath, *Evidence* (Thomson Round Hall, 2005) pp 303–310.

14. Such as the English Civil Evidence Act 1995, c 38.

15. Bankers' Book Evidence Act 1879, c 11.

16. See *Director of Corporate Enforcement v Bailey* [2007] IEHC 365 (1 November 2007).

17. Section 20(b).

18. See eg s 188 of the CJA 2006 (handling of forensic samples); s 6 of the Criminal Justice (Miscellaneous Provisions) Act 1997 (evidence of scene preservation); s 8(5) of the Criminal Assets Bureau Act 1996 (information obtained by CAB officers).

19. *Eastern Health Board v MK* [1999] 2 IR 99, [1999] 2 ILRM 321 (*per* Denham J): 'The fact that new exceptions have been made in recent times by the legislature to extend the list of exceptions to the rule does not per se exclude the jurisdiction of the courts.' (contd \...)

court statement of a party to the proceedings that is against that party's interest.[20] Similarly, hearsay statements that form an intrinsic part of the narration of the material events at trial will be admissible under the notoriously malleable *res gestae* exception.[21] There are also various instances in which parties may rely on the out-of-court statements of persons since deceased on the basis that the admission of such statements is necessary and the statements were made in circumstances which suggest they are reliable.[22] Finally, there are contexts in which the courts adopt a flexible attitude to the rule against hearsay, notably, where a party proffers an expert witness,[23] where the out-of-court statement is contained in a public document[24] and where hearsay is tendered in proceedings concerning the welfare of children.[25]

The incorporation into Irish law of the European Convention on Human Rights may place additional limits on the use by the prosecution of hearsay in criminal proceedings even where such evidence is otherwise admissible under an exception to the rule. Under the Convention, the legal issue is framed in case-specific terms, namely, whether the admission of hearsay in the particular proceedings would deprive the accused of his or her right to a fair trial under Article 6.[26] Nevertheless, the European Court of Human Rights (ECtHR) has set down certain general principles in cases such as *Laukkanen v Finland:*

---

19. (contd) But see *Director of Corporate Enforcement v Bailey* [2007] IEHC 365 (1 November 2007) (*per* Irvine J): '[T]here is no statutory mandate which would bring any of the documents concerned into a category to which the normal rules of evidence would not apply.' Some common law exceptions are largely of historical interest, eg a statement of a deceased as to the pedigree of a blood relative is unlikely to be invoked given the advent of DNA paternity testing.
20. See eg *Bord na gCon v Murphy* [1970] IR 301.
21. See eg *AG v Crosbie* [1966] IR 490.
22. *R v Woodcock* (1789) 1 Leach CC 500.
23. See **Chapter 4**.
24. See **6.08**.
25. *Eastern Health Board v MK* [1999] 2 IR 99, [1999] 2 ILRM 321; *Southern Health Board v CH* [1996] 1 IR 219, [1996] 2 ILRM 142.
26. As *DPP v Kelly* [2006] 3 IR 115 illustrates, this mirrors the corresponding inquiry undertaken by the Supreme Court under Art 38.1 of the Constitution.

> All the evidence must normally be produced in the presence of the accused at a public hearing with a view to adversarial argument. As a rule, a conviction should be based on the testimony of a witness whom the accused has had an opportunity to challenge and question. However, Article 6(3)(d) does not grant the accused an unlimited right to secure the appearance of witnesses in court. It is normally for the national courts to decide whether it is necessary or advisable to hear a particular witness.[27]

On a number of occasions, the ECtHR has found violations of Article 6(3)(d) where the prosecution relied exclusively or very substantially on out-of-court statements. For example, in *Van Mechelen v The Netherlands*, the applicants were denied a fair trial because their convictions rested essentially on the evidence of anonymous police officers whose testimony had been recorded in private outside the presence of the defence.[28] The Irish courts have faced a similar issue in repeated challenges to the propriety of s 3(2) of the Offences Against the State (Amendment) Act 1972[29] which permits a garda chief superintendent to give evidence of his belief that an accused is guilty of a charge of membership of an unlawful organisation.[30] In *DPP v Kelly*,[31] the Supreme Court held that a garda chief superintendent delivering such evidence was entitled to resist cross-examination as to the third-party source for his belief. The court held that the restriction on the right to cross-examine was proportionate to the need to protect third-party garda informers in the context of the fight against subversive crime. The conclusion that the applicant had not been denied a fair trial was consistent with the Strasbourg case law in so far as it was based in large measure on the existence in the case of prosecution evidence other than the chief superintendent's belief.[32] Moreover, the Supreme Court's emphasis on the special features of proceedings relating to offences against

27. App No 50230/99, 3 Feb 2004 at para 35. See also *R v Sellick* [2005] 2 Cr App R 15 (summarising the principles applied by the European Court).

28. (1998) 25 EHRR 647. See also *PS v Germany* (2003) 36 EHRR 61; *Lucà v Italy* (2003) 36 EHRR 46.

29. The constitutionality of s 3(2) was upheld in *O'Leary v AG* [1993] 1 IR 102.

30. Pursuant to s 21 of the Offences Against the State Act 1939.

31. [2006] 3 IR 115.

32 In a concurring judgment, Fennelly J suggested that an accused would have a 'powerful' argument based on denial of his rights where belief evidence was 'the sole plank in the prosecution's case' [2006] 3 IR 115. See also *Magnusson v Sweden (Admissibility)* App No 53972/00, 16 December 2003 (no violation where impugned evidence was not the only evidence); *Doorson v The Netherlands* (1996) 22 EHRR 330 (same). (contd \...)

the State echoes the European Court's determination in *SN v Sweden*[33] that restrictions on the right to cross-examination in the particular context of proceedings concerning sexual offences did not violate Article 6(3)(d).

The Convention may have a bearing on the rule relating to hearsay in a separate but related sense. The fair trial guarantee restricts the prosecution in the evidence it may adduce but conversely it may remove restrictions the law would otherwise place on the defence. The rights of the defence under the Constitution and the Convention include the right to present evidence that would exonerate the accused. The contours of this right have not been clearly prescribed, however, and neither the European nor the Irish courts have determined the circumstances, if any, in which it entitles the defence to rely on hearsay. In *R v Blastland,* the House of Lords expressed the traditional view that to admit the out-of-court statements of third parties confessing to the crime for which the accused is charged would create a 'very significant' and 'dangerous' new exception to the rule against hearsay.[34] However, the Court of Appeal, addressing the same issue in *R v Greenwood,* adopted the contemporary stance that the defence should be given wide latitude to produce evidence that would point to the possibility that another person committed the crime.[35]

6.02 THE DEFINITION OF HEARSAY

6.02.1 In general

As previously noted, the concept of hearsay is narrowly defined. Hearsay is an out-of-court statement offered in court to prove the truth of the matter stated. The term 'statement' is interpreted broadly and extends to oral assertions,[36] written assertions (in wide-ranging form including documents, diagrams, photographs and digital images)[37] and assertive, non-verbal

32. (contd) But see *SN v Sweden* (2004) 39 EHRR 13 (no violation even though statements were virtually the sole evidence).

33. (2004) 39 EHRR 13.

34. [1986] AC 41 (*per* Bridge LJ).

35. [2005] 1 Cr App R 7 (*per* Waller LJ).

36. *Doran v Cosgrove* (12 November 1999, unreported) SC; *Sparks v R* [1964] AC 964; *Teper v R* [1952] AC 480, [1952] 2 All ER 447.

37. *Director of Corporate Enforcement v Bailey* [2007] IEHC 365 (1 November 2007); *Re Family Law Act 1995, FP v SP* [2002] 4 IR 280; *Criminal Assets Bureau v Hunt* [2003] IESC 15; *DPP v Marley* [1985] ILRM 17.

conduct.[38] Evidence constitutes hearsay provided three conditions are met: (1) the evidence is an assertive statement or act; (2) the statement was made or the act committed out of court; and (3) the evidence is being offered to prove the truth of the matter stated.

6.02.2 The evidence is an assertive statement or act

(a) Assertive statements

Whereas there is general agreement that assertive statements fall within the definition of hearsay, it must be remembered that not all statements are assertive. As a practical matter, only declarative sentences ordinarily fall within the hearsay definition; they declare or assert facts, including states of mind. Imperative sentences giving orders, interrogatory sentences posing questions and exclamatory sentences voicing excited utterances, usually fall outside the definition of hearsay. If these sentences are relevant at all, their relevance is limited to the fact that they were uttered and, for that purpose, counsel can question the person who heard the declarant utter the sentence. There is little or no need to cross-examine the declarant of an imperative, interrogatory or exclamatory sentence about perception or memory.

If the proponent intends to offer evidence on the theory that it is a non-assertive statement, the foundation usually includes the following elements:

1. Where the statement was made.
2. When the statement was made.
3. Who was present.
4. That the tenor of the statement is non-assertive.
5. That the non-assertive statement is relevant to material facts in the case.

Our fact situation is a criminal proceeding. The prosecution alleges that Mr Adam Apple and Mr Paddy Plum conspired to sell and actually sold heroin. The witness is Garda Orla Orange. Garda Orange identifies herself. She then testifies that she is an undercover garda officer and that she infiltrated the meeting of a drug ring. The prosecution is the proponent.

P. Garda Orange, where were you on the evening of 17 January 2007? (1), (2)

38. *DPP v Bishop* [2005] IECCA 2 (27 January 2005) (handing over of keys); *Teper v R* [1952] AC 480, [1952] 2 All ER 447 (pointing); *Chandrasekera v R* [1937] AC 220 (nodding one's head).

W. I was at 4 Local Lane.
P. Who else was there? (3)
W. The two defendants, Adam Apple and Paddy Plum.
P. Where are they now? (3)
W. Here in court.
P. Specifically, where in court are they? (3)
W. (*Pointing at the defendant*) Over there.
P. Garda Orange, what happened during this meeting? (4)
W. The accused men made some plans.
P. What plans did they discuss? (4)
O. Judge, I object to that question on the ground that it calls for hearsay.
P. Judge, I think this matter requires to be addressed by way of *voir dire.*
J. Yes.
P. *(In the absence of the jury)* Judge, the witness will testify that the accused, Mr Adam Apple, ordered the accused, Mr Paddy Plum, to get some bags of heroin out of Mr Plum's car and that Mr Plum did so. (4) Mr Apple's statement is not hearsay because it is not assertive; the statement is not a declarative sentence but rather an imperative one, ordering Mr Plum to do something. (4) The only thing we are interested in is whether he gave the order. You might say that Garda Orange is an 'earwitness' to the fact that he gave an order. The statement is relevant to prove the existence of a conspiracy between them. (5)
J. Yes, I don't think that the objection is well-founded. You may continue with that line of questioning.
P. *(In the presence of the jury)* Garda Orange, let me repeat the question. What plans did they discuss? (4)
W. The plans for a drug sale. Mr. Apple told Mr Plum to get some bags of heroin out of Mr Plum's car to get them ready for sale.
P. What happened then?
W. Mr Apple left for a couple of minutes and then came back with some bags.
P. What was the appearance of the bags?
W. The bags themselves were transparent.
P. What, if anything, could you see in the bags?
W. There was a white, powdery substance in each bag.

In the final analysis, it is always a question of interpretation whether the statement is an assertion. Sometimes an exclamatory, imperative or interrogatory sentence contains an implicit assertion, and the proponent is interested only in the assertion. Assume, for instance, that in the above hypothetical, the two accused were charged with substantive drug offences rather than conspiracy and that the only question was whether the bags contained heroin. It is true that overall Mr Apple's utterance is an imperative sentence: 'Go out to your car and get the bags of heroin.' However, in this context, the prosecution would be interested only in the part of the sentence in which Mr Apple referred to 'the bags of heroin.' In fact, at trial, rather than questioning Garda Orange about the entire sentence, the prosecution might ask only: 'How did Mr Apple describe the bags?' or 'What did Mr. Apple say about the contents of the bags?' Although the overall classification of the sentence is imperative, the prosecution is attempting to elicit an assertion embodied in the sentence, and for that reason, the question calls for hearsay.

(b) Implied assertions

Further complexity surrounds the interpretation of assertive statements. In applying the rule against hearsay, do we take the statement in question at face value and assume that its meaning is limited to the express statement made by the declarant? Or should we also be concerned about any other inferences that might be drawn from the statement and offered in evidence? The common law does not distinguish between express and implied assertions for purposes of the rule, with the consequence that a party may not rely on an out-of-court statement to prove the truth of a matter inferred any more than it can use the statement to establish its expressive content. In *R v Kearley*[39] a majority of the House of Lords held that evidence that several individuals had telephoned the accused's residence looking for drugs was inadmissible to prove that the accused was a supplier of drugs. The statements of the telephone callers were relevant only in so far as they implied that the accused was a supplier of drugs. These implied assertions were caught by the rule against hearsay in the same way that an express out-of-court assertion that the accused was a supplier of drugs would have been.[40]

39. [1992] 2 AC 228, [1992] 2 All ER 345. In England, the common law position has been abrogated by s 115 of the CJA 2003 which limits the reach of the rule to intended assertions.

40. For reform in the UK, see s 1 of the Civil Evidence Act 1995, c 38 and s 115(3) of the CJA 2003, c 44.

(c) Assertive and non-assertive acts

Sometimes a person intends an act to be a true substitute for speech. For instance, persons sometimes nod or shake their heads in response to questions. In principle, these acts should be treated in the same fashion as verbal hearsay statements since they present the same probative dangers of perception, memory, narration and sincerity. For this reason, assertive acts or conduct fall within the definition of hearsay.[41]

In contrast, there is some disagreement over whether another category of evidence, namely non-assertive acts or conduct, constitutes hearsay. The classic English case of *Wright v Tatham*[42] is authority for the traditional common law view that evidence of a non-assertive act constitutes hearsay if: (1) the act is apparently prompted by a certain belief and (2) the proponent offers evidence to prove the truth of the belief. At issue in the case was the mental capacity of a testator. The proponent of the will attempted to prove the testator's mental competence by establishing that several persons had written business letters to the testator. Although the act of writing incidentally involved assertions in the letters, the act itself was non-assertive; the persons did not subjectively intend their act to constitute proof that the testator was competent. The authors of the letters assumed that the testator was competent, and the proponent of the will offered the evidence to show the truth of their assumption and belief. The proponent of the will reasoned that they would not have sent the letters to the testator unless they believed that he was competent; and if they, his close acquaintances, believed him to be competent, he probably was competent. The court held that the evidence fell within the definition of hearsay; even though the act of writing the letters was non-assertive, it presented probative dangers of perception and memory.

6.02.3 The statement is offered for a hearsay purpose

(a) Overview

A statement is not hearsay unless the proponent offers the statement to prove the truth of the assertion contained in the statement.[43] Offering the statement for that purpose creates the need to cross-examine the declarant about

41. *DPP v Bishop* [2005] IECCA 2 (27 January 2005); *Teper v R* [1952] AC 480, [1952] 2 All ER 447; *Chandrasekera v R* [1937] AC 220.

42. (1837) 7 Ad & E 313.

43. *Cullen v Clarke* [1963] IR 368.

perception or memory. The statement is deemed hearsay only when the immediate inference the proponent wants to draw is the truth of the assertion. If the proponent can demonstrate that the statement is relevant on any other theory, the statement is non-hearsay or original evidence. When the proponent offers the statement for a non-hearsay purpose, we are primarily interested in the simple fact that the statement was made. The fact *of* the statement is relevant; the truth of the facts *in* the statement is irrelevant. The only need to cross-examine is the need to question on the stand the witness who heard the statement made.

When the proponent intends to argue a non-hearsay theory for admitting a statement, the foundation includes the following elements:

1. Where the statement was made.
2. When the statement was made.
3. Who was present.
4. The tenor of the statement.
5. That the proponent intends to use the statement for a non-hearsay purpose.
6. That on a non-hearsay theory, the statement is relevant.

There are three common non-hearsay uses of evidence. First, the proponent may argue that the statement is circumstantial evidence of the declarant's state of mind. If the declarant's state of mind is relevant to the case, the proponent may use the declarant's statement as circumstantial proof of such states of mind as malice, hatred, premeditation and love. Sometimes, the mere fact that a person makes a certain statement gives us an insight into that person's frame of mind.[44] Second, the statement may be an operative fact or 'verbal act' in the case. In some situations, legal consequences flow directly from the use of certain words; examples include the words that comprise an offer in an action based on contract or the words that are alleged to constitute slander in an action in tort. Again, the mere fact that the declarant uttered the words is relevant; the words themselves have legal consequences. Finally, the proponent can prove the statement to show its effect on the state of mind of the person who heard or read the statement.[45] For example, if it is disputed whether the defendant knew of a certain dangerous condition, it is relevant to prove that someone told him of the condition. Quite apart from the truth of the third party's statement, the

44. *Ratten v R* [1972] AC 378.

45. *Subramaniam v Public Prosecutor* [1956] 1 WLR 965.

statement puts the defendant on notice. The following hypothetical situations illustrate these various uses of non-hearsay.

(b) The statement is circumstantial proof of the declarant's state of mind – mental output

Our fact situation is a dispute over real property. The deceased, Ms Betty Brown, formerly owned the land. Before she died, she gave her nephew, Mr Gary Gold, a deed to the property on 14 April 2005. The executor concedes that Ms Brown gave Mr Gold the deed but claims that she did not intend the deed to be immediately effective. The executor contends that since Ms Brown did not have the intent required by law, the deed was ineffective. Mr Gold calls Ms Phillipa Purple as a witness. Ms Purple identifies herself and states that she knew the deceased for several years. The nephew, Mr Gold, is the proponent.

P. Where were you on 13 April 2005? (1), (2)

W. I was visiting Betty Brown at her house on Leaf Lane.

P. Who else was there? (3)

W. Only the two of us.

P. What happened while you were there? (4)

W. We just had a nice chat.

P. What did you chat about? (4)

W. A lot of things, including Betty's nephew, Gary Gold.

P. What did Ms Brown say about her nephew, Gary? (4)

O. Judge, I object to that question on the ground that it calls for hearsay.

P. Judge, I expect Ms Purple to testify that Ms Brown said that her nephew was a man in a million. (4) I want to offer that testimony for a non-hearsay purpose, as circumstantial proof of Ms Brown's affection for Gary Gold. (5) The testimony is relevant to show that she had donative intent when she gave him the deed the next day. (6)

J. Very well. I am prepared to admit the evidence for that non-hearsay purpose.

P. Ms Purple, let me repeat the question. What did Ms Brown say about her nephew, Gary Gold? (4)

W. She said that he was a man in a million.

(c) The statement is an operative fact or 'verbal act'

The following situation involves a dispute over the sale by a bank of hay stored on a farm following a foreclosure. The plaintiff, Mr Farmer Frank, owned the farm which he leased to Mr Tommy Tenant. There were a number of large silos on the farm which were used for storing hay. When Mr Tenant fell behind in paying the rent, he agreed to give Mr Farmer the hay stored in two of the silos in lieu of the rent due for June and July. When they entered into the agreement, Mr Tenant said: 'That's grand with me. The hay in silos one and two is yours.' Mr Tenant subsequently obtained a loan from a bank, pledging 'my hay crop' as security for the loan. When Mr Tenant defaulted on the loan, the bank foreclosed and sold all the hay on the premises including the hay in silos one and two. Mr Farmer has instituted proceedings against the bank for conversion. The plaintiff, Mr Farmer, is the proponent. He has himself entered the witness box and is being examined by his own counsel. Mr Farmer has already identified himself, explained that he was Mr. Tenant's landlord and testified that Mr Tenant failed to pay his rent.

P. Mr Farmer, where were you on the afternoon of 6 July 2006? (1), (2)

W. I was at the farm, the one I rented to Mr Tenant.

P. Who else was there? (3)

W. Mr Tenant was the only one around. I didn't see his wife or children.

P. Why were you there? (4)

W. As I said, Mr Tenant had fallen behind on his rent. He was supposed to pay at the beginning of the month and he had missed the June and July payments. I asked him what he intended to do about the rent he owed.

P. What happened when you asked him that? (4)

W. He offered me a deal.

O. Judge, I'm asking that that last answer be disregarded on the ground that it is hearsay.

P. Judge, I expect that my client will testify that Mr Tenant offered to give my client the hay contained in two silos, silos one and two, in exchange for the outstanding rent. (4) I want to use the statement for a non-hearsay purpose, namely, as original evidence of the offer itself. (5) The words constituting the offer are an operative fact or verbal act; legal consequences flow simply from the fact that Mr Tenant uttered these words. (6)

J. I do not consider the objection to be well-founded. You may proceed with this line of questioning.

P. Mr Farmer, let me repeat the question. What happened when you asked him about the rent that he owed you? (4)

W. He offered to give me the hay in two silos in exchange for the rent.

P. What were his words? (4)

W. As far as I remember he said: 'That's grand with me. The hay in silos one and two is yours.'

P. What did you say then? (4)

W. I just said that I accepted the offer and we shook hands on it.

(d) The effect of the statement on the mind of the person who heard it or read it – mental input

Our scenario is an action in tort arising out of a road traffic accident. The plaintiff has alleged that the defendant was negligent in two respects: first, the defendant was speeding and, second, he drove the car knowing that its brakes were defective. In relation to the second claim, one issue is whether the defendant knew that the brakes were faulty. The plaintiff calls Mr Martin Mechanic who testifies that he manages a garage near the defendant's house. Mr Mechanic states that on 14 January 2006 the defendant brought his car to the garage for a regular service. The plaintiff is the proponent.

P. Mr Mechanic, where were you on 15 January 2006? (1), (2)

W. I was at my garage.

P. Who else was there? (3)

W. We had several customers, including the defendant.

P. Why was the defendant at the garage? (4)

W. He was there to pick up his car.

P. What happened while he was there? (4)

W. He collected the car and we talked for a while.

P. What did you talk about? (4)

W. We talked about his car mostly.

P. What did you tell him about the car? (4)

O. Judge, I object to that question on the ground that it would require the witness to give inadmissible hearsay evidence.

P. Judge, I expect the witness to testify that he told the defendant that the brakes in his car were faulty. (4) I want to use the witness's prior statement for a non-hearsay purpose, namely, to show its effect on the defendant's state of mind; it gave him knowledge that his brakes were bad. (5) This evidence is relevant to our claim that the defendant negligently drove the car when he knew that its brakes were defective. (6).

J. Yes, I consider that such question is permissible. Counsel, you may continue.

P. Mr Mechanic, let me repeat the question. What did you tell the defendant about his car? (4)

W. I told him that the brakes were bad and could fail at any time.

P. How close were you standing to the defendant when you told him that?

W. Only a foot or two away.

P. How noisy was the garage at the time?

W. It was very quiet.

P. How were you facing the defendant when you told him about his brakes?

W. I was talking directly to him.

P. Who else was talking to him at the time?

W. No one else. We were the only two people talking.

P. How did he react when you told him about the bad brakes?

W. He nodded his head, shrugged his shoulders and got into his car.

P. Thank you Mr Mechanic.

Of course, the proponent will have to introduce other, independent evidence that the brakes were defective. The plaintiff could call as a witness the person who actually worked on the brakes to describe the condition of the brakes. However, assuming that Mr Mechanic did not work on the car himself, it is clear that the proponent could use Mr Mechanic's testimony for the limited, non-hearsay purpose of proving that the defendant knew of the brakes' hazardous condition.

6.02.4 Electronic statements

Hearsay is routinely defined by reference to a statement made by 'a person.' Since the primary purpose of the rule against hearsay is that it safeguards the right to cross-examination, it follows logically that its application is limited to statements made by human declarants. Thus, for example, the rule applies to statements *stored* on a computer but not to statements *generated* by a computer.

Suppose that a business employee inputs data about a sale into the company computer. The input constitutes a statement by a human declarant, the employee. It is true that the statement is stored in the computer in electronic form. Yet, in the final analysis, the accuracy of the statement depends on the testimonial qualities of the human declarant who was the source of the input. If the company later prints out the data, the printout constitutes hearsay, and the proponent will need to lay a foundation for an exception to the rule against hearsay, such as the exception for the admission of business records in criminal proceedings.[46] This example may be distinguished from a statement generated by an instrument. For instance, assume that the accused is charged with drunken driving. The prosecution calls as a witness the garda officer who administered an intoxilyser to the accused. The garda officer is prepared to testify that when she administered the test to the defendant, the instrument displayed '0.17.' That display is elliptical; it amounts to the statement that the blood alcohol concentration of the person who blew into the instrument is 0.17. That statement is assertive but it was not made by a human declarant. Although it makes sense to give opposing counsel an opportunity to cross-examine a human declarant, counsel cannot cross-examine an intoxilyser. Consequently, the defence could not successfully object on hearsay grounds to the introduction of the testimony about the printout. Of course, the prosecution may have to contend with alternative challenges to the evidence, such as the accuracy and reliability of the intoxilyser technology.[47]

EXCEPTIONS TO THE RULE AGAINST HEARSAY

6.03 ADMISSIONS

6.03.1 In general

If the statement falls within the definition of hearsay, then the proponent of the statement must find an applicable exception to the rule against hearsay. One such exception is that for admissions made by an opposing party to the proceedings.[48] For example, in a negligence action, the plaintiff can prove that the defendant made an out-of-court statement acknowledging that he or

46. Sections 3–8 of the CEA 1992.

47. See eg *McGonnell v AG* [2006] IESC 64 (28 November 2006).

48. *Bord na gCon v Murphy* [1970] IR 310; *R v Blastland* [1986] AC 41; *R v Greenwood* [2005] 1 Cr App R 7.

she was at fault.[49] The same exception permits the prosecution in criminal proceedings to introduce a confession acknowledging guilt made by an accused during custodial detention.[50] The exception relating to admissions differs from most of the exceptions to the rule against hearsay and commentators have had some difficulty explaining it. Unlike most hearsay exceptions, admissions do not have a circumstantial guarantee of trustworthiness; although the admission is obviously disserving at the time of trial, the admission is admissible even if it was self-serving when made. Nor is there any need to show a necessity for resorting to hearsay; the opposing party is usually available and may be perfectly willing to testify about the subject matter of the earlier statement. The exception in relation to admissions is essentially the product of the adversarial system of litigation; the opponent can hardly complain since he or she can always take the stand to deny or explain the statement. Because of the unique rationale for this exception, there is some disagreement over whether admissions should be classified as hearsay at all. In contrast, there is general consensus on the foundational elements of the various types of admissions.

There are three basic kinds of admissions: express admissions, admissions by conduct and vicarious admissions. The basis of the classification is the reason for which we attribute the statement to the opposing party. In the case of express admissions and admissions by conduct, we attribute the statement to the opposing party because we find the statement in the party's own words or acts. In the case of vicarious admissions, a third party makes the statement but we attribute the statement to the opposing party by virtue of a legal relationship, such as agency, between the third party and the opposing party.

6.03.2 Express admissions

Courts will liberally admit the express admissions of an opposing party in civil and criminal proceedings. The term 'admission' is broadly defined to cover any statement which, having regard to the context in which it was made, is adverse to the party's cause.[51] The phrasing of the admission can be highly opinionated and the admission need not even be based on personal knowledge.

---

49. However, a party admission may not be used against other parties to the proceedings: *Doran v Cosgrove* (12 November 1999, unreported) SC.

50. *DPP v Shaw* [1982] IR 1; *People v Lynch* [1982] IR 64.

51. *DPP v Pringle* (1981) 1 Frewen 57.

In civil cases, the foundation for express admissions is straightforward and includes three elements:

1. The witness heard a declarant make a statement.
2. The witness identifies the declarant as the opposing party in the proceedings.
3. The statement is inconsistent with the position that the opposing party is taking at trial. In other words, the statement is relevant to an issue the proponent must prove in the case.

Our hypothetical situation involves an action in tort arising from a road traffic accident that occurred on 19 May 2006. The plaintiff, Ms Sandra Swan, alleges that the defendant, Mr Rory Robin, caused the collision by speeding. The speed limit in the particular area of the city is 30 kilometres per hour. The plaintiff calls the investigating garda officer, Grainne Gull. The witness has already identified herself and testified that she went to the scene of the accident. The proponent is the plaintiff.

P. What did you do when you arrived at the scene of the collision?
W. I investigated the accident.
P. How did you investigate the accident? (1)
W. I viewed the scene and interviewed the persons involved.
P. Whom did you interview? (2)
W. Ms Swan and Mr Robin.
P. Where is the defendant, Mr Robin, now? (2)
W. Here in the court.
P. Specifically, where in the court? (2)
W. (*Pointing at the defendant*) He's sitting over there.
P. Garda Gull, what did the defendant say about the accident? (3)
O. Judge, I object to that question on the basis that it would require the witness to give hearsay evidence that is inadmissible.
P. Judge, the statement is hearsay but it falls within the exception for admissions of an opposing party.
J. Yes, I am satisfied that the question is valid. You may continue.
P. Let me repeat the question. What did the defendant say about the accident? (3)
W. He said that he was very sorry and that he thought that he had caused the accident by driving too fast.
P. How fast did he say he was going? (3)
W. He said that he might have been going about 60 kilometres per hour.

6.03.3 Admissions by conduct

In some instances, courts will treat the conduct of a party as an admission of an allegation made in civil or criminal proceedings.[52] Examples include an offer by a party to settle proceedings,[53] a lie told by a party in connection with proceedings[54] and other forms of interference by a party with the course of proceedings.[55]

There has been some dispute over whether a party's silence in the face of an accusation may constitute an admission. In some instances courts have been willing to construe silence as an admission where the party would reasonably be expected to deny the accusation.[56] The party is deemed to have impliedly adopted the accusation by silence. The foundation includes the following elements:

1. The declarant made a statement.
2. The statement was an accusation against the opposing party.
3. The declarant made the statement in the party's presence.
4. The party heard and understood the statement.
5. The party had an opportunity to deny the statement.
6. The party remained silent.
7. Under similar circumstances, a reasonable person would have denied the accusation. (This element is a mixed question of law and fact.)

Our scenario is an action in tort arising out of a road traffic accident. The plaintiff, Mr Gregory Grey, alleges that the defendant, Mrs Barbara Black, caused the accident by disregarding a stop sign. The investigating garda officer was Sergeant Stephen Silver. The plaintiff calls Sergeant Silver to the stand. He has already identified himself and testified that he responded to the call to attend the scene of the accident. The plaintiff is the proponent.

P. What did you do when you arrived at the scene?

---

52. See generally McGrath, *Evidence* (Thomson Round Hall, 2005) pp 246–251.

53. *Tait v Beggs* [1905] 2 IR 525.

54. *DPP v Madden* [1977] IR 336.

55. *Moriarty v London, Chatham and Dover Rwy Co* (1870) LR 5 QB 314.

56. *R v Mitchell* (1892) 17 Cox CC 503; *Cleeland v M'Cune* (1908) 42 ILTR 202. On the drawing of inferences from an accused's silence in custodial detention, see eg s 30 of the CJA 2007.

W. I immediately sought out the two drivers.
P. Who were the drivers?
W. Your client, Mr Grey, and Mrs Black.
P. Where is Mr Grey now?
W. (*Pointing*) He is sitting over there.
P. Where is Mrs Black now?
W. (*Pointing*) She is sitting there.
P. Where did you find the plaintiff and defendant at the scene of the accident?
W. They were standing on one side of the junction.
P. How close were they to each other?
W. They were standing right next to each other.
P. What were they doing?
W. They were talking.
P. What were they talking about?
W. They were talking about the accident.
P. What, if anything, did Mr Grey tell Mrs Black about the accident? (1), (2)
O. Judge, I object to that question on the basis that to answer it the witness would have to give evidence that would be inadmissible hearsay.
P. Judge, I am trying to establish that Mr Grey told the defendant, Mrs Black, that she had failed to stop at a stop sign and that Mrs Black adopted the statement by remaining silent. In my respectful submission the statement is admissible as an exception to the rule against hearsay because it is an admission by conduct on the part of the defendant.
J. Yes, I consider that submission to be persuasive. You may continue with the line of questioning.
P. Sergeant Silver, let me repeat the question. What, if anything, did Mr Grey say to Mrs Black about the accident? (1), (2)
W. He told her that she had caused the accident by failing to stop at a stop sign. He said that she must be as blind as a bat.
P. How close was Mr Grey to Mrs Black when he made that statement? (3)
W. Two feet away at most. As I said, they were talking.
P. How much noise was there when Mr Grey made the statement? (4), (5)
W. It was fairly quiet. The traffic congestion had died down.

P. How many other people were talking to Mrs Black at the time? (4), (5)
W. No other people.
P. Who was Mr Grey facing when he made the statement? (4), (5)
W. He was looking directly at Mrs Black.
P. In what direction was she facing? (4), (5)
W. She was facing him.
P. What was Mr Grey's tone of voice when he made the statement? (5), (7)
W. He was animated.
P. Did Mr Grey threaten Mrs Black? (5), (7)
W. No. He was obviously upset but he didn't make threats. He didn't point a finger in her face or anything like that. He was just exasperated.
P. What was Mrs Black's demeanour immediately after Mr Grey made the statement? (4), (5), (7)
W. She looked nervous and anxious.
P. What, if anything, did she say then? (6)
W. Nothing.
P. Did she make any response to Mr Grey's statement that she had failed to stop at the stop sign? (6), (7).
W. No. She didn't say anything. She just looked at the ground and away from Mr Grey.

6.03.4 Vicarious admissions

In the case of vicarious admissions, the basis for imputing the statement to the opposing party is the party's relationship with the declarant. Thus, the statements of a predecessor in title may be admitted against the present titleholder, and the statements of an agent against the principal. The foundation consists of demonstrating the relation between the declarant and the opposing party. Once the relation has been demonstrated, the declarant's statements are vicariously admissible against the opposing party.

Most vicarious admissions are statements made by agents and admitted against the agent's principal in civil proceedings. The traditional view is that the declarant must have been expressly or impliedly authorised to communicate on behalf of the principal.[57] In addition, the statement in question must have been made to a third party and not merely to the principal.[58] The foundation includes the following elements:

1. The declarant was an agent of the opposing party.
2. The opposing party authorised the declarant to make the particular statement.
3. The statement was made to a third party.
4. The statement is inconsistent with a position that the opposing party is taking at trial; the statement is relevant to an issue the proponent must prove at trial.

The hypothetical situation is an action to recover on an insurance policy. Alpha Co Ltd is suing Beta Co Ltd. The Statement of Claim alleges that the defendant insured the plaintiff against fire; a fire occurred on the plaintiff's premises and caused €200,000 worth of damage and the defendant wrongfully refused to compensate the plaintiff. The insurance policy excluded cover for any fire caused by the negligence of the plaintiff's employees. During discovery, the defendant obtained a copy of a report prepared by the plaintiff's health and safety officer, Mr David Delta. The report includes the finding that one contributory cause of the fire was careless welding by the plaintiff's employees; the welders negligently cut into a furnace thereby permitting flames to escape. During its case-in-chief, the defendant calls Mr Delta. The defendant is the proponent. Mr Delta has already identified himself.

P. Where do you work? (1)
W. I work for Alpha Co Ltd.
P. How long have you worked for them? (1)
W. Seven years, give or take a few months.
P. What is your job with Alpha? (2)
W. I am the health and safety officer.
P. How long have you held that position? (2)
W. The last five years.
P. Where were you on 13 November 2006? (2)
W. At our factory.
P. What were you doing there? (2)

---

57. *Dwyer v Larkin* (1905) 39 ILTR 40; *Swan v Miller, Son and Torrance Ltd* [1919] 1 IR 151.

58. *Swan v Miller, Son and Torrance Ltd* [1919] 1 IR 151.

W. I was investigating the fire that had occurred the day before.
P. How long did you spend investigating the fire? (2)
W. The whole day.
P. What did you do when you finished the investigation? (2)
W. As is my normal practice, I prepared a report of the investigation.
P. Judge, I request that this be marked as defendant's exhibit F for identification.
J. It will be so marked.
P. Mr Delta, I am now handing you defendant's exhibit F for identification. What is it? (2)
W. It's my report on the fire.
P. How can you recognise it? (2)
W. I recognise my handwriting on the last page. I also recall the report's contents.
P. Again, what are your duties for Alpha? (2)
W. As I said before, I'm the health and safety officer.
P. In general terms, what is the subject of this particular report?
W. It relates to the fire I investigated as part of my duties.
P. Why did you prepare this particular report? (2), (3)
W. It's part of my job. The company is obliged by law to investigate any accidents at the factory. It's my job to prepare the report.
P. What did you do when you had finished the report? (3)
W. I made a photocopy of the report which I filed in my office. Then I put the original in a sealed envelope addressed to Alpha's Managing Director and left it in the factory's mailroom for posting in the usual way.
P. Judge, I now offer defendant's exhibit F for identification into evidence as defendant's exhibit F.
J. Very good.
P. Mr Delta, please turn to page 18 of exhibit F and read finding number four to the court. (4)
W. Finding number four reads: 'Another contributing factor may have been our own employees' carelessness. Some of our welders were evidently working next to a furnace on the second floor. Some eyewitness reports indicated that the welders accidentally cut into the furnace, releasing flames that started the fire.'

6.04 DECLARATIONS AGAINST INTEREST

The term 'declaration against interest' is used to refer to a particular kind of admission, namely, a statement by a deceased person that was against his or her pecuniary or proprietary interest at the time. Declarations against interest may be distinguished from admissions of a party to the proceedings, discussed above, in several respects. First, the declarant of an admission must be a party to the proceedings whereas any person can make a declaration against interest. Second, declarations against interest are admissible only if the declarant has since died; the declarant's unavailability supplies the necessity for resorting to hearsay. Finally, declarations against interest are admissible only if at the time of the statement, the declarant believed the statement was contrary to his or her interest; the declarant's belief is the guarantee of the statement's reliability. Thus, whereas admissions of a party are necessarily disserving to the declarant's interest at the time of trial, declarations against interest are disserving to the declarant's interest at the time they were made.

The foundation includes the following elements:

1. The declarant is deceased.
2. The declarant made a statement.
3. The statement was contrary to his or her pecuniary or proprietary interest at the time it was made.
4. The declarant believed that it was contrary to his or her interest at the time.

Our hypothetical situation involves a road traffic accident. The plaintiff, Mr Bob Basil is suing the defendant Mr Christopher Coriander for damages arising out of a collision between the plaintiff's van and the defendant's car. The defendant was not driving the car at the time and the driver of the car, Mr Paul Parsley, is now deceased. At the trial of the action, the plaintiff, Mr Basil, seeks to establish that Mr Parsley said that he 'never saw the van coming' before the collision. The deceased is alleged to have said this to Garda Tony Thyme who came upon the scene immediately after the collision. The plaintiff calls Garda Thyme. The witness has already identified himself and testified that he went to the scene of the accident. The proponent is the plaintiff.

P. How did you set about investigating the cause of the accident? (2)

W. I viewed the scene and interviewed both drivers.

P. Who exactly did you speak to? (2)

W. Mr Basil and Mr Parsley.

P. Is Mr Basil present in court today?

W. Yes, he was giving evidence just a moment ago.

P. Is Mr Parsley here? (1)

W. Mr Parsley died last year.

P. Garda Thyme, do you recall what Mr Parsley said to you about the accident? (2) (3)

O. Judge, I'm objecting to that question on the basis that answering it will involve the witness giving evidence that is inadmissible hearsay.

P. Judge, in my respectful submission, the statement is hearsay, but is properly admissible under the declaration against interest exception to the hearsay rule. Judge, I anticipate that the witness will say that the deceased made a statement that was contrary to his interest in so far as it would tend to establish that the deceased had been at fault and was responsible for the accident in question.

J. Very well. I consider that the proposed line of questioning is permissible. You may continue.

P. Garda Thyme, let me repeat the question. What did the deceased say to you about the accident? (2) (3)

W. He said that he 'never saw the other car coming' before the collision.

P. What did you understand the deceased to mean by that? (3) (4)

W. That he simply did not see Mr Basil's van before the collision took place.

P. Did the deceased say anything else? (3) (4)

W. He said that he was sorry and that he just hadn't seen the other vehicle.

6.05 *RES GESTAE*

Unlike the exception in relation to admissions, several of the exceptions to the rule against hearsay are grounded in a general assumption that the out-of-court statements that come within the exception are reliable. A common thread running through these exceptions is the accepted wisdom that the circumstances in which the statement was made raise an inference of the declarant's sincerity. The most famous of these exceptions relates to *res gestae*, ie 'the matter' or 'the transaction'.[59] This exception permits the admission of words which are 'so clearly associated with [the action or event] in time, place and circumstances, that they are part of the thing done, and so an item or part of real evidence and not merely a reported statement'.[60] The close association of the words with the underlying event provides the necessary safeguard against fabrication or distortion.

The courts have applied the *res gestae* exception over the years in several distinct contexts. Indeed, the ubiquity of the exception has had the negative consequence of creating some uncertainty and inconsistency in practice. As Lord Tomlin put it in *Holmes v Newman*, '[*res gestae*] is a phrase adopted to provide a respectable legal cloak for a variety of cases to which no formula of precision can be applied.'[61]

6.05.1 Spontaneous excited utterances

The case of spontaneous, excited utterances illustrates the common rationale of the various strands of the *res gestae* exception to the rule against hearsay. A startling event occurs, a participant or an observer becomes excited and the observer then makes a spontaneous statement about the event. The statement's spontaneity is the circumstantial guarantee of the declarant's sincerity. In *R v Andrews,* Ackner LJ couched the legal test in the following terms:

> (1) The primary question which the judge must ask himself is: can the possibility of concoction or distortion be disregarded? (2) To answer that question the judge must first consider the circumstances in which the particular statement was made, in order to satisfy himself that the event was so unusual or startling or dramatic as to dominate the thoughts of the victim, so that his utterance was an instinctive reaction to that event, thus giving no real opportunity for reasoned reflection. In such a situation the judge would be entitled to conclude that the involvement or pressure of the event would exclude the possibility of concoction or distortion, providing that the statement was made in conditions of approximate but not exact contemporaneity. (3) In other words for the statement to be sufficiently 'spontaneous' it must be so closely associated with the event which has excited the statement that it can

59. *Ratten v R* [1972] AC 378, [1971] 3 All ER 801 (*per* Wilberforce LJ): 'The expression *res gestae*, like many Latin phrases, is often used to cover situations insufficiently analysed in clear English terms.'

60. *Teper v R* [1952] AC 480, [1952] 2 All ER 447 (*per* Normand LJ), quoted with approval by Kenny J in *AG v Crosbie* [1966] IR 490.

61. [1931] 2 Ch 112.

fairly be stated that the mind of the declarant was still dominated by the event ...[62]

The foundation for a spontaneous excited utterance includes the following elements:

1. An event occurred.
2. The event was startling or stressful.
3. The declarant had personal knowledge of the event.
4. The declarant made a statement about the event.
5. The declarant made the statement while he or she was in a state of nervous excitement.

Our scenario here is an action in tort arising from a road traffic accident that occurred at a junction. The plaintiff was driving a blue car and the defendant was driving a red car. The issue is which car drove through a red light. The plaintiff calls Mr Barry Bystander as a witness. Mr Bystander has already identified himself. The plaintiff is the proponent.

P. Where were you on the afternoon of 13 March 2007?

W. I was in the Town Centre at the junction of Wide Street and Narrow Road.

P. Why were you there? (1)

W. I was walking my dog.

P. What, if anything, happened at the junction while you were there? (1), (2)

W. There was a car crash.

P. How did the crash come to your attention? (1), (2)

W. I was right there. I saw the two cars crash into each other with my own eyes and heard the sound of them colliding.

P. How noisy was the collision? (1), (2)

W. It was an awful, shattering sound.

P. How many bystanders were there? (1)

W. I'd say there were about 20 people in the immediate vicinity.

P. What was their reaction to the collision? (2)

62. [1987] AC 281, [1987] 1 All ER 513; *R v Carnall* [1985] Crim LR 944.

W. We were all shocked. It happened so fast, and the noise was so loud. And as soon as we looked, we could see that some people were injured and bleeding. It was an awful sight.

P. Who else besides yourself was in the crowd of bystanders? (3)

W. There were a number of people hanging around, but there was one guy in particular who stuck in my mind.

P. What was his name? (3)

W. I didn't catch his name.

P. What did he look like?

W. He was a young guy, maybe 25 or 30 years old, tall, with red hair and freckles.

P. Where was he at the time of the collision? (3)

W. Standing right next to me.

P. How was he facing? (3)

W. He was looking directly into the junction. He was waiting for the light to change so he could cross the road.

P. What was his demeanour right after the collision? (5)

W. He was just like the rest of us, shocked and frightened.

P. What was his facial expression? (5)

W. He had his mouth open as if he was shocked.

P. What was he doing? (5)

W. He was pointing at the crashed cars, gesturing wildly and shouting.

P. What was the tone of his voice? (5)

W. He was shouting loudly. He was excited.

P. What, if anything, did he say about the accident? (4)

O. Judge, I object to that question on the ground that what was said is inadmissible hearsay.

P. Judge, in my respectful submission, although the statement is hearsay, it is a spontaneous, excited utterance and falls within the *res gestae* exception.

W. I agree. The question is permissible. Please continue.

P. Mr Bystander, let me repeat the question. What, if anything, did this man say about the accident? (4)

P. He said that the fellow in the red car had gone right through the red light and caused the collision.

6.05.2 Contemporaneous statements

The spontaneity of the statement is the basic rationale for the *res gestae* exception in relation to excited utterances. The statement's contemporaneity can also serve as proof of the declarant's sincerity; the fact that the declarant makes the statement at roughly the same time as the event occurs is some evidence of the statement's reliability. The courts have tended to interpret the requirement of contemporaneity strictly.[63]

Where the declarant is a direct participant in the events at issue, the admission of the statement may be further justified on grounds of necessity; the declarant may be the only person who can shed light on his or her intentions or physical or emotional state.[64] Thus, the *res gestae* exception to the rule against hearsay extends to contemporaneous statements made by a person whose conduct is in issue. There are three variations on this theme: first, a contemporaneous statement made by a person performing an act explaining his or her intentions in performing the act; second, a contemporaneous statement made by a person as to his or her state of mind; and, third, a contemporaneous statement made by a person as to his or her physical condition.

Contemporaneous statements made by a person performing an act and explaining his or her intentions in performing the act are sometimes referred to as 'statements of present sense impression.' The foundation for these statements contains the following elements:

1. An event occurred.
2. The declarant had personal knowledge of the event.
3. The declarant made the statement during or very shortly after the event.
4. The statement relates to the declarant's own conduct.

To illustrate this exception, we will use the following variation on the last hypothetical involving the road traffic accident.

P. Where were you on the afternoon of 13 March 2007?

63. See eg *AG v Crosbie* [1966] IR 490 (statement made by victim 'immediately after he had been stabbed' admissible); *Sparks v R* [1964] AC 964 (statement made 'some time after' the assault inadmissible); *Teper v R* [1952] AC 480, [1952] 2 All ER 447 (rejecting evidence of an identification made from a distance and 26 minutes after the event).

64. *Ratten v R* [1972] AC 378, [1971] 3 All ER 801.

W. I was in the Town Centre at the junction of Wide Street and Narrow Road.
P. Why were you there? (1), (4)
W. I was walking my dog.
P. What, if anything, happened at the junction while you were there? (1)
W. There was a car crash.
P. How far were you from the crash when it occurred? (1)
W. I was about 30 feet from the point of impact or thereabouts.
P. In what direction were you facing? (1)
W. I was waiting for the light to change, so I was facing directly into the junction.
P. How clear was your line of vision to the collision? (1)
W. It was clear. I don't think there were any cars obstructing my view.
P. How much of the collision did you see? (1)
W. Pretty much all of it. I saw the cars approaching the junction and I saw them actually hit each other.
P. How many other bystanders were there? (2)
W. I'd say that there were about 20 people in the immediate vicinity.
P. Who were these bystanders? (2)
W. I didn't know any of them by name but one woman in particular stuck in my mind.
P. What did she look like? (2)
W. She was a young Chinese woman, maybe 20 or 25 years old.
P. Where was she standing at the time of the collision? (2)
W. She was standing right next to me.
P. In what direction was she facing? (2)
W. She was looking right into the junction. She was waiting for the light to change so she could walk across the road.
P. What did she do after the collision? (3)
W. She was pointing at the wreckage of the cars. We talked about the collision.
P. When did you and this bystander talk about the collision? (3)
W. Right after it happened.
P. How many minutes elapsed between the collision and your discussion of the collision with this bystander? (3)

W. It may have taken us a minute or so to get over the shock of what had happened, but it was no longer than that.

P. What, if anything, did this bystander say about the accident? (4)

O. Judge, I am objecting to that question on the basis that it calls for hearsay.

P. Judge, I concede that the question calls for hearsay but the statement is admissible as a contemporaneous statement or present sense impression under the *res gestae* exception.

O. Judge, I accept that the statement was roughly contemporaneous with the event. However, the exception for present sense impressions is limited to statements describing the declarant's own conduct. The bystander here was describing an event external to herself, namely the collision, rather than her own conduct.

J. Yes, I accept that submission. The objection is well-founded. That particular line of questioning is impermissible.

6.05.3 Declarations of state of mind or emotion

One of the most difficult things for counsel to prove is a person's state of mind. Counsel must usually rely on circumstantial proof such as conduct that implies a certain state of mind. Occasionally, a person openly declares his or her state of mind or emotion and these declarations often give us the best insight. Thus, the courts have developed a general rule that these declarations are admissible; if a person declares his or her then existing state of mind or emotion, the declaration is admissible to prove the existence of that state of mind or emotion.[65]

Ideally, the declarant will make the statement at the pivotal time under the relevant governing law. For example, under the law of property, the grantor must have the intention to pass title when handing the deed to the grantee. If at the very instant of handing the deed to the grantee, the grantor announces his or her intention to pass title, the statement is certainly admissible. What if the grantor makes such a statement shortly before or shortly after the manual delivery of the deed? The courts generally still admit the statement on the theory of continuity of state of mind; the time lapse between the

65. *Cullen v Clarke* [1963] IR 368; *Hanafin v Minister for the Environment* [1996] 2 IR 321.

statement and the critical event is so short that we may assume that the declarant's state of mind was the same at both times.[66]

The foundation for this doctrine is straightforward; the proponent need only establish the normal foundation for an event:

1. Where the statement was made.
2. When the statement was made. The declarant must make the statement at or near the pivotal time under the governing law.
3. Who was present.
4. Who made the statement.
5. The tenor of the statement.

The following hypothetical scenario is an action for quiet title. Ms Fiona Fork has instituted proceedings against the defendant, Mrs Siofra Spoon. Ms Fork claims title from the original titleholder, Mr Kieran Knife, her grandfather. She claims that on 25 December 2006, her grandfather gave her a deed to the property as a Christmas present. The plaintiff calls Mr Finn Fork, her brother, as a witness. The plaintiff is the proponent.

P. Where were you on 25 December 2006? (1), (2)

W. I was at our family Christmas party.

P. Who else was there? (3)

W. All the close relatives, including my grandfather, Kieran, and my sister, Fiona.

P. What, if anything, unusual happened during the party?

W. Grandad handed Fiona a deed to the family land in Coastal Cove. It was an unexpected Christmas present.

P. What, if anything, did he do when he handed her the deed? (4)

W. Well, he did say something.

P. What did he say? (5)

W. He said that he wanted her to have the land because ever since she was a little girl she had loved to holiday there.

In the next variation of the hypothetical, the grantor makes the statement shortly before delivery of the deed.

P. Where were you on 25 December 2006? (1), (2)

W. I was at our family Christmas party.

P. Who else was there? (3)

66. *Cullen v Clarke* [1963] IR 368.

W. All the close relatives, including my grandfather Kieran and my sister Fiona.

P. What, if anything, unusual happened during the party?

W. Grandad handed Fiona a deed to the family land in Coastal Cove. It was an unexpected Christmas present.

P. What, if anything, did he say about the deed during the Christmas party? (5)

O. Judge, I object. In my respectful submission that question calls for inadmissible hearsay evidence to be given.

P. Judge, I expect the witness to testify that his grandfather said that he wanted Fiona to have the land and that the grandfather made this statement only an hour before handing the deed to Fiona. The time lapse is so short that we may assume that the grandfather's state of mind was the same at both times.

J. Very well. I consider the question to be permissible. You may continue.

P. Mr Fork, let me repeat the question. What, if anything, did your grandfather say about the deed during the Christmas party? (5)

W. He said that he wanted Fiona to have the land because, ever since she was a little girl, she had loved to holiday there.

P. When did your grandfather say that? (4)

W. A little while before he handed the deed to her.

P. Specifically, how many minutes or hours before he handed her the deed? (4)

W. Just a few minutes.

6.05.4 Declarations of bodily condition

The courts are also willing to admit seemingly sincere statements about the declarant's bodily condition. Like statements relating to state of mind, these statements often provide the best available evidence of the declarant's physical state at the material time. Thus, for example, if a declarant proclaims that he or she is in good health or, conversely, is in bad health,[67]

67. *Donaghy v Ulster Spinning Co Ltd* (1912) 56 ILTR 33; *R v Black* (1922) 16 Cr App R 118.

the statement will be admissible to prove the declarant's physical condition.[68]

The foundation includes the following elements:

1. Where the statement was made.
2. When the statement was made.
3. Who was present.
4. Who made the statement.
5. To whom the statement was made.
6. The tenor of the statement. The statement must refer to the person's present bodily condition.

In this hypothetical fact scenario, the plaintiff, Ms Ashling Ailment, has brought a product liability action against the defendant, Dodgy Dosage Co Ltd. The plaintiff alleges that the defendant sold her defective medication and that the medication caused her serious physical injuries. She is seeking compensation including damages for pain and suffering. At the trial, the plaintiff calls Dr Mark Medic as a witness. Dr Medic identifies himself and states that he is a general practitioner.

P. Dr Medic, where were you on the afternoon of 28 January 2007? (1), (2)

W. In my surgery.

P. Who else was there? (3)

W. The plaintiff, Ms Ailment.

P. Where is the plaintiff now? (3)

W. Here, in the court.

P. Specifically, where in the court? (3)

W. (*Pointing*) She's sitting there.

P. What happened while the plaintiff was in your surgery? (3)

W. I conducted a medical examination of Ms Ailment.

P. During that examination, what, if anything, did she say to you about her physical condition? (4), (5), (6)

O. Judge, I object to that question on the ground that it calls for hearsay.

P. Judge, I concede that the question calls for hearsay. However, I expect that the witness will testify that the plaintiff said that she

68. The statement would be admissible to show the physical condition but not the *cause* of the physical condition. McGrath, *Evidence* (Thomson Round Hall, 2005) at 5.73 (citing cases).

was then in terrible pain. That statement qualifies as a declaration of present bodily condition under the *res gestae* exception to the rule against hearsay.

J. I consider that submission to be persuasive. You may continue with the line of questioning.

P. Dr Medic, let me repeat the question. During that examination, what, if anything, did she say to you about her physical condition?

W. She said that she was experiencing terrible abdominal pain.

6.06 DYING DECLARATIONS

There are various exceptional instances in which the courts will permit witnesses to testify about statements made in the past by persons who have since died. One of the most well known of these statements is the so-called 'dying declaration'. At early common law, the courts admitted the deceased's dying declaration explaining the cause of his or her death in a prosecution for the deceased's murder.[69] The circumstantial guarantee of trustworthiness is the declarant's sense of impending death; at the point of death, the declarant should have no reason no lie, and there is the theistic belief that the decedent will not want to face the Creator with a lie on his or her lips. Necessity serves as an additional rationale for admitting the hearsay statement given that the declarant is unavailable to testify at trial.

The common law doctrine includes the following foundational elements:

1. The case is a prosecution for the murder of the declarant.
2. The declarant made a statement at a time when he or she had a sense of impending death.
3. The statement relates to the event which caused the declarant's death.

The following hypothetical scenario is a prosecution for murder. The indictment alleges that the accused, Mr Aaron Assailant, murdered Mr Vincent Victim. The prosecution calls Dr Mark Medic as a witness. Dr Medic has already identified himself. The prosecution is the proponent.

P. Dr Medic, what is your occupation?

W. I am a general medical practitioner.

P. Where were you on the morning of 22 February 2007?

69. *R v Woodcock* (1789) 1 Leach 500; *R v Stephenson* [1947] NI 110; *Mills v R* [1995] 1 WLR 511.

W. I was in my surgery.
P. What happened that morning?
W. I received an emergency phone call.
P. What was the nature of the phone call?
W. Someone was badly hurt and needed immediate medical attention.
P. What did you do after you received this phone call?
W. I left my surgery and walked directly to 7 Cosy Crescent. That address is just around the corner from my surgery.
P. What did you find there?
W. I found several people surrounding a badly injured person.
P. Who was that person? (1)
W. Mr Vincent Victim.
P. How do you know that? (1)
W. He told me that was his name. Also, I checked a photo ID card that he had in his wallet.
P. What was his medical condition at the time? (2)
W. Very bad. He had several deep stab wounds and was bleeding profusely.
P. What did you do after you discovered these wounds? (2)
W. I helped him as best I could and when I realised that he was dying, I tried to make him as comfortable as possible.
P. What, if anything, did you tell him about his condition? (3).
W. I was honest with him. He asked, and I told him he was dying.
P. How did he respond? (2)
W. He looked frightened. Then he sighed very deeply.
P. What happened then? (2)
W. He asked that I contact a Catholic priest. He said that he wanted to receive the last rites before he died.
P. What happened then? (2)
W. The priest arrived and administered the sacrament. Then the priest and I accompanied Mr Victim in an ambulance to the hospital.
P. What happened in the ambulance on the way to the hospital? (1)
W. Mr Victim died in the ambulance. (1), (2)
P. What, if anything, did Mr Victim say before he died about the cause of his death? (3)
W. He said that someone had stabbed him with a knife.

P. Did he say who had stabbed him? (3)

W. Yes. He said it was Aaron Assailant.

6.07 BUSINESS RECORDS

Most of the exceptions to the rule against hearsay require some showing that the out-of-court statement is reliable. In the case of the various exceptions that fall within the old common law doctrine of *res gestae*, there is an inference of sincerity on the part of the declarant. This section and the following sections deal with two other exceptions that permit the admission of documentary statements, namely, business records and public records. In these instances, there is something about the process of generating the writing that creates an inference of the reliability of the statement.

In the case of business records, the circumstantial guarantee of trustworthiness is that since the entry is routine, the business's employees have developed habits of precision in gathering and reporting the data. The employees' habits help to ensure the reliability of the report. Necessity provides a further justification for relying on hearsay reports. If a business conducts hundreds or thousands of similar transactions during a year, it is doubtful whether any employee will remember the particular transaction recorded in the entry. Even when an employee remembers, the employee's memory is likely to be incomplete or hazy. Thus, the business entry is probably the most reliable evidence available.

The need for broader provision for the admission of business records was demonstrated by the landmark decision of the House of Lords in *DPP v Myers*.[70] Records compiled by employees of a car manufacturer in the ordinary course of business were held inadmissible on the ground that they were hearsay, notwithstanding that they were arguably the most reliable evidence available. The House of Lords famously declared that it was not the function of the courts to carve out new exceptions to the rule against hearsay. Parliament responded with legislation providing for the admission of a wide range of records in criminal and civil proceedings.[71] Although the Oireachtas followed suit with the inclusion in the Criminal Evidence Act 1992 of a business records exception to the rule against hearsay,[72] no

70. [1965] AC 1001.

71. Civil Evidence Act 1995, c 38.

72. See also s 8(5) of the Criminal Assets Bureau Act 1996 discussed in *Criminal Assets Bureau v Hunt* [2003] 2 IR 168, [2003] 2 ILRM 481.

equivalent general provision has been enacted in relation to civil proceedings.

Under s 5 of the Criminal Evidence Act 1992, 'information contained in a document shall be admissible in any criminal proceedings as evidence of any fact therein of which direct oral evidence would be admissible' provided that the information was compiled in the ordinary course of business, was supplied by a person who had personal knowledge of the matters dealt with and appear in legible form.[73] Under s 8, the trial judge shall refuse to admit the documentary evidence in question where he or she is of the opinion that in all the circumstances the interests of justice demand it.[74]

Given the persuasive justifications for the exception, it is perhaps surprising that in civil proceedings there is no equivalent general statutory exception. There are certain specific exceptions in law. First, business records may qualify under the common law doctrine in relation to declarations in the course of duty. Under this doctrine, a record made by a person in pursuance of a duty owed to another to record the performance of an act is admissible provided that: (i) the declarant is since deceased; (ii) the record was made contemporaneously with the performance of the act; (iii) the person making the record had personal knowledge of the facts recorded; and (iv) the person making the record had no motive to misrepresent the facts.[75] Second, under the Bankers' Books Evidence Act 1879, as amended, copies of records used in the ordinary business of a bank are admissible as evidence of their contents.[76] Similarly, the Companies Act 1963, as amended, makes limited provision for the admission of business records.[77]

The absence of a general statutory exception notwithstanding, business records are often admitted in civil proceedings usually with the agreement of

---

73. *DPP v Byrne* (7 June 2000, unreported) CCA. Various documents are expressly excluded such as information compiled for the purposes of a criminal or other investigation, information protected by privilege, and information taken on oath: s 5(3).

74. Section 8(2) sets out certain factors which the judge shall consider including whether it is a reasonable inference that the information is reliable.

75. *Malone v L'Estrange* (1839) 2 Ir Eq R 16; *Dillon v Tobin* (1879) 12 ILTR 32; *Miller v Wheatley* (1891) 28 LR Ir 44; *Ryan v Ring* (1889) 25 LR Ir 184; *Mulhearn v Clery* [1930] IR 649.

76. Bankers' Book Evidence Act 1879, c 11; *JB O'C v PCD* [1985] IR 265.

77. See *Director of Corporate Enforcement v Bailey* [2007] IEHC 365 (1 November 2007).

the parties. The foundation for the introduction of a business record might include the following elements:

1. The record was compiled in the ordinary course of a specified business.
2. The person who supplied the report had personal knowledge of the facts or events reported.
3. Where the information was in non-legible form and has been reproduced in permanent legible form, the information was reproduced in the course of the normal operation of the reproduction system concerned.
4. The information is not privileged from disclosure in the proceedings and was not supplied by a witness who would not be compellable at the instance of the proponent.
5. The information was not compiled for the purposes of, or in contemplation of, any investigation, inquiry or proceeding.

The hypothetical example that follows is based on a civil action in which the plaintiff company sues the defendant for moneys allegedly due and owing. The plaintiff, a company providing hotel accommodation for business executives, alleges that the defendant company block-booked a number of rooms at the plaintiff's premises to be used by visitors attending a management conference organised by the defendant. The defendant has asserted that the plaintiff is seeking to overcharge the defendant and that fewer rooms were booked than claimed by the defendant. The plaintiff calls as a witness an officer in its Accounting Department to verify that the plaintiff's records of bookings are an accurate reflection of the bookings actually made.

P. I am now handing you the plaintiff's exhibit number 1 for identification. Do you recognise it?

W. Yes it's a booking form that we produce weekly to reflect the level of bookings that have been made for the next fortnight.

P. Are you the custodian, or otherwise in a position to know what this document is? (2)

W. I am the Accounts Manager and would frequently prepare and examine this type of document.

P. Was this document prepared in the ordinary course of business? (1)

W. Yes, this document would be prepared and generated as a matter of routine.

P. Were the entries in the exhibit made at the time of the bookings that the document reflects?

W. Yes, the way our system works, as soon as a booking is made, this is processed into the system so the entry onto the system is virtually instantaneous.

P. Who would physically have made the entries for these bookings in question? (2) (4)

W. I made the entries myself. You can see on the documents that I initialled it 'PM1' and dated it. The person making the entry always initials it and dates it in this manner.

P. Was this document prepared in contemplation of any legal proceedings?

W. Absolutely not. It was generated as a matter of course almost as soon as the bookings in question were made.

6.08 PUBLIC RECORDS

A second important documentary exception to the rule against hearsay is the public records exception. Just as business employees presumably are careful in gathering and recording information for their employers, public employees presumably are diligent in performing the same tasks for their employer, the government.[78]

The proponent of an official record rarely presents live testimony to authenticate the record. In most instances, the judge will accept the statute, regulation or custom as a matter of judicial notice. In addition, if the attested copy is fair on its face (ie complete and with no deletions), the document's face creates a permissive inference that the official followed the proper procedures in preparing the particular record.

At common law, the foundation for the official records exception to the rule against hearsay contains the following elements:

1. The record contains matters of a public nature.
2. The record was intended to be open to public inspection.
3. The record was prepared by a public official acting under a duty to record the fact or event.

---

78. *The Irish Society v the Bishop of Derry* (1846) 12 Cl & Finn 641; *R (Lanktree) v McCarthy* [1903] 2 IR 146; *Minister of Defence v Buckley* [1978] IR 314.

The common law exception for public documents has also been extended by statute. A wide range of documents such as Acts of the Oireachtas[79] and the registration of births and deaths[80] are admissible under various statutory provisions. The foundational requirements vary in accordance with the provisions of each statute.

The following hypothetical situation is based on a constitutional challenge instituted by Mr Billy Blue, a prospective general election candidate in the constituency of Anytown. Mr Blue argues that the constituency does not have sufficient representation because of the recent rapid increase in population. The plaintiff wishes to introduce into evidence the results of a recent census conducted by Anytown County Council. This was the first occasion on which the County Council conducted a census and the plaintiff is concerned that the trial judge might not take judicial notice of its terms. Consequently, the plaintiff calls the Chief Executive of the County Council, Mr Walter White, to give evidence. The plaintiff is the proponent.

P. Mr White, what is your occupation?

W. I am Chief Executive of Anytown County Council. I have held that position since 2002.

P. I am now handing you the plaintiff's exhibit number 2. What is it?

W. This is the census conducted for the Dublin Electoral Constituency of Anytown in 2006.

P. What information does this document contain? (1)

W. It contains thorough information regarding the population of the constituency, the electoral register, the age profile of the local population etc.

P. Does it contain information of a public nature, in your view? (1)

W. Yes.

P. Did you have any involvement in the preparation of this document? (3)

W. Yes, I had a central involvement in its preparation. As Chief Executive of Anytown Council, I was responsible for overseeing the production and completion of this report. I headed up a steering committee which included five other people.

P. Why was the report prepared? (3)

79. Section 2 of the Documentary Evidence Act 1925.

80. Section 68 of the Civil Registration Act 2004.

W. It was required to be prepared under the provisions of the Local Government (Amendment) Act 2003.

W. Was the report available for public inspection?

P. Yes, a copy of the report was posted on the Anytown Council Website, and hundreds of free copies were available in the Anytown Council civic offices.

6.09 PREVIOUS WITNESSES STATEMENTS

6.09.1 The law

The Oireachtas recently created a substantial new statutory exception to the rule against hearsay in criminal proceedings. Section 16 of the Criminal Justice Act 2006 facilitates the admission of a previous out-of-court statement made by an unco-operative witness. The exception rests on the twin justifications of necessity and reliability. First, as regards necessity, s 16(1) provides that the previous witness statement is admissible as evidence of the facts stated therein where the witness: (a) refuses to testify, (b) denies making the statement or (c) gives evidence which is inconsistent with the statement.[81] Second, s 16(2) speaks to reliability by requiring the proponent to demonstrate that: (a) the witness made the statement, (b) that direct oral evidence of the statement would be admissible, (c) the statement was made voluntarily, or (d) the statement was made on oath or affirmation or in circumstances in which the witness understood the requirement to tell the truth. Section 16(3) sets out certain factors which the court shall consider when deciding whether the statement is reliable. These factors include whether the statement was video-recorded (where relevant) and whether the witness has an explanation for his or her failure to co-operate.

6.09.2 Elements of the foundation

The relevant provisions of the 2006 Act have yet to be interpreted by the Court of Criminal Appeal and the Supreme Court. Nevertheless, on a literal, common-sense reading of the text and surrounding law, an appropriate evidentiary foundation might contain the following elements:

1. The witness is unco-operative:
   a. the witness refuses to testify; or

81. Section 16(1).

b. the witness denies making the statement; or

c. the witness gives evidence which is inconsistent with the statement.

2. The witness made the statement.
3. The statement was made voluntarily.
4. The statement was made on oath or affirmation or in circumstances in which the witness understood the requirement to tell the truth.
5. The statement was properly recorded.
6. The witness has been given an opportunity to explain his or her failure to co-operate. (Where the witness denies making the statement or gives evidence inconsistent with it, the statement should be put to the witness and the witness given an opportunity to justify the denial or explain the inconsistency.)

6.09.3 Sample foundation

The hypothetical case is based on a murder trial in the Central Criminal Court. The accused, Gary Green, is charged with the murder of a young man, Wayne White. The killing took place in a park in Notown on a summer's evening. A friend of the accused, Paul Purple, is a key witness. He was with Gary Green on the evening in question and was initially suspected of involvement in the material events. He was arrested on suspicion of murder, but no charges were ever proferred against him. During the course of arrest, Paul Purple made a statement to the gardaí in which he stated that Gary Green stabbed Wayne White during a heated argument.

At trial in the Central Criminal Court, Mr Purple is called as a witness by the prosecution. He takes the stand but denies ever having made such a statement, and states that he knows nothing about the death of Wayne White. This satisfies the first element of the foundation as stated above. The prosecution seeks to have Mr Purple's statement admitted into evidence in accordance with the provisions of the 2006 Act. The trial judge permits the prosecution to call Garda Ben Black to the stand. Garda Black has identified himself and testified that he is assigned to Main Street Garda Station in the City Centre. The proponent is the prosecution.

P. *(In the absence of the jury)* Garda Black, where were you on the afternoon of 1 February 2008?

W. I was on duty at Main Street Garda Station.

P. What happened that afternoon? (2), (4)
W. Two of my colleagues brought a person in for questioning.
P. Who was that person? (2), (4)
W. Paul Purple.
P. Where is Paul Purple now? (2), (4)
W. He is here in the court; he was giving evidence a few moments ago.
P. What happened after Mr Purple was brought into the station? (2), (4)
W. Myself and Sergeant Brian Brown brought him into the main interview room in the station.
P. What happened then? (2), (4)
W. We began questioning him in connection with the murder of Wayne White.
P. What promises or inducements did you make to Mr Purple during the questioning? (3)
W. None whatsoever.
P. What threats did you make to him? (3)
W. Absolutely none.
P. What force did you use during the interview? (3)
W. None.
P. Garda Black, I'm now handing you the State's exhibit number six for identification. What is it? (2)
W. It's a statement that Paul Purple made whilst in custody.
P. Do you remember his making this statement? (2)
W. Yes, I do.
P. Garda Black, without reading from the statement, would you tell the court the gist of what Mr Purple said? (2)
W. Judge, he said that Gary Green stabbed Wayne White during the course of an argument in The Public Park on the evening in question. He was quite clear about Mr Green's involvement in the killing, and that the deceased had died as a result of stab wounds inflicted by Mr Green.
P. Garda Black, was this statement electronically recorded? (5)
W. Yes, it was.
P. Is that recording available to be examined should the court so direct? (5)
W. Yes, Judge, a copy of the recording is here in court.

The 2006 Act is silent on the procedure that should be applied in a situation where a witness denies making a statement (as Paul Purple does here) or gives evidence that is inconsistent with the statement and a party (in this case, the prosecution) then seeks to have the statement admitted into evidence. Nevertheless, it is reasonable to assume that the party would be required to follow the traditional common law procedure for impeaching a witness with a previous statement discussed at **2.14** above. In *AG v Taylor*[82] the Court of Criminal Appeal set out the procedure that applies where a witness has been declared hostile and counsel is seeking to admit evidence of the fact that the statement was made for the limited purpose of impugning the credibility of the witness. The case involved a prosecution for murder in which the deceased's widow was called to testify for the prosecution. When she gave evidence which contradicted a previous statement she had made to the guards, the prosecution sought and was granted permission to treat her as a hostile witness. Walsh J stated:

> This particular witness had been allowed to be treated as hostile and, when the jury were recalled to court, the proper procedure for the prosecution was to have put to the witness that she had on another occasion made a statement which differed materially from or contradicted the one she was making in the witness-box. If she were to deny that, then the proper procedure would have been to have her stand down from the box, and to prove in fact that she did make a statement by putting into the box the person who took the statement, proving it in the ordinary way without revealing the contents of the statement at that stage. The earlier witness should then have been put back in the box and the statement put to her for identification, and then her attention should have been directed to the passage in which the alleged contradiction or material variation appears.[83]

Of course the 2006 Act provides for the admission of the statement into evidence as proof of the matter stated (and not merely for the limited purpose of impugning the credibility of the witness by establishing the fact that the previous statement was made). Nevertheless, the stated procedure might be adapted to accommodate the need to give a witness who denies making a previous statement an opportunity to justify the denial or a witness who concedes making a statement but offers inconsistent testimony an opportunity to explain the inconsistency. Thus, in the hypothetical set out above, the prosecution might recall Paul Purple to the stand after Garda

82. [1974] 1 IR 97.

83. [1974] 1 IR 97 at 99.

Black had stepped down and afford Paul Purple an opportunity to retract his denial or, alternatively, reassert his denial in response to Garda Black's evidence.

Chapter 7

UNLAWFULLY OBTAINED EVIDENCE

7.01 BACKGROUND

The admissibility of evidence in the Irish courts is conditioned by the well-known requirement that the evidence be obtained by exclusively lawful means. This position is at odds with the historical stance of the common law. As Lord Goddard stated in *Kuruma v R:*

> [T]he test to be applied in considering whether evidence is admissible is whether it is relevant to the matters at issue. If it is, it is admissible and the Court is not concerned with how the evidence was obtained.[1]

The Supreme Court broke with the common law tradition in the landmark case of *AG v O'Brien.*[2] The rule was revised and strengthened some years later in *DPP v Kenny.*[3] In relation to evidence obtained in breach of the constitutional rights of a citizen, Finlay CJ cast the exclusionary rule in the following terms:

> I am satisfied that the correct principle is that evidence obtained by invasion of the constitutional personal rights of a citizen must be excluded unless a court is satisfied that either the act constituting the breach of constitutional rights was committed unintentionally or accidentally or is satisfied that there are extraordinary excusing circumstances which justify the admission of the evidence in its (the court's) discretion.[4]

The scope of the exceptions to the rule recognised by Finlay CJ became the focus of the subsequent case law. The concept of an unintentional or accidental breach of constitutional rights is objectively defined with the consequence that in practice the prosecution can plead neither that the breach was *de minimis* nor that the law enforcement authorities acted in good faith. Similarly, the extraordinary circumstances that might justify the admission of the evidence have been narrowly construed. The relatively

---

1. [1955] AC 197 quoted with approval in *AG v McGrath* (1960) 98 ILTR 59.
2. [1965] IR 142.
3. [1990] 2 IR 110, [1990] ILRM 569.
4. [1990] 2 IR 110 at 134, [1990] ILRM 569.

absolute tenor of the exclusionary rule has been the subject of controversy and debate.[5]

7.02 UNCONSTITUTIONALLY OBTAINED EVIDENCE

In the following scenario, Oliver Orange is on trial for drug offences. The accused was arrested at his home following a garda search of the premises. He is charged with possession of cannabis and the prosecution evidence includes a quantity of cannabis which the gardaí found hidden in an upstairs bedroom during the search. The defence are challenging the admissibility of this evidence on the ground that it was procured in breach of the accused's constitutional right to the inviolability of his dwelling.[6] Although the gardaí had a warrant to search the premises, the date for the completion of the search, as stated on the warrant, had lapsed.[7]

7.02.1 Elements of the foundation and sample foundation

The defence (the opponent) is seeking to establish the following:

1. The gardaí entered the accused's residence for the purpose of conducting a search.
2. The entry was deliberate and intentional.
3. There was no lawful authority for the entry and search.
4. The evidence in question was obtained during the search.

The garda who conducted the search has given evidence by way of examination-in-chief. He is now cross-examined by counsel for the defendant.

O. *(In the absence of the jury)* You've stated that the defendant's home was searched because of the suspicion that drugs were on the premises, is that correct? (1)

---

5. See eg *DPP v Ryan* [2005] 1 IR 209; *DPP v Cash* [2007] IEHC (28 March 2007); *Final Report of the Balance in the Criminal Law Review Group* (March 2007) at p 166 and Note of Dissent by Gerard Hogan SC at pp 287–88.
6. Article 40.5 of the Constitution.
7. See *Curtin v Dáil Éireann* [2006] 2 IR 556. On defects in warrants, see generally *Competition Authority v Irish Dental Association* [2005] 3 IR 208; *DPP v Ryan* [2005] 1 IR 209; *DPP v McGartland* (20 January 2003, unreported) CCA; *DPP v Balfe* [1998] 4 IR 50.

W. That's correct.

O. And am I correct in thinking that the reason you entered the defendant's residence was for the purpose of carrying out a search to see if any drugs were indeed present? (1) (2)

W. Correct, yes.

O. You went to the defendant's residence with the intention of entering inside, isn't that so? (2)

W. Yes.

O. But the warrant on which you entered the accused's residence was bad on its face, isn't that correct? (3)

W. I now know that to be the case, but I didn't know that at the time.

O. I didn't ask you whether you knew at the time; I was putting it to you that the warrant on foot of which you purported to enter the defendant's residence was in fact defective, isn't that so?

W. Yes.

O. That warrant was defective because the date for completion of the search as stated on the warrant had lapsed, isn't that so? (3)

W. Yes.

O. You state that you seized a quantity of cannabis resin in the course of the search, is that correct? (4)

W. That is correct.

O. And no illegal substances of any nature were found to be in the possession of the accused, or found in his residence, at any other time, isn't that so? (4)

W. That is correct.

O. *(By way of submission to the judge)* Judge, in my respectful submission, the position is relatively clear having regard to the decided case law. The search of the accused's residence was carried out in breach of the accused's constitutional rights, since the warrant was bad on its face, Judge. It had lapsed, and it follows that the gardaí had no lawful authority to enter the accused's residence. It equally follows, Judge, that any evidence found in the course of such unlawful search is inadmissible, as it is contaminated by virtue of having been obtained during an unlawful search. The crucial evidence, Judge, was obtained as a direct result of the violation of the accused's constitutional rights. In those circumstances, Judge, I submit that the accused has no case to answer, and is entitled to be acquitted by direction.

7.03 CAUSATIVE LINK

Even where a party establishes that evidence was obtained by unconstitutional or unlawful means, a trial judge will not apply the exclusionary rule nor exercise his or her exclusionary discretion in the absence of a causative link between the impugned action and the evidence obtained. The party must establish that the evidence was obtained as a result of the unconstitutional or unlawful action.[8]

7.03.1 Elements of the foundation and sample foundation

In the following scenario, the accused is charged with an offence under s 49 of the Road Traffic Act 1961. The accused was found to have had excess alcohol in his blood whilst driving a car. Counsel for the accused challenges the admissibility of this evidence, on the basis that there was a breach of the accused's constitutional right of access to a solicitor. The State, although accepting that there was such a breach, argues that the evidence is nonetheless admissible because it was not causally linked to the fact that the accused was denied access to a solicitor, in breach of his constitutional rights.

Counsel for the State (the proponent) is seeking to establish that, although the evidence was obtained subsequent to the accused's rights having been breached, thc evidence was not obtained as a result of the breach of the accused's rights.

Counsel for the State is conducting the examination-in-chief of Garda Brian Brown, who interviewed the accused. The garda has identified himself and given preliminary background evidence.

P. (*In the absence of the jury*) Garda Brown, was the defendant properly informed of his right of access to a solicitor, and were sufficient steps taken to enable him to exercise that right?

W. Although the defendant was informed of his right of access to a solicitor, I accept that the defendant's rights in this regard were not properly respected.

P. Please elaborate further on this, Garda Brown.

---

8. *DPP v Buck* [2002] 2 IR 268; *Walsh v O'Buachalla* [1991] 1 IR 56; *DPP v Healy* [1990] 2 IR 73; *DPP v Shaw* [1982] IR 1; *DPP v Pringle* (1981) 2 Frewen 57.

W. When the defendant informed me that he wanted to see his solicitor, I did not act on that request because I did not think that the request was genuine. I believed, that the defendant was merely using this as a stalling or delaying tactic, and I informed him that he could contact his solicitor after a urine or blood sample had been obtained.

P. Do you acknowledge that you were wrong in this respect, Garda, and that the defendant's request to see his solicitor should have been facilitated and complied with?

W. I do.

P. What sample was taken from the accused and when was it taken?

W. A urine sample was taken almost immediately after the defendant had requested to speak to his solicitor.

P. Garda, suppose that the defendant had consulted with his solicitor prior to being asked to provide a sample. Could the defendant then have refused to give the sample?

W. No. The defendant was bound to provide a sample, and we would have to have taken a sample regardless of any advice that the defendant was given by his solicitor.

P. *(By way of submission to the judge)* Judge, in my respectful submission, this is a case in which there is no causative link between the breach of the accused's rights and the evidence sought to be admitted against him. It is plain that the constitutional rights of the accused were breached, Judge, and that is regrettable, to say the least. But I say, Judge, that the law is clear that evidence is nonetheless admissible once it has not been obtained as a direct result of the breach of the accused person's constitutional rights. Fundamentally, Judge, in the instant case the accused was required by statute to provide a sample, and so there is no connection between the breach of his right of access to a solicitor and the taking of that sample. I wish to rely in this context, Judge, on the decision of Mr Justice Blayney in the case of *Walsh v District Justice O'Buachalla*.[9]

7.04 EXTRAORDINARY EXCUSING CIRCUMSTANCES

The exclusionary rule in relation to unlawfully obtained evidence is subject to an important exception. As Finlay CJ stated in *DPP v Kenny*, evidence

9. [1991] 1 IR 56.

obtained in breach of constitutional rights may be admitted at the discretion of the trial judge where the breach was justified by the existence of 'extraordinary excusing circumstances'.[10] The concept of extraordinary excusing circumstances had been elucidated by the Supreme Court in the earlier *O'Brien* case, with Walsh J providing three examples: the need to prevent the imminent destruction of evidence, the need to rescue a victim in peril and the need to conduct a warrantless search incidental to and contemporaneous with a lawful arrest.[11]

7.04.1 Elements of the foundation and sample foundation

In the following hypothetical situation, the accused is charged with a number of serious offences including counterfeiting offences, being in possession of illicit goods and handling stolen property. The background is that the gardaí went to the home of the accused and observed him acting suspiciously with other men, unloading goods and boxes from a lorry and bringing them into the house. When the men saw the gardaí, they ran into the house and slammed the door. The gardaí then burst into the house and found a considerable amount of alcohol, counterfeit goods and cigarettes.

At trial, the accused challenges the admissibility of this evidence on the basis that it was obtained in breach of his constitutional right to inviolability of the dwelling. Counsel for the State concedes that the gardaí acted in violation of the accused's right to inviolability of the dwelling, but argues that the evidence is nonetheless admissible because it qualifies under the extraordinary excusing circumstances exception to the rule that evidence obtained in breach of constitutional rights is inadmissible.

The State (the proponent) is seeking to establish the following:

1. That the gardaí acted in response to an apprehension that vital evidence was going to be imminently destroyed.
2. That there was a reasonable justification for this apprehension.

The garda who led the investigation, Garda William White, is giving his evidence-in-chief. Garda White has introduced himself and has given evidence on preliminary matters.

---

10. [1990] 2 IR 110 at 134.

11. *AG v O'Brien* [1965] IR 142 at 170. See also *DPP v Dillon* [2002] 4 IR 501; *DPP v Delaney* [1997] 3 IR 453; *Freeman v DPP* [1996] 3 IR 565.

P. *(In the absence of the jury)* Garda White, please describe the scene that you encountered on arrival at the defendant's home. (1)

W. I saw the accused and three other men unloading a large quantity of goods from the back of a white Hiace van.

P. What did you think as you observed this?

W. I thought it was highly suspicious. There was clearly a very large amount of goods in the van, and the men appeared anxious to move the contents of the van indoors as quickly as possible.

P. Did you approach the men? (1)

W. No, but one of the men, whom I know to be an associate of the defendant, spotted me and I heard him say to the others 'guards'. The men then ran into the house and slammed the door behind them.

P. What did you do then, Garda White?

W. I ran to the front door of the house and knocked on it. I identified myself as a member of An Garda Síochána and requested to be let into the house.

P. Why were you seeking to enter the house at this point, Garda White? (1) (2)

W. I was concerned that the men would seek to destroy evidence and otherwise set about frustrating garda efforts to investigate what appeared to be a serious criminal offence.

P. Why did you have that concern, Garda White? (2)

W. Because of how suspicious the entire scene appeared, and the way in which the men ran when they saw me.

P. *(Addressing the judge)* Judge, in my respectful submission, this is a case in which, notwithstanding that there was breach of the defendant's right to inviolability of the dwelling, the evidence is still admissible. It is clear from Garda White's evidence that the gardaí acted on the basis of a reasonable apprehension that it was necessary to make an immediate entry onto the premises to prevent the imminent destruction of vital evidence.

7.05 ILLEGALLY OBTAINED EVIDENCE

In relation to evidence obtained by illegal, as opposed to unconstitutional means, the trial judge retains a discretion to exclude the evidence on a consideration of all the circumstances. As Kingsmill Moore J stated in *O'Brien:*

> On the one hand, the nature and extent of the illegality have to be taken into account. Was the illegal action intentional or unintentional, and, if intentional, was it the result of an *ad hoc* decision or does it represent a settled or deliberate policy? Was the illegality one of a trivial and technical nature or was it a serious invasion of important rights the recurrence of which would involve a real danger to necessary freedoms? Were there circumstances of urgency or emergency which provide some excuse for the action?[12]

The reach of constitutional rights is such, however, that situations in which the admissibility of evidence is challenged with reference to alleged illegal conduct, falling short of unconstitutional conduct, are rare. Consider a variation of the fact pattern set out in **7.02** above. Following his arrest, Oliver Orange was taken to the local garda station where he was questioned about the cannabis found in his residence. The prosecution intend to call Garda Brian Brown who interviewed Oliver Orange in custody. Garda Brown has testified that Oliver Orange admitted that the cannabis was his. The defence are contesting the admissibility of the confession: Oliver Orange denies making the confession and argues, in the alternative, that even if the confession was made, it was made as a direct consequence of breaches of the Custody Regulations committed by the gardaí during the course of his detention.[13] Specifically, the defence contend that Oliver Orange was questioned by three gardaí[14] between the hours of midnight and 8 am[15] and that the fact of the interview was not entered in the custody record.[16] The admissibility of a confession is a matter of law for the determination of the trial judge in the absence of the jury. Although proof of these breaches of the Custody Regulations would not lead to the automatic exclusion of Oliver Orange's confession, the defence might argue that it

12. [1965] IR 142 at 160.
13. Criminal Justice Act 1984 (Treatment of Persons in Custody in Garda Síochána Stations) Regulations 1987 (SI 199/1987).
14. Regulation 12(3) specifies that not more than two gardaí shall question the arrested person at any time and not more than four gardaí shall be present at any one time during the interview.
15. Regulation 12(7) prohibits questioning during these hours unless authorised by the member in charge. Such authority shall not be given other than on limited, specified grounds.
16. Regulations 6 and 12(11).

constitutes a basis on which the trial judge may exercise his or her discretion to exclude the evidence.

7.06 CIVIL PROCEEDINGS

The exclusionary rule in relation to unlawfully obtained evidence also applies in civil proceedings. The courts have recognised the entitlement of a party to the exclusion at trial of evidence obtained in breach of that party's constitutional rights.[17] Furthermore, where the evidence was obtained by unlawful as opposed to unconstitutional means, it may be excluded at the trial judge's discretion.[18]

7.06.1 Sample foundation

The following scenario is based on a civil action brought by the plaintiff company, which carries on business as a film distribution company. The plaintiff alleges that the defendant has been making and selling and generally 'hawking about' pirated DVDs in which the plaintiff owns the copyright.

The plaintiff has purported to rely on evidence of illicit materials and pirated DVDs that were seized during a garda search of a van owned by the defendant. The defendants are challenging the admissibility of the evidence obtained, on the basis that no search warrant was produced for the search of the van. Counsel for the plaintiff, whilst accepting that the search of the van may have been unlawful, submits that the search was not in breach of the defendant's constitutional rights and should be admitted.

The plaintiff calls Garda Jack Jug who conducted the impugned search of the van. Elementary evidence of an introductory nature has already been given. The plaintiff is the proponent.

P. Garda Jug, you have said that you personally went to search the van in question.

W. That's correct.

17. *Competition Authority v Irish Dental Association* [2005] 3 IR 208.

18. *Kennedy v Incorporated Law Society of Ireland (No 3)* [2002] 2 IR 458; *P McG v AF* (28 January 2000, unreported) HC; *Universal City Studios v Mulligan (No 2)* [1999] 3 IR 458.

P. Was that search conducted on foot of a valid warrant?

W. The position is that on or about 1 February 2008, I duly endorsed the necessary warrant at Centre Street Garda Station and left it there for forwarding to Market Street Garda Station. I was subsequently unable to trace the warrant.

P. Garda Jug, have you any recollection of the said warrant?

W. I recall that it was in the standard form of warrant. I do not recollect what District Court the warrant would have gone back to with the endorsement of execution on it.

P. Garda, do you recall the events later on the day of 1 February 2008?

W. I do. I was on duty in the vicinity of Centre Street, wearing plain clothes. At approximately 1 pm I observed a man I know to be Conor Cup sitting in a parked van, registration number 06 D 007 on Centre Street.

P. Garda, is Mr Cup present in court today?

W. Yes, he's sitting in the second row over there wearing a navy overcoat and a red tie.

P. Did you speak with Mr Cup on 1 February 2008?

W. Yes, I approached the van and identified myself to Mr Cup. I showed him the search warrant and I told him that I was going to search the van.

P. Did Mr Cup object in any way?

W. No, he was fully co-operative.

P. Did you find anything of note in the van?

W. I found a very large quantity of DVDs, which I believed to be pirated materials.

P. What was Mr Cup's attitude at this point?

W. Fairly relaxed, I'd say. He told me that I could take everything. I duly seized approximately 350 DVDs – 353 to be precise.

P. *(Addressing the judge)* Judge, the position would appear to be that the lawfulness of the search effectively cannot be proven in the absence of the warrant on foot of which the search was carried out. However, in my respectful submission, it is still appropriate in all the circumstances for the evidence arising from the search to be admitted into evidence. It is plain, Judge,

> that Garda Jug acted *bona fide* in the discharge of his duties, and it is equally plain that the search did not involve an invasion of the constitutional personal rights of the defendant. In all the circumstances, I say that the evidence is admissible.

7.07 CONFESSIONS

An admission by a party to legal proceedings is admissible as an exception to the rule against hearsay. Where that admission is a confession made by a criminal defendant while in custodial detention, the foundation is more complicated. Aside from the conditions to the hearsay exception, the prosecution must comply with constitutional and human rights requirements.[19] Where the admissibility of a confession is challenged, the prosecution must demonstrate that the confession was voluntary[20] and that it was obtained through the use of fair procedures.[21] The prosecution has the burden of proving all elements of the offence[22] beyond a reasonable doubt.[23] If the accused pleads not guilty, the accused takes the general position that all the facts alleged by the prosecution are false.

7.07.1 Elements of the foundation

The foundation includes the following elements:

1. The witness heard a declarant make a statement.
2. The witness identifies the declarant as the accused.
3. The statement was voluntary.
4. The statement was the product of fair procedures.

---

19. See generally McGrath, *Evidence* (Thomson Round Hall, 2005) chs 8 and 11; Healy, *Irish Laws of Evidence* (Thomson Round Hall, 2004) chs 10 and 13; Walsh, *Criminal Procedure* (Thomson Round Hall, 2002) ch 9B.

20. See eg *DPP v Shaw* [1982] IR 1; *People v Lynch* [1982] IR 64; *People v Hoey* [1987] IR 637; *DPP v Madden* [1977] IR 336.

21. *DPP v O'Loughlin* [1979] IR 85; *DPP v Shaw* [1982] IR 1; *DPP v Ward* (27 November 1998, unreported) Special Criminal Court.

22. *Hardy v Ireland* [1994] 2 IR 550; *O'Leary v AG* [1993] 1 IR 102; *Woolmington v DPP* [1935] AC 462.

23. *AG v Byrne* [1974] IR 1; *Miller v Minister for Pensions* [1947] 2 All ER 372.

5. The statement is inconsistent with the position the accused is taking at trial and is relevant to an element of the offence which the prosecution must prove.

7.07.2 Sample foundation

Our hypothetical situation is a prosecution for robbery. The accused is Mr Charlie Carpet. The prosecution calls Garda Richard Rug as a witness. Garda Rug identifies himself and then testifies that he is assigned to the River Street Garda Station. The proponent is the prosecution.

P. (*In the absence of the jury*) Garda Rug, where were you on the afternoon of 20 January 2006?

W. I was on duty at the River Street Station.

P. What happened that afternoon?

W. Some other officers brought a person in for questioning.

P. Who was that person? (2)

W. Charlie Carpet.

P. Where is Charlie Carpet now? (2)

W. He is here in the court.

P. Specifically, where in the court? (2)

W. (*Pointing*) He is sitting over there.

P. What happened after the officers brought Mr Carpet into the station? (3)

W. Myself and Garda Matthew Mat took him into an interview room.

P. What happened then? (3)

W. We began questioning him.

P. What promises did you make to him during the questioning? (3)

W. None.

P. What force did you use during the interview? (3)

W. None.

P. What threats did you make? (3)

W. None.

P. What requests did he make during questioning? (3)

W. He asked for a cup of tea and to go to the bathroom.

P. How did you respond to these requests?

W. I granted them. I gave him a cup of tea. I let him go to the bathroom. I tried to make him as comfortable as possible.

P. What, if anything, did you say to Mr Carpet?

W. I informed him of his rights.

P. How did you inform him of his rights?

W. I read them to him and then handed him a written copy.

P. Garda Rug, I am now handing you prosecution exhibition number three for identification. What is it? (4)

W. It's the written copy I just referred to.

P. How can you recognise it? (4)

W. I initialled it, and I asked Mr Carpet to initial it as well. I see the initials and the date which we wrote in pencil on the card.

P. How did you use the card during the interview? (3)

W. I read from it verbatim to make certain that Mr Carpet was correctly informed of his rights.

P. What happened after you read this information to Mr Carpet?

W. I asked him whether he understood his rights. (4)

P. What was his answer? (4)

W. He said that he did.

P. What happened next?

W. I asked him whether he wanted a lawyer.

P. What was his response?

W. He said no.

P. What happened then?

W. I asked him whether he was willing to talk about the robbery.

P. What was his response?

W. He told me about the robbery. (1), (2)

P. What did he say about the robbery? (5)

W. He said he had taken money from the shop in the train station and that he was very sorry that he had done it. He said that he needed money and couldn't figure out any other way to get it.

At common law, it was open to a court to convict an accused where the only admissible evidence offered by the prosecution was the accused's confession. It remains the law today that corroboration, ie independent, supporting evidence, is not required. However, s 10(1) of the Criminal Procedure Act 1993 provides that where at a trial on indictment the prosecution relies on the uncorroborated confession of an accused: 'the trial judge shall advise the jury to have due regard to the absence of corroboration.'[24]

The constitutional and statutory rights of criminal suspects are supported by administrative regulations governing custodial detention. Under the auspices of the Criminal Justice Act 1984, regulations for the treatment of persons in custody were issued in 1987.[25] The Custody Regulations cover wide-ranging aspects of detention including the maintenance of a custody record,[26] the right of the suspect to be informed of various matters,[27] the conduct of interviews[28] and provisions relating to juveniles[29] and foreign nationals.[30] A breach of the custody regulations does not 'of itself' render a confession inadmissible at trial.[31] However, it may influence the trial judge in exercising his or her discretion to exclude evidence obtained through illegal (as opposed to unconstitutional) means.[32] Moreover, it may also have some

24. Section 10(2) states that it shall not be necessary for a judge to use any particular form of words when cautioning the jury. See *DPP v O'Neill* (28 January 2002, unreported) CCA; *DPP v Connolly* [2003] 2 IR 1; *DPP v Murphy* [2005] 2 IR 125.

25. SI 199/1987. See also Criminal Justice (Forensic Evidence) Act 1990 Regulations 1992 (SI 130/1992).

26. Regulations 6 and 7.

27. Regulation 8.

28. Regulation 12.

29. Regulations 9 and 13.

30. Regulation 15.

31. Section 7(3) of the CJA 1984; *DPP v Darcy* (29 July 1997, unreported) CCA; *DPP v Spratt* [1995] 1 IR 585, [1995] 2 ILRM 117.

32. *DPP v Spratt* [1995] 1 IR 585, [1995] 2 ILRM 117. See **7.05** above.

bearing on the judge's determination as to whether, having regard to the totality of the circumstances, the confession was voluntary and procured using fair procedures. The Custody Regulations have not displaced the operation of the so-called 'Judges Rules', a set of protections fashioned at common law for the protection of persons questioned by police officers.[33]

The benefits of electronic recording as a safeguard in the interviewing of suspects are well established. Nevertheless, it was not until 1997 that regulations facilitating the introduction of electronic recording were issued.[34] The Electronic Recording Regulations require the electronic recording of interviews[35] but undercut that requirement through the inclusion of liberal exceptions: electronic recording is not mandatory where the equipment is functionally faulty,[36] already in use[37] or otherwise not practicable.[38] In the years following the promulgation of the Regulations, the courts became increasingly impatient with delays in the practical implementation of electronic recording. In *DPP v Connolly,* Hardiman J warned:

> The courts have been very patient, perhaps excessively patient, with delays in this regard. The time cannot be remote when we will hear a submission that, absent extraordinary circumstances (by which we do not mean that a particular garda station has no audio visual machinery or that the audio visual room was being painted) it is unacceptable to tender in evidence a statement which has not been so recorded.[39]

---

33. *DPP v Spratt* [1995] 1 IR 585, [1995] 2 ILRM 117; *DPP v McCann* (1981) 2 Frewen 57.
34. Criminal Justice Act 1984 (Electronic Recording of Interviews) Regulations 1997 (SI 74/1997).
35. Regulation 4(1).
36. Regulation 4(3)(a)(i). The functional fault must be sufficient to render the equipment 'unavailable' and, moreover, the member in charge must consider on reasonable grounds that the interview should not be delayed until the fault is rectified.
37. Regulation 4(3)(a)(ii). Here also, the member in charge must consider on reasonable grounds that the interview should not be delayed until the equipment becomes available.
38. Regulation 4(3)(b). See eg *DPP v Holland* (15 June 1998, unreported) CCA.
39. [2003] 2 IR 1.

Recent case law makes plain that the courts will no longer excuse failures to electronically record interviews other than for very good reasons.[40] The Electronic Recording Regulations enjoy a status equivalent to the Custody Regulations and, consequently, a failure to electronically record will not lead automatically to the exclusion of a confession at trial.[41] Nevertheless, in any particular case the trial judge retains a discretion to exclude the confession on this ground.[42]

The following hypothetical situation is based on a case in which the gardaí failed to comply with the Custody Regulations during the period of the accused's arrest and detention. The accused was arrested on 1 February 2008 and held for a period of 22 hours. On three occasions during his detention the accused was interviewed by members of An Garda Síochána for periods in excess of four hours. The accused had no sleep during the period of his detention. Ultimately, the accused made a statement to gardaí admitting his guilt. At trial, defence counsel argues that the inculpatory statement was taken in breach of the Custody Regulations and that, accordingly, the statement should not be admitted in evidence.

The investigating garda is being cross-examined by defence counsel. The defence is the proponent.

P. *(In the absence of the jury)* The accused was in custody for a total of 22 hours, isn't that correct?

W. That is correct.

P. And the first interview that was conducted with the accused lasted for 5 hours and 40 minutes, isn't that correct?

W. That is correct.

P. And you are fully aware Garda, aren't you, that, section 12, sub-section 4 of the Custody Regulations provides that if an interview has lasted for four hours, it be either terminated or adjourned for a reasonable time?

W. Yes, I am aware of that.

---

40. *DPP v Michael Murphy* [2005] 4 IR 504; *DPP v O'Neill* [2007] IECCA 8 (16 March 2007).

41. CJA 1984, s 27(4).

42. CJA 1984, s 27(4). Section 30 of CJA 2007 permits the drawing of inferences at trial from the failure of an accused to mention particular facts during a custodial interview. However, s 30(6) sets down the precondition that the interview be electronically recorded or that accused consented in writing to it not being recorded.

P. And are you also aware that that provision is mandatory in nature?
W. Yes.
P. You accept then that whilst the accused was in garda custody, a mandatory provision of the custody regulations was breached?
W. I accept that.
P. Why were two further interviews conducted with the accused that also went on for more than four hours?
W. I don't have a satisfactory explanation for that and I accept that a break should have been taken after four hours.
P. Isn't it also the case that the accused was denied the opportunity of sleeping during his period in custody?
W. Yes.
P. At what time was the confession made by the accused?
W. At 11 pm.
P. In other words, virtually at the very end of the accused's period of detention?
W. Yes.
P. And after the accused had been questioned repeatedly for periods in excess of four hours?
W. Yes.
P. And without his having been given the opportunity to sleep?
W. Yes.
P. (*Addressing the judge*) Judge, in my respectful submission, this is a case in which the confession is inadmissible. The authorities are clear that in circumstances where there has been a breach of the Custody Regulations, the trial judge enjoys a discretion to exclude an inculpatory statement made by an accused. I accept, Judge, that the fact that the Regulations were breached does not automatically render the confession inadmissible. However, in my submission, the totality of the circumstances in this case, given the nature of the breaches, and the fact that the accused was not given the opportunity to sleep, bear on the voluntariness and fairness of the confession. This is a case in which it would not be safe to admit the confession into evidence.

Chapter 8

SUBSTITUTES FOR EVIDENCE

8.01 INTRODUCTION

The previous chapters analyse the legal restrictions on the process of admitting evidence during a trial. However, there are substitutes for conventional evidence: for example, a party may make a formal admission as to a fact, the judge may take judicial notice of a proposition, or the finder of fact may be taken outside the courtroom to view a scene or object that is relevant to the case. This chapter addresses these substitutes for evidence.

8.02 FORMAL ADMISSIONS

8.02.1 The law

A party to a proceeding, whether civil or criminal, may make a formal admission before or during a trial that a certain fact existed or that a certain event occurred.[1] The effect of the formal admission is that the other party is not required to prove the fact or event in question. Once the fact or event has been formally admitted, ordinarily neither party can introduce evidence to contradict it. What would motivate a party to admit a fact that the other party would otherwise have to prove? There may be certain tactical benefits to making a formal admission; for example, the party may reduce the length and cost of the proceedings and may create the impression in the minds of the judge and/or jury that the party is a reasonable, fair person.

In criminal proceedings, the making of formal admissions is governed by s 22(1) of the Criminal Justice Act 1984:

> [A]ny fact of which oral evidence may be given in oral proceedings may be admitted for the purpose of those proceedings by or on behalf of the prosecution or the accused, and the admission by any party of such fact under this section shall as against that party be conclusive evidence in those proceedings of the fact admitted.

An admission may be made before or at the hearing but, if made otherwise than in court, it must be made in writing and signed by the person making

1. *Urquhart v Butterfield* (1887) 37 Ch D 357.

it.[2] An admission shall be treated as such for the purposes of the proceedings and also any subsequent proceedings relating to the same matter including any appeal or retrial.[3] It may be withdrawn subsequently with the leave of the court.[4]

In civil proceedings, formal admissions of fact are made in various ways.[5] Order 32, r 1 of the Rules of the Superior Courts establishes the general proposition that '[a]ny party to a cause or matter may give notice, by his pleading or otherwise in writing, that he admits the truth of the whole or any part of the case of any other party.' Formal admissions are frequently sought and made during the exchange of pleadings. The admission may be made explicitly in a party's pleading.[6] If not, it may be implicit in the party's failure to deny a fact asserted in the pleading of another party by virtue of Ord 19, r 13:

> Every allegation of fact in any pleading, not being a petition, if not denied specifically or by necessary implication, or stated to be not admitted in the pleading of the opposite party, shall be taken to be admitted, except as against an infant, or person of unsound mind.

In addition, one party may seek an admission from another party by serving on that party a notice to admit.[7] Order 32, r 2 makes provision for the admission of documents[8] and r 4 for the admission of specific facts. These procedures further judicial economy by relieving a party of the burden of proving facts that the other side is willing to admit.[9] A formal admission made in writing in advance of trial has the merit of reducing the possibility

---

2. Section 22(2). An admission made by a body corporate must be signed by an officer such as a director or manager. An admission by an accused person must be made or approved by his or her counsel or solicitor.
3. Section 22(3).
4. Section 22(4).
5. See generally McGrath, *Evidence* (Thomson Round Hall, 2005) para 13.05; Delany and McGrath, *Civil Procedure in the Superior Courts* (2nd edn, Thomson Round Hall, 2005) pp 501–04.
6. Rules of the Superior Courts, Ord 32, r 1.
7. Rules of the Superior Courts, Ord 32, r 4.
8. Ord 32, r 3 states that a notice to admit documents shall be in the Form No 13 in Appendix C.
9. With this rationale in mind, the rules require a party who fails to serve a notice to admit to pay the cost of proving the document or fact (Ord 32, rr 2 and 4).

of disagreement at trial over the content of the admission. Nevertheless, there is nothing to prevent the making of an oral admission by a party in court during the course of the proceedings.[10]

8.02.2 Elements of the foundation

The procedure for entering a formal admission includes these steps:

1. Counsel representing one of the parties announces to the judge that there has been a formal admission.
2. The judge then asks counsel for the other party to confirm that this is true.
3. Counsel for the other party gives the necessary confirmation.
4. The proponent establishes the content of the admission. If the admission is oral, the proponent simply states the nature of the admission on the record. If the stipulation is in writing, the proponent introduces the writing.
5. When required, the judge personally questions the party or parties before accepting the formal admission. The judge ensures that the party understands the nature and consequences of the formal admission.

In a jury trial, after the judge accepts the stipulation, the judge informs the jury of the stipulation and instructs the jury on the legal effect of the stipulation.

8.02.3 Sample foundation

This hypothetical scenario is an action for breach of contract. The plaintiff, Maple Industries Co Ltd, alleges that on 10 January 2006 it entered into a contract with the defendant, Beech Co Ltd. The Statement of Claim alleges that under the terms of the contract, Beech Co Ltd promised to excavate a site, lay a foundation and build a two-storey shopping centre for the plaintiff. In its Defence, the defendant raises the defences of impossibility and financial impracticability. The Defence alleges that a week after beginning

[10] Regardless of the procedure that is used, a party to a civil action is generally free to withdraw a formal admission at any subsequent stage in the proceedings. *H Clark (Doncaster) Ltd v Wilkinson* [1965] Ch 694. However, a party may be estopped from withdrawing a formal admission in certain circumstances.

excavation, the defendant discovered a subsoil condition that made it prohibitively expensive for it to complete the promised construction work. The proponent is the defendant.

P. Judge, I would like to announce that the plaintiff has made a formal admission in relation to its knowledge of the existence of the subsoil condition that the defendant discovered in March 2006. (1)

J. (*To counsel for the defendant)* Is that true? (2)

O. Yes, Judge. (3)

J. What is the nature of this formal admission? (4)

P. The formal admission is that before the defendant's discovery of the layer of granite in March 2006, neither the plaintiff nor any of the plaintiff's employees had actual, subjective knowledge that the layer of granite existed.

J. *(To counsel for the plaintiff)* Is that the tenor of the formal admission?

O. Yes.

J. And does your client consent to this formal admission?

O. Yes, Judge.

J. Has this agreement been reduced to writing?

P. No, Judge.

O. No – it is an oral admission, Judge.

J. Very well. If that is the case, I shall accept the formal admission of fact.

8.03 JUDICIAL NOTICE

8.03.1 The law

Judicial notice is another substitute for formal evidence. The judge relieves the parties of the duty to present evidence by noting a fact and, in a jury trial, instructing the jury of the fact's existence.[11] What type of facts may be judicially noticed? Typically, the fact must take one of three forms: (1) the fact is generally known within the territorial jurisdiction of the court;[12] (2) the fact is capable of accurate and ready determination by resort to sources

---

11. *Greene v Minister for Defence* [1998] 4 IR 464.

12. See eg *State (Gilsenan) v McMorrow* [1978] IR 360; *State (Taylor) v Circuit Judge for Wicklow* [1951] IR 311.

whose accuracy cannot reasonably be questioned;[13] or (3) the fact is the subject of a statutory requirement of judicial notice.[14]

The procedure for judicial notice varies depending upon the basis for judicial notice that the party is invoking. When the party claims that the fact is a matter of common knowledge, the request can be informal. Similarly, the procedure is straightforward where judicial notice is required by statute. On the other hand, if the party claims that the fact is a readily verifiable certainty, the request might be put in writing and supported by documentary material. For example, when the party requests judicial notice of a scientific principle, the party might submit documentary proof of the principle's validity. Courts may relax the rule against hearsay when the parties are contesting the propriety of judicial notice; the judge may permit the parties to use affidavits, declarations and letters that would usually be considered inadmissible hearsay.

8.03.2 Sample foundation

The following scenario illustrates the first basis for judicial notice: namely, matters of common knowledge. The situation is a proceeding in tort arising out of a road traffic accident. The plaintiff, Ms Charlotte Cream, alleges that the defendant, Mr Graham Grey, was speeding and carelessly struck her as she was walking across the street. The plaintiff has already called Mr Barry Brown as a witness. Mr Brown testified that he observed the accident. He testified that the defendant's car struck the plaintiff at the junction of Main Street and River Road and that the defendant was driving at 50 kilometres per hour just before the accident. Mr Brown leaves the witness box and the following occurs. The plaintiff is the proponent:

P. Judge, I'm requesting at this point that you take judicial notice of two facts.

J. What are the facts?

P. The first is that the speed limit in the town centre is 40 kilometres per hour. The second is that the junction of Main

13. See eg *State (O'Connor) v Ó Caomhanaigh* [1963] IR 112; *R v Botrill, ex parte Kuechenmeister* [1947] KB 41.

14. See eg s 6(1) of the Interpretation Act 1937; s 18 of the Jurisdiction of Courts and Enforcement of Judgments Act 1998; s 4 of the European Convention on Human Rights Act 2003.

Street and River Road is located in the town centre. Both facts are common knowledge in this area.

J. I agree. I will take judicial notice of both facts.

8.04 JURY VIEW

8.04.1 Background

Occasionally, a lawyer acting in a case will want the judge and members of the jury to view an object or location that cannot feasibly be brought into the courtroom. In most cases, a lawyer will be content to offer either a witness's oral description of the object or location, a diagram of the object or location, or a photograph of the object or location. However, in some exceptional cases, the object or location is so complex or plays such a pivotal role in the case that the lawyer wants the finder of fact to observe it personally. The procedure whereby the finder of fact observes the object or location outside the courtroom is known as a view.[15] The sensory impressions that the finder of fact gathers during the view do not qualify as substantive evidence. The purpose of the view is to assist the finder of fact in assessing the credibility of the evidence offered by the witnesses in the case.[16]

8.04.2 Elements of the foundation

The proponent may bring a motion for a view, which motion is grounded on affidavit. The affidavits should show that:

1. Certain property exists.
2. The property is logically relevant to the pending case.
3. It is impossible or inconvenient to bring the property into the courtroom.
4. The features of the property are so complex or detailed that an oral description, diagram or photograph would be inadequate.
5. The property is in substantially the same condition as at the time of the relevant event. If the property has changed materially, the judge usually exercises his or her discretion by denying the

---

15. *Buckingham v Daily News* [1956] 2 QB 534; *Molumby v Kearns* (19 January 1999, unreported) HC; *McAllister v Dunnes Stores* (5 February 1987, unreported) HC.

16. *DPP v Maguire* [1995] 2 IR 286.

motion. (In a jury trial, if the property has changed markedly, a view might mislead the jury.)

8.04.3 Sample foundation

The scenario that follows is a personal injuries action arising from a collision in February 2006 on a stretch of road on the outskirts of Centreville. The plaintiff requests that the trial judge view the section of road where the collision occurred. In support of this application, the plaintiff opens two affidavits, both of which refer to the same section of road mentioned in the pleadings. For that reason, both of the affidavits lay the first three elements of the foundation. The date of the hearing of the application is 2 March 2008.

THE HIGH COURT

Record No 2007/6475P

BILLY BOTTLE

Plaintiff

-and-

CIARAN CARAFE

Defendant

AFFIDAVIT OF GARY GLASS

I, Gary Glass, photographer, of East Street, Centreville, aged eighteen years and upwards, MAKE OATH, and say as follows:

1. I say that I am a professional photographer and the owner of Glass Photography, East Street, Centreville.
2. I beg to refer to the pleadings already had herein, when produced.
3. I say that on 3 September 2006, a solicitor, Ms Claire Canister, contacted me by telephone. She asked me to meet her on Outer Avenue just east of the junction with Inner Road, on the outskirts of Centreville. (1), (2), (3) She stated that she was the solicitor on record for the plaintiff in a civil action arising from a collision on that stretch of Outer Avenue.
4. I say that I met Ms Canister at the junction of Outer Avenue and Inner Road at 11 am on 4 September 2006. I say that while Ms Canister and I were at the junction, she explained that she was interested in showing the judge at the trial of the action the 100 metres of Outer Avenue immediately to the east of the junction with

Inner Road. I say that Ms Canister asked whether I could photograph or videotape that section of the road.

5. I say that I carefully inspected the 100 metres of the road in question. I walked the stretch of road twice and drove the stretch of road twice. I then advised Ms Canister that in my professional opinion, neither still photographs nor a videotape would be adequate. I say that the section of the road in question is not only winding, the road is also uneven. I say that even if I took 100 still photographs and submitted them to this Honourable Court, the stills would not adequately convey to the court the sense of travelling down that stretch of road. In addition, since the road is both curvy and uneven, even a videotape would convey only a limited sense of the perspective of a driver on that stretch of road.
6. Accordingly, I humbly aver that in my professional opinion, it will be necessary for the trial judge to physically inspect the junction in question in this case.

SWORN by the said Gary Glass
this day of 2008 before me
commissioner for oaths/practising
solicitor and I know the Deponent.

THE HIGH COURT

Record No 2007/6475P

Between:

BILLY BOTTLE

Plaintiff

-and-

CIARAN CARAFE

Defendant

<u>AFFIDAVIT OF VICTORIA VAT</u>

I, Victoria Vat, office manager, of The Green Gables, Perimeter Road, Centreville, aged eighteen years and upwards, MAKE OATH and say as follows:

1. I say that I am an office manager and that I reside at The Green Gables, Perimeter Road, Centreville.
2. I make this affidavit from facts within my own knowledge save where otherwise appearing, and whereso appearing I believe the same to be true and accurate.

3. I beg to refer to the pleadings already had herein, when produced.
4. I say that I have lived at that above-mentioned residence for the past 14 years. I say that I am intimately familiar with the junction of the Outer Avenue and Inner Road on the outskirts of Centreville, as this is the junction closest to my house. I say that I have driven through this junction thousands of times.
5. I say that I can recall the condition of the 100 metres of Outer Avenue immediately to the east of Inner Road as of February 2006. I generally remember the condition of the road and the foliage on both sides of the road. I inspected that area again today. I say and believe that, to the best of my recollection, the condition of the road and foliage today is substantially the same as the condition in February 2006.
6. Accordingly, I humbly aver that, in the event that the learned trial judge in the above entitled action was to visit the junction of Outer Avenue and Inner Road, the condition would be virtually identical to the condition which would have been operative in February 2006.

SWORN by the said Victoria Vat
this day of 2008 before
me commissioner for oaths/practising
solicitor and I know the Deponent.

INDEX

[all references are to heading number]

G

H